WALKING THROUGH
SPAIN

OTHER BOOKS BY
ROBIN NEILLANDS

The Road to Compostela
Walking Through France: From the Channel to the Camargue
Cycletouring in France
Cycletouring in Spain & Portugal
Britain by Bicycle
Walking in France

Military History
The Hundred Years War 1337–1453
By Sea & Land: The Royal Marines Commandos 1942–82
The Raiders: The Army Commandos 1940–45
The Desert Rats: The 7th Armoured Division 1939–45

Fiction (As Robin Hunter)
The Fourth Angel
Quarry's Contract
The London Connection

WALKING THROUGH

SPAIN

From Santander to the Mediterranean

ROBIN NEILLANDS

Macdonald
Queen Anne Press

A QUEEN ANNE PRESS BOOK

First published in Great Britain in 1991 by
Queen Anne Press, a division of
Macdonald & Co (Publishers) Ltd
Orbit House
1 New Fetter Lane
London EC4A 1AR

A member of Maxwell Macmillan Pergamon Publishing Corporation

Maps drawn by Terry Brown

British Library Cataloguing in Publication Data
Neillands, Robin *1935–*
    Walking through Spain.
    1. Spain. Description & travel
    914.60483

    ISBN 0–356–17978–8

Typeset by Selectmove Limited, London
Printed and bound in Great Britain by
BPCC Hazell Books
Aylesbury, Bucks, England
Member of BPCC Ltd.

CONTENTS

ACKNOWLEDGEMENTS

A lot of people helped me with this walk, so thanks are due to Geoff Cowen, for planning the route and for his company in Andalucía, and the Brittany Ferrets, Toby Oliver, Peter Chambers, Keith Howell and John Lloyd, for their support on this and other occasions. Thanks also to Toby Oliver and Ian Carruthers of Brittany Ferries for help with transportation and the more comfortable accommodation. Pauline Kirkman of Air Europe was another staunch friend, as was Richard Parker of Daisy Roots, who provided that most comfortable of walking footwear. In Spain, Piedad García and Lito, Pilar and the Lopez family were a constant support, while back in England my secretary, Estelle Huxley, kept the typewriter working and deciphered my notes. I could not have put this trip together without the advice of 'Champ' Champion of Tenerife and the staff at the London Library who dug out a great range of useful books. Thanks are also due to some shops, particularly Stanford's Map Shop in Long Acre, London, and MacCarta Ltd in King's Cross Road, London. I would also like to thank Peter Orrin of Waymark Holidays for his help in Jimena de la Frontera, and Ken Ward of Lord Winston's Walking Tours for a lot of useful advice.

THIS ONE IS FOR
GEOFF COWEN
Most generous of friends

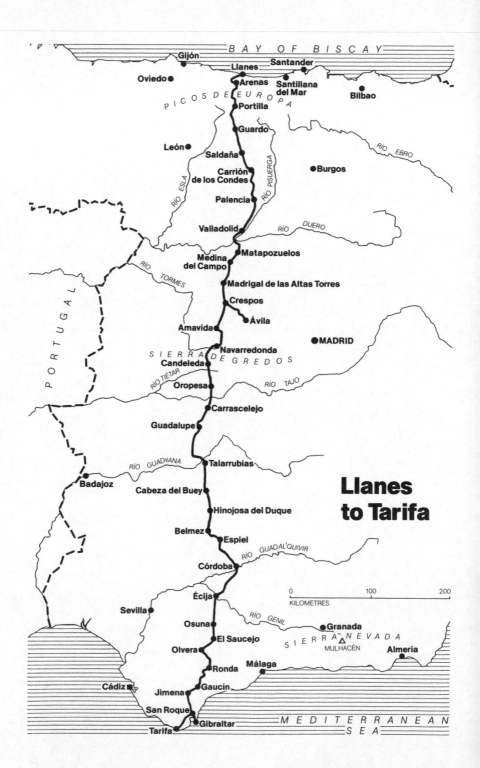

BAY OF BISCAY

Gijón
Llanes   Santander
Oviedo   Arenas
           Santillana
           del Mar   Bilbao
PICOS DE EUROPA
           Portilla
           Guardo
León
           Saldaña
           Carrión
           de los Condes   Burgos
RÍO ESLA
RÍO PISUERGA
RÍO EBRO
           Palencia

           Valladolid   RÍO DUERO
           Matapozuelos
           Medina
           del Campo
RÍO TORMES
           Madrigal de las Altas Torres
           Crespos
           Amavida   Ávila
PORTUGAL
           SIERRA DE GREDOS   MADRID
           Navarredonda
           Candeleda
RÍO TIÉTAR   Oropesa   RÍO TAJO
           Carrascelejo
           Guadalupe

RÍO GUADIANA   Talarrubias

Badajoz
           Cabeza del Buey

           Hinojosa del Duque   **Llanes
           Belmez   to Tarifa**
                   Espiel
                   RÍO GUADALQUIVIR
           Córdoba

           Écija
                      RÍO GENIL
Sevilla   Osuna   Granada
           El Saucejo   SIERRA NEVADA
Olvera   MULHACÉN   Almería
           Ronda   Málaga
           Gaucín
Cádiz   Jimena
       San Roque
     Tarifa   Gibraltar   MEDITERRANEAN
                              SEA

0   100   200
KILOMETRES

CHAPTER ONE

PREPARATIONS

'Take a piece of paper,' said Uncle Podger – he always began at the beginning – 'and put down on it everything you can possibly require; see that it contains nothing you can possibly do without. Imagine yourself in bed; what have you got on? Very well, put it down. You get up; what do you do? Wash yourself. What do you wash yourself with? Soap; put down soap. Then take your clothes. Begin at your feet; what do you wear on your feet? Boots, shoes, socks; put them down. Put down everything, then you don't forget anything.' The list made, he would go over it carefully, to see that he had forgotten nothing. Then he would go over it again, and strike out everything it was possible to dispense with. Then he would lose the list.

Jerome K. Jerome *Three Men on the Bummell*

Late in the afternoon, somewhere south of Medina del Campo, I ran out of water. This can be a serious matter on the wide, hot *meseta* of Castile, but I could see a small village a short distance away and there I headed, anticipating a tap, a little shade and, with luck, a glass of cold beer. Little things mean a lot on a walk through Spain. When I arrived, walking in down a narrow, dusty street, the village seemed deserted. The trees were dozing in the heat, and even the dogs lacked energy to do much more than pant. I found the bar, indicated by the usual plastic curtain over the entrance, but it was, inevitably, shut. This was pointed out to me by an old man sitting on the steps outside, who rapped the door behind with his cane and said briefly, *'Cerrado'*. Well, I could do without the beer, but water I had to have.

When I asked the old man, he pointed away into the trees with his stick and said there was a tap, *un grifo*, over there. When I went off to find it, he heaved himself up from the steps and followed, hobbling along at my side to ask who I was, where I came from, and what I was doing, in a most un-Spanish fashion, relaying this information to a number of other people who started to appear from the surrounding houses. These included three aged crones in black, who came hurrying from a house like a flock of crows, wiping wet hands on their aprons. By the time I got to the tap, there must have been a dozen people with me. When I saw the tap I realised why.

The tap was on a standpipe, backed by a wooden post, and the whole of it was seething with bees. Whether it was a swarm or a nest, I do not know, but the brass tap projected sharply from a brown, droning mass. Clearly, if I wanted any water, I must brave the bees. That fact, and more, was obvious when I glanced back at the spectators. They were now gathered in a group, all eyes upon me, and the issue between us was clear. Did 'el inglés' have 'cojones' or not? Everyone looked interested and the old bastard who had put me in this situation looked positively gleeful.

I usually work on the theory that most dangers are either avoidable or imaginary. If, for example, a dog is running about freely, it probably does not bite. It is the chained-up ones you have to watch out for. If the bees were left to occupy the village tap in peace, they might be amiable, or then again they might not. Well, I would soon see. I reached forward, gingerly, fingers spread, and turned on the tap. To my horror it began to vibrate violently under the water pressure, the pipe shaking against the post, and a deeper menacing drone came from the bees. Some took flight and buzzed about my head. I snapped the tap off again and leapt back, sweating. Being set upon by a swarm of bees is not something to relish. For a moment, standing there in the leaf-dappled sunlight under the trees, I thought of beating a retreat, out of this village and away from these people, but I needed water and I was not about to ask the villagers for it. From their faces it was not on offer anyway. For more than a moment I hated them and understood, perhaps for the first time, why the Spanish find the bullfight so fascinating – because it's dangerous for somebody else. So there we waited, me, the bees, and the village people, while I made up my mind. Then I stepped back to the tap and turned it back on, full blast.

*   *   *

This is an account of a walk across Spain, from Santander on the northern coast of Cantabria, at the southern end of the Bay of Biscay, south to Tarifa and the Rock of Gibraltar, on the shores of the Mediterranean, but this is not a book about walking. This is a book about Spain. Like millions of people, I have often been to Spain on holiday, staying along the Costas or in the Balearics, nosing about Madrid, *parador*-hopping by car or, several times, riding about the remoter parts on my bicycle. Compared with most people, I know Spain well and, having a Chilean wife, I speak more than adequate Spanish. On this journey, though, I saw Spain at an eye-to-eye level and at a snail's pace, which is the best way to see any country. I would agree with Evelyn Waugh's remark that, 'The human eye receives the most intense images when the observer's feet are planted firmly on the ground.' Besides, I like walking. If there is time to spare there is no pleasanter way to travel – up to a point. Long distance walking is not for everyone, as I shall presently reveal. Before we depart on this journey, though, let me tell you a little about myself. It won't take long.

About ten years ago, I sold a business that was breaking my heart and bank balance at a roughly equal rate, and found myself suddenly unemployed. If you have worked all the hours God sends for years, that can take a little getting used to. To help the process of adjustment along, and while deciding what to do next, I got on my bicycle one summer's day and rode it for a thousand miles or so, across France and Spain, down the Pilgrim Road from Le Puy to Santiago de Compostela in Galicia. I'll tell you something about that later, when we come to Carrión de los Condes on the *campo* of Castile.

Two years after going to Compostela, I got on the bicycle again and rode it across Turkey, Syria and Jordan, down the Crusader Trail to Jerusalem. I could tell you a lot about that trip, but already you will see the emergence of a pattern. If a thing is worth doing, it is worth doing twice. Then, in 1987, I walked across France, from the Channel coast to the Camargue, and you can read a book about that. It then seemed only natural that a couple of years later I would be looking about for a fresh country and a new challenge. Since I prefer Europe to anywhere else, my eye soon fell upon the wild and desolate hinterland of Spain.

There are various reasons for this. To begin with I speak Spanish, which certainly helps. Secondly, a walk across Spain, north to south, is roughly the same distance as the one across France – about a thousand kilometres or six hundred miles as the crow flies, though rather more on foot. I could therefore fit the journey into the same sort of time scale, say about six weeks. Then, although I have been to Spain many times, I hardly know the interior at all, so this would be a journey through a *terra incognita*. Spain enjoys a huge tourist trade, but for the most part the tourists flock to the Balearic Islands or settle round the Costas. This leaves the vast central heartland of the country virtually unexplored, certainly by the foot-powered traveller. Lastly, there was a ferry from Plymouth to Santander to get me to the start, and an airport in Gibraltar to get me home again, so I already had the start and finish of my journey. For the bit in the middle, I gathered up some maps of Spain and went to see Geoff Cowen.

Geoff has been a friend of mine for over twenty years, and he plans my trips. If possible, for he is a busy fellow, he then joins me for part of the way and this is our way of keeping in touch. All that apart, Geoff is an organiser.

If Geoff says something will work, it will work. If he says, 'Don't do it,' it is as well to listen. Then you can do it anyway, but at least you will have been warned. I told Geoff the start and finish points, gave him a time scale, mentioned that I'd like to see some castles and must not miss the shrine at Guadalupe, handed over the maps and let him get on with it while I went off to gather more information. I am a great believer in soliciting help wherever I can find it, and for this walk accurate information seemed essential. The centre of Spain remains largely an unknown territory, certainly for walkers. One of the replies was the following letter from a gentleman in the Canary Islands:

Dear Robin Neillands,

I am glad that you found my notes helpful. While I can understand your giving up a tent in order to save weight, finding accommodation in rural areas is certainly going to be a problem. Your only predecessor, who walked across Spain (San Sebastián to Barcelona), had great problems in finding inns and most of those he found were filthy. This was in 1876. Since then I am sure they are much cleaner but, apart from the tourist areas, not more frequent.

The Spanish Government publishes a book, *Guía de Hoteles* (or *Guía de Alojamientos Hoteleros*), which lists all the hotels in the country down to 'one-star hostels', which are pretty primitive. A proportion, perhaps about a quarter of the villages included in small type on the Michelin 1:1,000,000 scale map I mentioned in my last letter, are included but as villages are rather far apart they are clearly thin on the ground. Apart from this, finding accommodation in remote areas could be difficult and time-consuming. The Guide should be available from bigger London booksellers. Failing this, consult the Spanish National Tourist Office in St James's St, or the Library of the Spanish Institute. You probably would not want to take the book with you but could make a list of the villages near your route.

If you don't already know Spanish, *do* make an attempt to learn a little. In remote areas you are unlikely to find English spoken (except a few words by schoolchildren).

The book I mentioned above is *On Foot in Spain* by J.S. Campion (Chapman & Hall 1879). It would be worth your reading; try a good secondhand bookseller, or a good public library could probably get it through their exchange system. Failing that, there is always the British Museum.

I look forward to hearing how you get on and in due course to adding *your* book to my library.

Yours sincerely,

'Champ' Champion

P.S.   With the rise in the standard of living, Spanish village shops have improved a great deal but the variety of food is still limited. Water supply has also improved, but it is wise to take some purifying tablets. *¡Feliz viaje!*

I found this information very accurate, and I am very grateful to Mr Champion for it. In the months before the trip I read everything I could lay my hands on about Spain, but even the real travellers' books, while full of good advice on food, heat, lack of water and so on, were not much help on the thorny question of accommodation. This is the critical question for a walker, as it affects how you travel; do you have to backpack and carry a full range of hard-hitting gear, or can you manage with a spare shirt and lots of socks? The problem is compounded by the fact that rural Spain has changed out of all recognition in recent years, with all the usual effects of growing prosperity. People are leaving the land, abandoning their farms and villages, so that the hinterland of Spain is, if anything, more empty than it was when Laurie Lee wandered across it in the 1930s. Regarding Laurie Lee, almost everyone who heard about the walk asked, 'Are you going to do a Laurie Lee and follow the path he took in *As I Walked Out One Midsummer Morning*?' Would that I had the time. I made the time for extensive reading before the trip, making the rather surprising discovery that there are a great many books on Spain, some by walkers, others by distinguished travellers, quite apart from a mass on the Peninsula's complex history. Laurie Lee's books are essential reading, as is Michener's *Iberia* and H.V. Morton's *A Stranger in Spain*, though both these concentrate largely on the cities. For good background on the walking, I had V.S. Pritchett's *Marching Spain*, an account of his walk from Badajoz to Vigo, published in 1928. Penguin does an excellent paperback, *History of Spain and Portugal*, and a lot of accurate detail on places that might otherwise be overlooked comes in Richard Ford's *A Handbook for Travellers in Spain*, published in three volumes by John Murray as long ago as 1855, and even that was the third edition. My desk began to groan under the weight of books and guides, and an expanded list of titles will be found in the bibliography. Most of these are based on city to city hops, or wandering by car, or even stagecoach. My project was rather more physical.

My aim was a *diretissima*, a walk straight across the Peninsula, north to south, in as direct a line as possible and, wherever possible, on footpaths. Geoff reported back that the direct route from Santander to Málaga, via Madrid, could be achieved by following the main road. To avoid this he decided I should swing off a little and start my trip in the little port of Llanes, which lies west of Santander. Llanes is the major lobster port of Spain, and I am always partial to a lobster with a bottle of chilled Torres, so Llanes sounded like a good starting point. From there I also had direct access to one of the great walking areas in Spain, the soaring mountains of the Picos de Europa, an outcrop of the Pyrenees, which bar the wide Atlantic from the hot plains of Castile.

Spain is not really a walker's country. By and large the Spanish do not walk at all and the facilities available for walkers reflect this. There is no great waymarked footpath network to rival the twenty thousand miles or more of the *Grande Randonnée* in France. There is no intricate inheritance of footpaths such as walkers can enjoy in Britain, where many paths date back to the time of the Saxons. On the other hand, Spain certainly has areas where keen walkers can go, and I had already been to many of them. I have often walked in the Pyrenees, from little Nuria to the top of Mont Canigou in Roussillon, and up through the marvellous Ordesa Canyon, north of Jaca and Torla in Aragón, and so over the range into France. I have walked in Mallorca and Cataluña, ridden across Spain on my bicycle and skied in the Sierra Nevada of Andalucía and on the Sierra de Guadarrama, north of Madrid. The big difference between Spain and other 'walkers' countries', like Austria, France, or Britain, lies in the lack of organisation. This may seem a boon, a chance to escape the well-followed, eroded tracks and really strike out into the unknown, but the snag is that Spain can be – and often is – a hot, hard, rugged and inhospitable country. Walking in Spain is not EASY.

Spain certainly has great outdoor areas and is marvellous for riders on horseback or bicycle, but the facilities for walking are minimal to say the least. The secret of a good walking trip is preparation, but the secret of preparation is reliable information. Reliable information on walking across Spain was hard to come by because no one had walked across Spain for the last fifty years. I got a lot of suggestions from motorists, but this was hardly relevant, and as the American proverb has it: 'It is better to know nuthin', than know what ain't so'. Amen to that.

*   *   *

By now, some months into the planning phase, my search for information had spread wide, especially to the Spanish Embassy and Tourist Board, but here I met with little more than apathy. I could get no information worth having on the available accommodation, or any advice on what to take. The need for this is interlinked because anything I needed on the ground and couldn't find, I would have to take with me. That meant weight and weight is the bane of the walker's life. More important still was the question of good, up-to-date maps, and this was getting critical, for by now Geoff had come up with the route.

'These Spanish maps you gave me are so ancient some of them have "*Here be dragons*" written on them, but you begin here,' he said, tapping the 1:1,000,000 scale Michelin map he was using for the outline plan, 'at Arenas, on the north side of the Picos, just inland from the coast at Llanes. From there you take the path through the Cares Gorge to Caín, here. That is one of the most spectacular walks in Spain, or so they say. You then go on to Posada de Valdeón and Guardo, and then follow the Río Carrión down to Carrión de los Condes, where it cuts your Road to Compostela, as requested. Then comes the flat bit, the *meseta*, so on you go, through Palencia to this place, Vallydolid – how do you pronounce that?'

'Va-ya-doh-lid,' I told him. 'Not Vallydolid.'

'Yeah, well, Vallydolid to Medina del Campo, which has a castle. You wanted castles, right? Then – God help you – across the plains to Ávila. There will be lots to write about there. Then comes the tricky bit. The Sierra de Gredos – I think there is a path across to Candeleda – and so to Oropesa, here. Then there is damn-all for fifty miles or so to that place you wanted put in . . .?'

'Guadalupe. Gwah-dah-loop-eh.'

'Right . . . Guada-thing. So, after that, more damn-all, heat, dust, thirst, all the stuff you like, until Córdoba. Look, are you quite sure you want to do this?'

'Wherever I go, I must go through Guadalupe. I've never been there and I want to see it.'

'Your problem. Well, after Córdoba you go more or less south and west through Écija and so over the hills to Ronda – a beautiful town. Perhaps I'll join you there. Then we go down through the White Towns either to Tarifa here, or to Gibraltar. Why not the one or the other? Why both?'

'Gibraltar is the place the British know, but the Spanish can get huffy about it. Besides, Tarifa is on the actual southern tip of Europe, so that's the logical place to stop.'

So, to sum up, Geoff had planned a walk that would take me a long way from the Costas, an arrow-like journey through the heart of Spain. I would begin in the mountains of the green and misty north, hacking through the hills to the *tierra de campos*, the flat grain and sheep country of Castile, the doormat to the wide *meseta*, that great tableland of Central

Spain. This would lead me to the west of Segovia and Madrid and across the Sierra de Gredos, which forms part of the Central Cordillera of Spain, and so, eventually to Extremadura, the country of the *conquistadores*, a place wise walkers will avoid. I would go there because I wanted to see Guadalupe, the great shrine of the Spanish-Americas. Then I would have fearsome arid country to cross before I reached the dark heights of the Sierra Morena, beyond which lay mighty Córdoba, that great city of the Moors in the valley of the Guadalquivir. From there, a more rapid, staccato succession of plains and sierras, moving from olives to oranges, across Andalucía, around the Sierra de Ronda and – God willing – down at last to the Mediterranean at a point where, just across the Straits, lay Africa. This was a journey indeed.

*   *   *

According to Geoff, this walk, of about seven hundred miles, would take six weeks, allowing for the occasional day off, at an average of seventeen miles per day. This seemed reasonable. I walk at about three miles an hour, and six hours' walking a day, plus an hour or so supporting the local economy in some shady bar, looked about right. The trip fitted the time scale, so I was delighted. I am always delighted at the first sight of a plan and the fact that the plans *never* work out as planned doesn't seem to discourage me. If I was bright I wouldn't do this sort of thing at my age. The underlying problem at the moment was that we needed up-to-date, accurate, large-scale maps of say 1:50,000 scale ($1\frac{1}{4}''$ to 1 mile), to plan the daily stages. The ones I wanted were not available in England and Geoff could do no more until I had them so, brooding on this problem, I went off to see Toby Oliver and the Brittany Ferrets.

For the last twelve years I have been going on walks and various capers in France and Spain with a group of journalist friends, known collectively as the Brittany Ferrets, because our journeys always start with a trip on a Brittany Ferry. Toby Oliver handles the Public Relations for Brittany Ferries, but he also walks. The other regular Ferrets are Peter Chambers, once of the *Daily Express* and now the doyen of our little group; John Lloyd, a tall, quiet fellow, who always turns up with the *dernier-cri* of camping and walking kit; and Keith Howell of the London Broadcasting Company, my personal hero. Keith spends his working life in a dark radio studio under the paving stones of Fleet Street, and this is not the best training ground for the outdoor life, but Keith is indomitable. To see him trudging up a mountain path under a heavy pack, tired out but totally determined to continue, is to see guts in action. Any walk, long or short, is all the better for the presence of my fellow Ferrets, because we always have a good time and have been known to do a little drinking.

One of the decisions we made at this meeting was to go down to Mallorca for a week and do a little walking in the rugged hills of the northern sierra. This little saga should have given me a glimpse of the larger picture. Two days before we were to leave for Spain, the airline cancelled the flight. It took forty-eight hours of screaming threats before they put it on again. Clutching the tickets – for I was in charge – I set out to meet the others at Gatwick and, to avoid the evening rush hour on the M25, decided to go by train from Reading. The 16.15 would have been ideal, but when I got to the station the 16.15 had been cancelled. No worries, catch the 16.50. When the 16.50 arrived, the driver walked off . . . an overtime ban was in action. No problems, catch the 17.03 via Clapham Junction. When the 17.03 came in, three train-loads of commuters crammed onto it and the driver refused to take it out as it was overloaded. In the end I had to take a taxi round the M25 – the one thing I had been trying to avoid – and we just caught the plane. The taxi ride alone cost £70!

Mallorca is a good place for a gentle walking holiday, but even there the terrain can be rugged and the weather extreme. We climbed the second highest mountain, getting down just before dark, strolled from Puerto Pollensa down the Boquer Valley to the sea, and finished our week with the five hour hike down the Pareis Gorge to Sa Calobra, which only the Spanish would call a walk at all. Much of it lies along a river-bed and involves clambering over great rocks. We returned to England a little fitter and rather thoughtful.

*   *   *

The Ferrets decided to come with me for the first few days of my walk, as they had done on the walk across France, which would provide a level of support and companionship until I got going, while Geoff would join me at the start and meet me again at the finish. Provided we could get some sort of organisation set up in Spain to find a route and some accommodation at the start, this would be perfect, but it proved difficult. An ever more urgent stream of messages went out to our contacts in Santander, requesting help with overnight accommodation and a guide across the barren bits, but the replies, if soothing, were somehow unconvincing. As Toby said to me some weeks before the start, 'There is an air of incredulity about the whole project. I don't think they believe you are serious.'

CHAPTER TWO

SETTING OUT

If a man cannot catch glory when his knees are supple, he had better not try when they grow stiff.

General Sir Charles Napier (1841)

All the above took several months. Geoff and I had many other things to do with our time apart from planning this journey, but even so, as the day of departure drew near, two thoughts began to loom ever larger in my mind. What was I doing it for and, having done it, what was I going to write about? In the beginning is the plan but in the end is the book. I do this sort of thing for a living. 'Because it is there' may be a good enough reason to climb Everest, but it can hardly hold true for a walk across Spain. After all, Spain is in Europe, and we all know Spain. By now I had most of the books, and although no one had walked at some speed from north to south, plenty of people had wandered about the Peninsula. Spain is a country that attracts the wanderer, and many wanderers write books. There was nothing new about that. Therefore, what I needed was a theme. Going to Compostela I had enjoyed the background of the Pilgrimage to the Shrine of St James, which has been going on since AD 949. Crossing France on foot meant planning a footpath journey, and that definitely was a first and therefore notable, but what was my theme to be for Spain? Worry, worry. Other people, like my wife, considered that this journey might be dangerous. The prospect of danger perked me up a bit. A little danger here and there would be something to write about. My attitude to danger is simple. If I think something is going to be dangerous, I don't do it. Anyway, danger is relative; a result of the odds. More people die each year on the Matterhorn than have died on Everest since that mountain was first climbed in 1953. But then again, thousands swarm up the Matterhorn every season while only a few attempt Everest. It's all relative.

The day of the explorer is over, at least on dry land, and the day of the adventurous traveller is coming to a close. Modern adventurers now have to rack their brains to come up with a trip which is new, exciting, different or simply promotable. Rumour has it that coming down the Amazon on roller skates is just about the last big adventure, for what counts today is not where you travel but *how*. I have elected to do my wandering in Europe on foot or by bicycle, and although many people will never believe me, this can prove more than adventurous enough for me, and for most people.

Spain and France are populated, civilised Western European states, yet – let me assure you – if you cross the wild parts of France and Spain alone and on foot, it is quite remarkably easy to get into serious trouble. This comes not from the people but from a combination of weather, weariness and terrain that can easily be overwhelming and, in Europe, so unexpected. Well, I've done this before, so I know what I'm about. I don't worry about it too much. I just go and do it.

My main worry then was not the risk but that there would not be enough to write about when the trip was over. The walking day, enhance or romance it how you will, actually consists of getting up early and putting one foot in front of the other until the day and the distance is done. Then you eat and sleep in tent or dosshouse, before getting up to do it all over again, day after day, until the end of the trip. Things may happen along the way, but I have not been too lucky in this respect over the years. I've had my ups and downs to be sure, but someone else is hogging my share of colourful, adventurous incidents – or so it would seem.

Other travel books are full of meetings with the great and the good, or detailed accounts of how this traveller from a foreign land, usually a lesser light in every way, chances upon some local lord or international celebrity to whom he is at once well known and an immediate intimate. I wish that sort of thing happened to me. I never seem to meet any of these aristocrats or those well-rounded intellectuals, awash with years and Nobel prizes. Neither have my travels been overburdened with village Hampdens, sage rustics or even homespun philosophers. This is not for want of trying. Meetings are the very stuff of travel, and since I speak adequate Spanish at the sub-philosophical level, I flung myself like a rug on anyone I met, but to no real avail. Most of the people I met walking across Spain were shepherds, cowherds, barmen: country people. The country people of Spain are far too concerned with their own affairs to worry about passing strangers or the Meaning of Life. They also display a curious preoccupation with manure. This may seem unlikely but, as an example, consider this conversation in a bar in the village of Santa Marina, on the south side of the Picos de Europa, where I stopped for a rest and a beer. Two men were going five rounds with a cow in the street outside and this provided an excuse for conversation.

'The *vaca* is very important, *sí, señor*. She gives us *leche* . . . *y queso*, cheese, *y mucha mierda. ¿Qué es el inglés por mierda, señor?*'

'Cow-shit', I said briefly. I had quickly realised there was no homespun philosophy on offer here. On the other hand, my father-in-law owned a ranch in Chile. We had mountains of manure, and I am something of an expert on the subject.

'*Sí* . . . *eso*. Now this we put on the fields for to grow the crops, the wheat, and every day, *gracias a la vaca*, we have more *leche*, more *queso*, more. . . .'

'*Mierda*', I said.

'*Sí*. An' when she is dead, we have the skin of the *vaca* for to make shoes an' handbags. *Señor* . . . *es muy útil, la vaca.*'

Absorbing stuff, eh? Not quite what might give a reviewer, reading these words over his pipe and glass of port, any reason to nod sagely at this country sense and sensibility, but the best I can come up with at the moment. Why can't I meet someone *famous*. The snag was, and is, that I don't know any Spanish grandees. I've never been introduced to any great writers or famed intellectuals. If I were to chance on any by accident, they would hardly be lurking in some fly-blown bar on the Castilian *meseta* on the off chance that I might stop by. It may happen to others; they say it does and I will believe anything, but I *hae me doots*.

So, with such fascinating contacts not readily available, what theme should I choose to underpin this journey? Nobody in their right mind would walk across Spain just to go for a walk. No one in their right mind would walk across Spain. Even so, a walk of hundreds of miles across this wild and beautiful land must provide more than exercise and by the end of it I would have learned something. I had been puzzling over this question of a theme for some weeks before I saw the answer staring me in the face. On foot I would surely have a chance to see a different Spain from the one found on the Costas. After all, what did I *really* know about Spain? Hardly anything. I got out some books and looked up a few facts and figures.

Spain, I discovered, was the third largest country in Europe after Russia and France. That was a surprise. I had nursed the idea that Spain, even without Portugal grossed into the Peninsula, was larger than France, but not so. Spain, I read, covers an area of 194,885 square miles, or nearly 505,000 square kilometres. Spain is big. Into this space are crammed some thirty-eight million people, most of whom live in the big cities or around the coast. The centre of Spain is quite empty.

Spain is the most mountainous country in Western Europe. Even the flatlands which occupy much of the Central Peninsula are high, at an average of 600 metres or just under 2,000 feet, and they are not all that flat either, being seamed with steep hills or sierras. Even so, as my maps had already revealed, the great feature of Spain is this central plain, the *meseta*, which occupies most of the Peninsula between Cantabria and Andalucía. This is split by several mountain ranges, most notably the Sierra de Gredos and the Sierra de Guadarrama, which straddle the *meseta* of Castile, north of Madrid; the Sierra Morena, the Black Mountain, north of Córdoba, which divides Andalucía from Castile, and the Sierra Nevada, which lies above the Mediterranean. This last contains the highest mountain in Spain, the Mulhacén, which soars to over 11,000 feet (3,478 metres). The average height of the main sierras is about 6,000 feet, one third higher again than Ben Nevis, Britain's highest mountain, but these main sierras are just extreme examples of the breed. In Spain, on foot, you will find sierras everywhere, so that the hinterland can be best imagined as either a flat ironing-board plain, or a tumbled mountain range, or a mixture of both. I thought about this carefully, for terrain is the first limitation on the walker. I then turned my attention to the weather.

Millions of people go to Spain for the summer weather, but the weather of Spain is not always necessarily benign. In fact, it can get very cold and rainy in Spain, a point on which the Spanish Tourist Boards are remarkably reticent. Spain has a harsh climate and that pleasant, if scorching, day by the hotel pool will present quite a different picture to the thirsty walker frying out on the dusty *meseta* during the same daylight hours. I have been scourged by the Spanish sun while riding to Compostela in July and nailed down by a blizzard in the Pyrenees in the early days of October, so I know about the Spanish weather. Most of all, I know it is unreliable and has become especially so in recent years.

I had elected to time my walk across Spain in the period between mid-September and early November, hoping for mild autumnal days and the occasional drop of rain after the heat of high summer and the equinoxal storms of early autumn had passed. It was not to turn out like that. There is much truth in the remark that Africa begins at the Pyrenees. Crossing the *meseta* and sierras, I thought how much this central part of Spain resembled Africa, how much the Moors must have felt at home here, how the greener, cooler country of the north must have seemed so desirable, how different this heartland of Spain was from the Spain of the Costas. Tourism has simply nibbled round the edges of Spain, and spread itself only a few miles from the sea. Out in the middle of Spain lies another country and another world, one which I knew nothing about. The purpose of this journey, then, was to see it, learn about it, write about it. The heart of Spain would be my stage.

*   *   *

For characters to people this stage, I can summon up the past. Spain is a land with much history, some might say too much. 'Happy is the land that has no history', indeed, but Spain is not that kind of land at all. Unlike France or England, Spain is not a collection of former dukedoms and territories banded together by time into a whole, but an amalgamation of kingdoms: Castile, León, Aragón, Cataluña, Navarra, the Asturias, a melting pot of Christian and Moor. This burden of history has an effect today. As I ambled across Spain, I noticed again and again that I was meeting a quite different kind of people, sometimes in the space of a few miles. As I moved from Cantabria to Castile, from Castile to Extremadura, and so on to Andalucía, I met people as different from each other as the Scots are from the Welsh. I would have the chance and the time to learn all about these separate kingdoms of Spain and how they came together during the long process of the Reconquista. The Reconquista, the long march of the Christians from the Asturias to the Mediterranean, would give me a theme for my journey. With a theme to underpin my travels, things were looking up. I began to get quite excited. Other than countless kings there was Pelayo, that half-legendary Gothic hero who first turned back the Moors at Covadonga and so began the long process of the Reconquista; Rodrigo Díaz de Vivar, better known to history as El Cid; Juana la Loca (the Mad); Cesare Borgia; Cristóbal Colón (Christopher Columbus); Miguel de Cervantes and his creation Don Quixote; Al-Mansur the Moorish conqueror . . . and hundreds more. Thinking and learning about these people would take my mind off my problems as I plodded across the golden land of Spain.

*   *   *

This background settled, practical matters intruded once again. We were now in mid-July, with the departure date looming ever nearer. Going on such a journey requires a high degree of preparation, and since I was to go on foot, I took Uncle Podger's advice and began with my feet. The secret weapon of the walker is loop-stitched socks, so I bought six pairs of those. Then came the problem of boots. On my walk across France I wore a marvellous make of boots called Daisy Roots, which worked wonderfully well and never once gave me a blister, though my feet were often very sore and tender at the end of a twenty-mile day. Since the terrain of Spain promised to be much rougher than that of France, I felt the need for something rather more substantial, but when I consulted an American friend of mine, Joe Diedrich, who has walked about the world a bit, he thought rather differently.

'I've walked in the Himalayas and in Patagonia,' he said, 'and all I've ever worn are trainers. They're light, which is a great factor, and they're comfortable. Take a pair and try them. Heavy boots can really weigh you down, you know.'

That seemed good advice, so I put a pair of trainers on my list. At heart though, I'm a boot man, so I went to see Richard Parker down at the Daisy Roots factory at Midsomer Norton, and we spent an entire afternoon in his warehouse, where I tried out several models and took two pairs home for a test. In the end I chose a new pair of the lightweight Vettas I had worn across France, with the addition of a shock-absorbing inner-sole and a tough Sky-Walker sole. These boots worked excellently, so there only remained the problem of maps and weight, and both proved insuperable. The maps of Spain cannot yet rival the detail of the Ordnance Survey maps or those of the *Institut Géographique National* in France, and even up-to-date Spanish maps are said to be inaccurate, which always makes me nervous. My main problem was to obtain any maps at all of the appropriate scale. These must be 1:100,000 or less (bearing in mind that the smaller the scale the greater the detail; the 1:50,000 scale is more detailed than the 1:100,000). My usual source, Stanford's Map Shop in Long Acre, London, had a few of the 1:100,000 and some 1:50,000 scale, but not those of the areas I needed, and they said that to obtain more could take months. During our visit to Mallorca I tried all the shops in Palma, but they had maps of the Balearics only. This was getting tricky. I was running out of time and I didn't have the necessary maps, so I rang one of our former au pair girls, Piedad García, who now lives in Madrid, and asked her to investigate. She came back with the news that I would need at least *sixty* 1:50,000 scale maps to walk across the Peninsula, which I calculated would weigh a lot and take up most of the space in my rucksack. More problems . . . decisions, decisions! I finally decided to take twelve Peninsula-spanning, 1:400,000 scale maps for the main axis of my walk. This is a large-scale map and far from suitable for walking, and some of them were thirty years old or more, but what can you do? I decided to buy the 1:50,000 scale maps wherever I could. These were only seventeen years old, but what other option was there? Finally, for the Picos and the Gredos, I bought the guidebook and maps published by Editorial Alpina, who offer 1:25,000 scale maps for the high country. With those, a compass, and a bit of luck, I ought to get by. This wasn't Africa, after all.

My plans were given a further boost by another letter from Mr Champion:

Dear Rob,

I read your remarks on your coming walk across Spain with considerable interest. It recalled memories of my own first experience of pedestrian camping in Spain. That was in 1924 and things have changed a lot since then.

I am glad that you have found a source for the 1:50,000 military maps but you will find them very poor compared with the Ordnance ones and unreliable for footpaths. The main roads have been brought more or less up to date but footpaths are shown that must have disappeared years ago and many good ones are omitted. Incidentally, I checked the weight of a bundle of eight sheets and made it 12oz. As you will presumably need well over fifty sheets, they will make some inroads in your 20lb target.

Spain provides some of the best and some of the worst country in the world for walking. In some areas there is no alternative to the main roads and everywhere in Spain motor traffic has increased enormously in the last few years. Fortunately many roads have very wide verges, originally intended for driving animals, but there is not much fun slogging for twenty miles along a straight road and then finding that the scenery has hardly changed since you started. *The moral is to avoid the plains of Castile* (I tried).

I suggest that the best way of route planning would be to get the general Michelin map of Spain and Portugal No. 990 – 1:100,000. This shades in green all the areas that are mountainous or wooded and the idea would be to pick out a route passing mainly through green areas and to select un-numbered roads, many of which are really only tracks. This would, of course, involve quite a lot of mileage as compared with the direct highways but should provide a lot of very enjoyable walking and camping. The Spanish Tourist Office has useful material; I recommend their booklet, *Nature in Spain*. There should be no problem in finding overnight camp spots in the mountain areas. Organised sites in urban areas are comparatively few. Remember that in autumn it rains in Spain. How much in a particular year is a matter of luck. Also it can be very cold, particularly at higher altitudes.

I wish you the best of luck. I only wish I were young enough to do the same thing myself. Please write if you think that I can give any useful advice. I will be interested to learn how your plans develop.

Yours sincerely,

C.L. Champion

My final worry was weight. I hate to labour the point, but if I don't, I'll get a lot of those letters written in green ink on recycled paper, pointing out the error of my ways. If I could have obtained accurate, up-to-date information on accommodation, I could have dispensed with much of the camping gear, all of which I had taken to France and never used once. Spain, I rather fancied, would be a different proposition. I was still determined, from bitter experience, to travel as light as possible. This meant cutting my kit to the bone; one spare shirt instead of two, one camera, a lightweight tent, no sleeping mat, no spares. There are those who slip in small items on the theory that they weigh nothing, but they fool themselves; everything weighs something. The greatest weights were two notebooks, one in which to write the travelling draft of this book, and another in which I would attempt to work out the plot of my next novel. This was to be my intellectual exercise, for I decided to go without something to read. In the end, I put in a paperback copy of *Poetry, Please*, which contains a hundred poems, but leaving out books was among my biggest mistakes. I will never again travel without something to read. Poetry is a good choice for the weight-conscious traveller, because it offers a choice of entertainment. You can read it, or declaim it, or try to learn it. To learn a hundred poems by heart would provide a diversion from the problems of plot. I also took my horn-handled walking stick, the companion on my walk across France and a most necessary aid in fending off dogs, probing the depths of bogs or streams, or simply helping me hobble down rocky mountain paths. In the event, it came to have more uses than that; but for the fortunate presence of my heavy walking stick, I might never have completed this journey.

Even so, deciding to write a book rather than read one seemed like a good idea at the time. That is what the cowboy said when they asked him why he had taken his clothes off and jumped into the cactus. The weight was still crushing. When I heaved the Karrimor rucksack onto the bathroom scales, the needle swung round to a hefty 37lb, and that was without food and with an empty water bottle. I purged the rucksack of three pairs of socks and half-a-dozen tent pegs. A full kit list is given at the end of the book and, basic as it is, it still weighed far too much for a hot, twenty-mile day across the plains and sierras of Spain. The decision on when to go walking had largely been decided by other work and the time needed for preparation, but when the day of departure finally arrived, I can't say I was ready. I had the kit packed and the book contracted, but I was not remotely fit and our Spanish contacts, who had been charged with setting up the Ferret support section of the walk over the first four days, were still remarkably silent.

*   *   *

Even so, we were as ready as we could be, and something should be left
to chance. Geoff had finally elected to join me in Ronda. 'Outside the
bullring on the 20th at four o'clock and don't be late!' The four Ferrets
were going to walk with me from Arenas, when we would, with luck, have
a support vehicle for the rucksacks plus the chance to get fit and have a
few laughs before they turned back and I was finally on my own. I don't
mind being on my own because, to quote Thoreau: 'The man who goes
alone can start today; but he who waits for another, must wait till that
other is ready'. It is often better to go alone simply because it is easier,
but having a companion gives you someone to talk to and someone to
write about. The word 'I' is almost as boring to write as it is to read if
you are forced to employ it all the time. Besides, I like the Ferrets and,
a final worry, I was starting to feel unwell. My wife occupies the position
of resident hypochondriac in our household, so I kept quiet about this
feeling of unease, until I finally decided to creep off and see a doctor.
This was done in Mallorca where the doctors seem to have time and call
you by your first name, which makes bad news less alarming. He listened
to my chest, pumped up my arm, drained off a phial or two of blood,
and when all the tests were completed suggested a holiday. I pointed
out that I was already on holiday, three whole weeks of it. He said he
was thinking of something longer. 'How much longer?' I asked. 'Say a
year', he suggested. A year! I did have a regular buzzing and tingling
sensation in my chest and left arm, which is said to be a Bad Sign. I also
felt like death, but a year was impossible. He shrugged his shoulders and
shook my hand, and I went off to walk across Spain. Doctor Footpath can
cure almost anything.

*   *   *

We left Plymouth on the *Bretagne*, the new flagship of the Brittany
Ferries fleet. It was a bright morning, full of late summer sunshine,
and if there is a better way to go walking than by sailing to the start in
a comfortable, well-run ship, I have yet to find it. We ate and drank and
put the world to rights for the next twenty-four hours, and all seemed set
fair. Then we arrived in Santander and met the first big setback.
    Santander is a good spot to make a landfall in Spain. The bay of
Santander is wide and beautiful, backed by the Picos mountains and

flanked by long golden sandy beaches. This is the capital of Cantabria, the Green Land of Spain, a far cry from the hot and dusty Mediterranean Costas. Santander was almost destroyed by a great fire in 1941, but it has been carefully rebuilt and the beach suburbs have an almost Edwardian air of leisurely grace and charm. This part of Spain is where the Spanish choose to go on holiday, and it has long been a stamping ground of the Ferrets. We were itching to go back to our favourite haunt hereabouts, the little village of Sotres in the Picos de Europa. Other people visit Cantabria to see the prehistoric cave paintings at Altamira – if they are allowed in – or to stay at the *Gil Blas parador* at Santillana del Mar, which is a jewel of the Romanesque, set in golden stone, but for the Ferrets there is no place like Sotres.

Sotres has four bars, one television set, low prices and a great quantity of manure. Manure is indeed the main export of Sotres, and the place is awash with it, quite literally if it should rain, and it rains rather a lot in Sotres. Some people might regard Sotres as ghastly, but there is nothing the Ferrets like better than to slog over the hills from Fuente Dé to Sotres, getting soaked to the skin along the way, and finish up in the *fonda*, where a very good evening costs very little money. A tour of Sotres by night would be rather brief, but if you like to get away from the madding crowd and visit a spot where the other, wiser, travellers never go, Sotres is a definite must. I had included Sotres as one of my essential places on this walk, but events were to keep us apart.

None of the arrangements we had asked for had been made. Even worse, the local people had arranged something quite different. I have to say that I then experienced a severe sense-of-humour crisis. Paco, our guide-to-be, declared that as the country south of the Picos was both flat and boring, he had decided to save us from ourselves and arranged something much more interesting; a series of day walks from a central point. I could have strangled him. For the record, there are some sixty miles of beautiful hill country south of the Picos, long before the *campo* of Castile, but since all the arrangements had already been made, we were in a quandary. Well, I was in a quandary.

'We appear to have two incompatible plans here,' said Peter, when Paco revealed his intentions that evening. That was the first time I knew we even had two plans, but if they were incompatible, I could easily make them fit. Paco had decided that our first day walk would be through the Cares Gorge to Caín. This fitted in with Geoff's route and would take us south. Therefore, we could walk together for a while and then, when the others turned back at Caín, I would simply continue on my way, as intended, towards the south. Toby suggested that I might stay with the Ferrets and walk about the Picos for a few days and they would run me south by car before leaving and so make up my lost time and distance. I was against this for various reasons. Firstly, it was not what we had spent months planning. Secondly, if I walked anywhere at all it would be in my declared direction: south. A step anywhere else was a step in the wrong direction. Thirdly, I was well aware what the yah-boo brigade back in Britain would say if the Ferrets returned to London and said I had started my walk across Spain with an eighty-mile car ride. Anyway, I was walking south.

Even so, I enjoyed meeting Paco, one of the real mountain men. Over dinner, he confided that if he was going to walk across Spain, he would allow a couple of years for the journey. I pointed out that that meant about a mile a day, but I took his point. There is a lot to see in Spain but the walker is limited by the fact that the feet and legs will refuse to function after twenty miles. The most beautiful spot, perhaps just five miles off your path, will take half a day to get to and back again, so although much is gained by walking, much has to be left for another time. Anyway, we had a pleasant enough evening and I got my sense of humour back.

Pique apart – and it was largely my own fault for not doing a reconnaissance first – you need to be prepared for a caper like this. You have to decide what you are going to do, and how you are going to do it. You can't let your plans and decisions be sidetracked by other people's ideas and alternatives or you will never get anywhere. There used to be a saying in the Commandos: 'It's all in the heart and the mind', and very true it is. My mind was made up and I wasn't about to change it.

*   *   *

All things considered, we spent a rather pleasant afternoon and evening in Llanes, a pretty little port on the green coast of Cantabria. When I got up next morning it was raining. Great wreaths of clouds were slipping down over the north face of the Picos and the day looked dreary, not at all the ideal conditions for the start of a walk. Rather to my ill-concealed surprise, the new arrangements seemed to be working. One of Paco's young assistants was actually outside the hotel with his Land Rover, all set to take us up to the start of the walk at Arenas, the northern entrance to the famous gorge, the *garganta de Cares*. We had breakfast, a rather silent meal, then piled ourselves and our rucksacks into the Land Rover and set off at great speed on a white-knuckle ride to the mountains. Half an hour later we skidded headlong into the front of a bus.

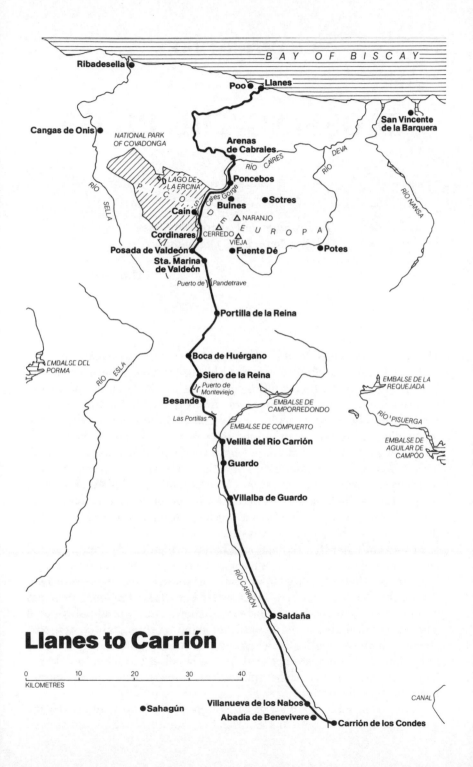

BAY OF BISCAY

Ribadesella
Poo • • Llanes
San Vincente
de la Barquera
Cangas de Onis •
NATIONAL PARK
OF COVADONGA
Arenas
de Cabrales
RÍO DEVA
RÍO CAIRES
RÍO
RÍO NANSA
RÍO SELLA
P I C O S
LAGO DE
LA ERCINA
Poncebos
Cares Gorge
Bulnes • Sotres
Caín
△ NARANJO
D E
△ CERREDO △
Cordinares
E U R O P A
VIEJA
Posada de Valdeón
• Fuente Dé • Potes
Sta. Marina
de Valdeón
Puerto de) (Pandetrave
Portilla de la Reina
EMBALSE DEL
PORMA
RÍO ESLA
Boca de Huérgano
EMBALSE DE LA
REQUEJADA
Siero de la Reina
Puerto de
Montevivejo
EMBALSE DE
CAMPORREDONDO
RÍO PISUERGA
Besande
Las Portillas
EMBALSE DE COMPUERTO
EMBALSE DE
AGUILAR DE
CAMPÓO
Velilla del Río Carrión
Guardo
Villalba de Guardo
RÍO CARRIÓN
Saldaña

Llanes to Carrión

0   10   20   30   40
KILOMETRES

CANAL
• Sahagún
Villanueva de los Nabos •
Abadía de Benevivere •
• Carrión de los Condes

CHAPTER THREE

CROSSING THE PICOS

Tres Espagnoles; quatro opiniones
(Three Spaniards; four opinions)

Old Spanish Saying

The impact was considerable. Fortunately we were so packed in with rucksacks and swaddled in our hard-hitting outdoor clothing, that no one was hurt, give or take a few bruises. We climbed out and inspected the two vehicles. The Land Rover was firmly embedded in the coach, so we recorded the incident with our cameras and then stood about in the rain while the two drivers examined the damage and looked gloomy. All things considered, I thought they took it very well. The normal course of events following a collision in Spain is that the drivers leap from behind their steering wheels to engage in a bout of fisticuffs. This pair seemed too pacific for that and settled for an exchange of cigarettes and, while a crowd of locals assembled from nowhere to admire the damage, we drifted down to the village of El Cerezo and into the bar.

El Cerezo is hardly a village and barely a hamlet. As Peter pointed out, it can only boast 'a byre, a barn and a bar', but the bar was at least interesting. This was a real Asturian bar, selling dusty bottles of beer and local cider. In rural Spain this sort of bar is also the local shop and it sold galvanised buckets, cowbells, bellows, curious knobbly-soled clogs of the kind clearly most useful for skipping through cowpats, plus sharpening stones and balls of string; a utilitarian kind of pub, the bar at El Cerezo. Mine host appeared from a hovel at the back to dole out bottles of beer, clearly of the opinion that a few crashes on the corner might be good for trade.

Here we stayed for an hour or so, with periodic forays out to view the growing traffic jam, until the approaching sound of sirens announced the arrival of the Guardia Civil. After that, the road block vanished as if by magic. Our transport, however, was clearly in no state to move, the radiator smashed, the front wings forced back upon the tyres. When we attempted to start the engine, a menacing cloud of oily black smoke crept from under the bonnet. The Ferrets were fairly philosophical about this, but I was getting anxious. Time was wasting, I had a long way to walk that day, and my expedition seemed to be stalled yet again. Then a friendly hotel owner appeared, also complete with Land Rover, and offered to drive the luggage to his hotel at Poo, where the Ferrets were to stay, and then take us on to our start at the northern end of the Cares Gorge at Poncebos. This gentleman drove at a much more sedate pace, and by just after noon we had dropped off the luggage and bumped up the track to our starting point, already high in the Cares Gorge. We were about to set off at last. The only current snags were that Peter was erupting with explosive sneezes every few minutes, declaring that he got colds like other people got the Black Death, and it was raining. For my part, since it was already early afternoon and I still had about twenty miles and a mountain range between me and my first stop, I was anxious to be off.

*   *   *

There are two ways through the Cares *garganta* between Poncebos and Caín. A flat lower path runs fairly near the river, while the true *senda*, which climbed and climbed high above the torrent, runs over a series of ever higher ridges, set hundreds of feet above the sheer drop into the gorge itself. This is a fairly vertiginous path until it falls away at last, after several miles, onto level ground. As an introduction to a walk across Spain, this route through the Cares Gorge could hardly be bettered for spectacular scenery and soaring views. Much to my surprise, this being late September and a terrible day to boot, the path was fairly crowded. French, German, Spanish, even English walkers, were out there enjoying the challenge of this classic trail, some clad in the most unsuitable garments for a spot of serious walking. We even met, and swiftly passed, a group of mountain bikers, all struggling uphill over the badly broken ground, pushing their laden machines. Now with the walk finally under way I had, at last, a little time to think.

*   *   *

Quite apart from any geographical convenience, a walk north to south follows the path of the Reconquista, the Reconquest of Spain by the Christians from the Moors. Although the process itself took centuries, it began hereabouts in the Picos de Europa, from the cave at Covadonga.

Spain (*Hispania*) enters history with the Romans. Although it had already been known and partly colonised by the Phoenicians and the Greeks, their settlements usually lay around the coast and they made little impact on the interior. Hannibal brought his Carthaginians here during the Punic Wars of the 2nd century BC, and the Romans duly followed, founding Córdoba as their capital in 151 BC. The Romans stayed until the 5th century AD, when they in turn were overrun by the Visigoths who, having sacked Rome, advanced across southern France into Spain and established their capital in Toledo. Their rule was somewhat brief, less than a hundred and fifty years. Then the Moors came across the Straits of Gibraltar in AD 711 and swiftly overran all but this small corner of the entire Peninsula. The only portion of the country to resist effectively was in the Picos de Europa, where a local Visigothic lord, Pelayo, set up a centre of resistance and beat them back. After ten years of guerrilla warfare the Moors withdrew from Cantabria and flooded north across the Pyrenees into France, where they were defeated and repulsed by Charles Martel at the Battle of Poitiers in AD 732. Pelayo defeated the Moors in pitched battle at Covadonga in 718, and was crowned king of the Asturias before his death at Cangas de Onis in AD 737.

Cangas de Onis is therefore one of the essential places to see in the Picos. It lies on the Río Sella, just a little place of solid yellow-tiled houses, but it was the first capital of a recognisable Spain. The Spanish like to move their capitals about, and a number of towns held the honour before it settled on Madrid in the 16th century. The Asturian kings set up their capital at Onis about AD 740. They worshipped in the Church of Santa Cruz, and buried their kings and nobles here.

Looking around these bleak northern mountains (and bleak they were indeed on that dull, grey, rainy day), it is not hard to imagine why Pelayos' resistance was so hard and so successful. This is a land shaped by nature for guerrilla warfare. There are few roads and a great shortage of tracks, just a few rough, ankle-twisting mule trails and hump-backed Roman bridges to provide a means of communication between the isolated mountain communities which lie along the rushing torrents of the Cares or the Deva. Years ago, when I visited little Bulnes, which is one of the more notable villages in the Picos, the population was just eight, including a newborn baby. A few years later, when the Ferrets walked to Sotres, we arrived just after electricity and just before the telephone. If you want to step back in time in Western Europe, the Picos is a good place to visit. If you want to travel even further back, you can visit the caves at Altamira. The prehistoric paintings at Altamira rival those of Lascaux and, unlike the ones in France, may even be seen from time to time if you ask nicely at the local tourist office, or have a quiet word with the porter at the *Gil Blas parador* in Santillana del Mar. There are a few such places here, suitable for the motorist and package tourists, but these high hills of the Picos are more suited to the botanist, the caver and climber, and the birdwatcher. These are no gentle hills, but sheer-sided, jagged mountains, cleft by deep gorges where eagles soar in the thermals. The eagles were there, circling high above the mountains, but even down in the Cares Gorge the views are imposing, especially the one across to the great rocky spike of the Naranjo de Bulnes, the most spectacular of all the Picos summits.

*   *   *

A lightly-laden walker would take about three hours to walk from Poncebos to Caín, on the switchback mountain footpath. This runs first across the high shoulder of the mountain before descending to a cart-wide ledge cut out of the sheer cliff. Here the rock comes down to brush your hair in places, as you duck through tunnels or cross little bridges like the *Puente de los Rebecos*, the Bridge of the Ibex, high above the noisy, rushing torrent.

The early part of the walk passed pleasantly enough until about mid-afternoon. Then the others decided to stop for their picnic lunch, taken from a goodly number of plastic bags supplied by the hotelier at Poo. Since we had started late and I wanted to make Posada de Valdeón that night, I decided to press on, but stayed for a moment before departure to record a message for Keith's radio programme. While we were doing this, John was attacked by a goat.

The spot selected for this picnic lunch was clearly well used by walkers and equally well known to goats. A large nanny-goat was lying in ambush behind a rock and shot into view as soon as the sandwiches appeared. This was no ordinary goat. She went after John's lunch with all the enthusiasm and agility of a basketball player, her head shooting at his sandwiches over his shoulder, round his back, across his knees and under his arm, while he fought her off with one hand and tried to eat a large cheese roll with the other. This is not easy. When her initial assault failed, the goat drew back a few feet, snorting with exasperation, dropped her horns and butted John full in the back. She then turned her attention to Toby. Toby, who had been watching this performance with crammed mouth and bulging eyes, appeared to be having a fit.

'I'm no good with animals,' John grumbled, as the Ferrets hurriedly packed up their sandwiches and fled to goat-free ground. I left them to it and marched on for Caín.

By the time I got to Caín, I was drenched with sweat, spray and rainwater. I still had a long way to go before I reached my night-stop at Posada, so I took only a brief look round before the next leg, which began with a gruelling uphill slog to the viewpoint or *mirador* at Tombo. On a good day this gives great views of the surrounding peaks, and also marks one of the entrances to the National Park of Covadonga, the first nature park established in Spain, back in 1918, long before the present heyday of conservation. It covers much of the Picos, with peaks soaring to over 2,400 metres or 7,872 feet. Although the locals' claim that there are still wild brown bear and wolves in the Picos may or may not be true, there are certainly lynx, wild cats, otters and ermine, and a great quantity of deer, which I could hear roaring away in the woods as I plodded up the road from Caín.

Spain is not over-blessed with National Parks. At the moment there are only four, at Ordesa and Aigües Tortes in the Pyrenees, on the Coto Doñana in the estuary of the Guadalquivir south-west of Sevilla, at Las Tablas de Daimiel in La Mancha, and this one here at Covadonga. The Covadonga park lies at the western end of the Picos and although the region is rich in wildlife, it was originally established in 1918 as a memorial to the battle of Covadonga, which took place 1,200 years earlier in AD 718.

Before I made my first trip to the Picos many years ago, I asked a mountaineering friend about these peaks and he told me only that, 'They go straight up and down, just like the Dolomites'. In fact, although there is a similarity, the Picos, like the Spaniards, are rather more harsh than their Italian counterparts. The banana-like Naranjo de Bulnes is probably the most spectacular peak, but there are several more over the 2,400 metre mark; the highest one, the Peña de Santa de Castilla, rises to 2,592 metres (8,503 feet), the Torre Cerrado to 2,648 metres (8,687 feet), and here in the centre the Peña Vieja to 2,613 metres (8,572 feet). The Naranjo de Bulnes rears up out of this mass for over 400 metres. The west face was first climbed as recently as 1974 by a team of four Spaniards, who got to the top with the assistance of two hundred and twenty pitons, ninety expansion bolts hammered into the face, and great quantities of rope. Chris Bonington once told me that if the team was big enough and you used enough aids, you could get up anything. The Naranjo is the Eiger of the Picos; the first ascent up the north-east face was made in 1904, and not many climbers have scaled it since, although the long west face route is becoming steadily more popular.

I am not a climber, so for me the appeal of the Picos is the walking and the wildlife. The rock is limestone and the walking is hard, but the rewards are considerable. Rocky mule trails are the main means of travel, and from late May to October the Picos are a delight. If there are bear and wolf hereabouts, I have seen neither, but there is certainly a great variety of birds — eagles, griffon vultures, buzzards, alpine choughs — which rest on the sheer cliffs behind the *parador* at Fuente Dé, and a great quantity of warblers, flycatchers, game birds and thrushes. Browsing along with a field guide, the botanist can find oxlip, orchids, all kinds of heath and heather, Spanish gorse, bellflowers . . . the list is endless. There are trout in the lakes at El Enol and La Ercina, and salmon come to spawn in the Ríos Cares, Deva and Nansa, which cut the Picos into several parts. For those who like walking and wildlife, the Picos are quite wonderful, and Paco was right to recommend a stay here.

*   *   *

Once past the Mirador del Tombo another steep little climb took me through the pretty village of Cordinares, and with one final push, very weary now, I reached the head of the Valle de Valdeón and into my reward. Suddenly, the steep grey mountains moved back, and lower hills, clad now in golden autumn bracken, swept up from the fields ahead to frame a wide, green, rolling country, quite beautiful in the slanting evening light, a fine sight at the end of a very long day. On the way down the hill to Posada, I had a shouted conversation with a lady wielding a hoe in a field, and then with another plying an axe in her garden. The women seem to do most of the manual labour hereabouts. Both assured me there was plenty of room in the village and so it proved. Within half an hour I had found a small, very small, room in a *fonda* for just 900 pesetas (about £5), and by nightfall I was sitting in a bar writing up these notes. Only 680 miles still to go, if Geoff's estimate was accurate. If that glimpse of the country ahead in the evening light was anything to go by, I had some glorious walking to look forward to over the next few days. I had also discovered the Spanish *fonda* and I was to become addicted to it in the weeks to come. This one at Posada was typical of the breed, and is worth describing.

I had still not solved the accommodation problem, which meant that part of the load on my back consisted of a tent. No one is less averse to a spot of luxury than I am, so where a *parador* lay on my route I had booked a room. This, apart from ensuring that I had a bed for the night, gave me a periodic contact point in the event of disasters at home, and if I could maintain my rate of advance, a series of pegs to hang the journey on. I don't mind camping, but after this first *fonda* at

Valdeón, I intended to get a roof over my head wherever possible. The sign to look out for in Spain is *Comidas y Camas*, meals and beds. The bed may be small and the food simple, but who needs more? My room at this *fonda* was the kind you might describe as adequate. About the size of four telephone boxes, it contained a four-foot bed, a wardrobe, a desk, a chair and a bedside table. A naked lightbulb hung from a wire on the ceiling. When I put the rucksack down there was nowhere else to stand. The walls were green, the floor bare boards, but at the end of a hard day it was paradise. There was a bar downstairs, and dinner in the offing. I had a cold-to-tepid shower in the bathroom down the corridor and counted my blessings. Day one had passed with no great difficulty and my walk had finally begun.

*   *   *

The mountains of the Picos de Europa are split between two northern provinces of Spain, the Asturias and Cantabria. The Asturias is the hardy, working-class corner of the Peninsula, the equivalent of Yorkshire, full of no-nonsense people, many of them in mining communities. During the Civil War of 1936–39 the miners of Asturias fought Franco's tanks with sticks of dynamite and his infantry with their bare hands; they suffered for their resistance after the Civil War was over. It remains a poor land, but proud of its tenacity in the face of adversity, natural and man-made, and proud of its history. In 1388, during the reign of Juan I of León, the region of Asturias became a Principality and the title Prince of the Asturias is borne by the eldest son of the King of Spain to this very day.

Cantabria, on the other hand, is the Green Coast of Spain: the Spanish Cornwall. To maintain the comparison, this is a place of sea and mountains, rather wet from the Atlantic winds and devoted to agriculture, which is no easy option in this land of small fields set on relentlessly sloping hillsides. Travel on any road in the Picos and you will find a farmer leading a cow, and when not employed in moving his cow about, he sits in a field and watches it. The point to bear in mind is that Spain is one of the few countries in Western Europe which still has peasants. These are small farmers, who wrest a living from a few fields and live in a way that has hardly changed for centuries, give or take a lightbulb. The peasants of the Asturias have a particularly rugged terrain to cope with and get most of the finer things of life, such as meat, milk and cheese, from their cows, whom they love with a passion that amounts to adoration. The local breed is the Tudanca, a type of Friesian, and they live cheek-by-jowl with their owners, in small barns and byres. You will not often see them in the fields, partly because the fields are small and sloping, partly because a byre-kept cow produces richer milk. What you will see in the fields, often close to the little farms, are the typical Asturian *hórreos* or granaries, where the corn is stored until planting time. These are said to date back to Celtic times and have hardly changed at all down the centuries. They are small, snug, sloping structures, typical of the rural situation. The overriding architectural form hereabouts is the Romanesque. Some places, like Potes and Santillana del Mar consist of little else, but if you have the time and patience, poke about in the valleys of the Picos and you will find beautiful, glowing Romanesque churches everywhere tucked away in the green hillsides. The Gothic style came into Spain down the *Camino Francés*, the Pilgrim Road to Compostela, and we will not meet it for a while yet. Meantime, we have the cow, and must not mock it.

The cow does produce all manner of useful things, as my informant had noted, but my favourite of these is a local pudding called *leche-frito*, or fried milk. Only a Cantabrian would even *think* of frying milk, but since I have wandered on to food, the local seafood is splendid and very varied. The Ferrets like their food and we once ate plates of oysters and whole lobsters at Santillana del Mar for a negligible amount of money, though our evenings in Sotres, the Pearl of the Picos, tend to go on rather longer and cost even less. Ah, I shall miss Sotres this time round. That, in a way, is the snag with walking; you are limited by time and distance in the places you can visit. I would have liked to go back to Sotres on this walk, hell-hole though it is, or maybe travel west to see Oviedo, a marvellous city from all I've heard tell, but my feet will only take me so far, and my time is not limitless. I have to get on at twenty miles a day, and if I keep that up I will eventually reach Tarifa. Meanwhile, I must dine.

Mountain regions are not usually noted for *haute cuisine*, and the general fare on offer in the Picos tends to be of the simple, ample, rib-sticking variety. They make a good cheese around Arenas de Cabrales, and serve it with a rather flat kind of cider, *sidra*, which waiters froth up by pouring it into your glass from a great height. The fish is good, but the real local speciality is *pote asturiano*, which consists of ham, blood sausage and pig's ears, and does take a little getting used to. In Potes, which is the main town and a very pretty spot, the great dish is *cocido labaniego de Potes*, which is a stew of pork and vegetables. The local wine is the fearful Chacoli, which is definitely an acquired taste. The other great Asturian dish is *fabadci*, which is based on those white beans, *fabes*, which grow hereabouts, mixed with various parts of pig. A good meal in the Picos would be a soup, or a trout, followed by a thick stew, a dish of *leche-frito*, and that blue cheese from Cabrales, the

Spanish Roquefort, with a bottle of Rioja. That's what I had in Posada de Valdeón, and I dined like a king.

*   *   *

Posada is a tiny place, very popular with walkers, a fact indicated by the piles of rucksacks resting on every café terrace and at all the street corners. This is a point worth making. Your property is quite safe in the little villages of Spain. You can leave it unattended for hours and no one will touch it. In the cities they will steal the shoes off your feet. There are three or four *fondas* in Posada, all full on the night I was there, plus one adequate restaurant and a small supermarket. The nightlife is therefore minimal. The town lies at 900 metres (2,952 feet) and that night it got very, very cold.

Next morning, getting away early proved a problem. I felt like a *café con leche* to warm me up, and the waitress flatly refused to serve me before nine o'clock on the dot. Then there was a further delay because while my map indicated a footpath heading south out of the village, I could not locate it and no one in the village knew where it began. Various suggestions followed, including that I should take a taxi, wait for the bus, or go back to Caín. No one walked south, so why should I? The good walking hereabouts was in the Picos. I think they were all related to Paco. Even so, by nine-thirty I was at last on the road south, first towards Prada, a small suburb of Posada, then climbing steadily, up and up yet again, to Santa Marina de Valdeón, where a huge, grey-green rock occupied one side of the road, and another, crowned with a church, stood opposite, both guarding the entrance to the village. Like all the other villages hereabouts, Santa Marina smelt of cows, and I picked my path carefully up the main street, through steaming piles of manure. I'm not all that fond of manure. Past Santa Marina the road makes two massive swings up the mountain, but here the footpath to the Puerto de Pandetrave Pass (1,562 metres, 5,092 feet) definitely begins. Always willing to swap roads for footpaths, I followed it up the steep grass and bracken-covered hillside over the two road bends and so into the Reserva de Riaño, one of the many hunting reserves on the south side of the Picos. It was quite a climb. Dripping with rivers of perspiration – no, let's not be mealy-mouthed about it, sweat – I reached the Puerto de Pandetrave Pass. There are great views from here in either direction, back to the soaring grey cliffs of the Picos or south along the valley of Valdeón. Over to the east, hidden from view behind the hills, lies the little town of Potes with its beautiful Romanesque church, a great quantity of old bridges (which give the town its name), and the vilest wine in Europe. When the Ferrets visited Potes some years ago, we were royally entertained by the *alcalde* (mayor), who presented us with a case of his local brew as we were leaving. The Ferrets will drink almost anything, but the wine of Potes was beyond us. Hoping it would be stolen, we left the case of wine outside our hotel and it duly disappeared. Next morning, minus one bottle, it was back.

The mountains are spectacular around the Pandetrave Pass, but to my mind the southern view from here is rather more beautiful, a touch of the Scottish Highlands in the wilds of Spain, but a Scotland writ large and full of striking colours. Great green rocks stood cloaked with lichen, the hillsides were draped in purple autumn heather and golden bracken. Deer appeared round every bend, plunging off down the hillside at the crunch of my approaching footsteps, while great buzzards and eagles rose in the thermals. This is truly a magical land, and quite empty of people. On a more prosaic note, the sun came out to dry the wet socks hanging on the back of my rucksack, and even on day two of the walk, I was already an unlovely sight.

The sun soon came out to drive away the mists on this delightful morning. From the Pandetrave col the road swoops and swerves down the south side of the mountain, offering a clear route south and plenty of sunny corners even in the deep valley. I hate road-walking and soon took to the valley floor on the right of the road, which gave me the advantages of soft earth for the feet, and by cutting the corners I could reduce the distance. Following the path beside the stream, which was often difficult but never impossible, I stayed here until the path rejoined the road six miles down by the little Río Puma, a green, gurgling stream, full of fish, a tributary of the larger Río Bayones. I had been walking for five hours, so it was now mid-afternoon and time to cross the river bridge in Portilla de la Reina and stop for a beer at the *Bar Tirso*. I sat in the sun there, sipping *San Miguel* beer and chatting to señora Edelvira and her son Amador, until it was time to move on again. One of señora Edelvira's other sons is the porter at the *parador* at Fuente Dé, so we had a good chat about that, for jobs in the Picos are hard to find. Señora Edelvira was doing pretty well as her four sons and three daughters were all off her hands and working locally.

I had stormed here over a fairly long day and could happily have dozed off in the sun on the bar terrace for a spot of Iberian yoga. The siesta is a declining institution in Spain and was never popular in the cooler industrious north, but if you are hot and weary it has a lot to recommend it, not least because not much happens in Spain between two and five. So, unless you are eating, you might as well sleep. I have this antic urge within me so, after letting my socks dry out on the railings of the bar, I put them on again, said goodbye to the señora, and set off, gently strolling, for Huérgano.

Portilla de la Reina is not very big. In fact, Portilla is downright tiny, but it is very pretty and the southern gateway to the Picos. Apart from the *Bar Tirso*, it boasts a *fonda* and a couple of roadside restaurants. I could have stopped here but, especially in the early days of a walk, I like to get on. I also changed my Daisy Root boots for a pair of trainers to give any blisters a chance to heal and struck out west, down the wide green valley of the Río Bayones, for my night-stop at Boca de Huérgano, twelve kilometres to the south-west. When I got there I would have come over twenty miles from my starting point that morning at Posada de Valdeón. As with the morning, so went the afternoon. It was more of a stroll now, on flat ground beside the river and down a valley that widened by the mile to offer deep grassy meadows and orchards on either side, a distinct change from the barren mass of the Picos that lay just a day at my back.

Boca de Huérgano is also rather small, practically minute in fact, but it has a pleasant bar and what appeared at first to be a rather grubby *fonda*. It is set in more of that gloriously green Spanish countryside, with a ruined castle tower at one end of the village and the solid block of a mountain jammed into the pass at the other. Boca is a little oasis in which to spend the night, and since there was a *fonda*, my rucksack full of camping gear remained untouched. As a bonus my grubby *fonda* offered a real surprise, for once past the bar and through a storeroom piled with fruit and vegetables, I found that the rest of the building had been transformed into a glittering small hotel, with stripped pine walls, marble floors and brass light fittings. God alone knows where the money came from as the price was just 1,300 pesetas the night for dinner, bed and breakfast. They even had piping hot water in the showers and a line outside my window on which to dry my socks. I sat in the evening sun on the wooden bench outside the *fonda* and thought, not for the first time, how lucky I am.

CHAPTER FOUR

CROSSING LEÓN

León lies in torpid lethargy,
shrouded in the magnificence of
her past, and taking, it would
appear, an eternal siesta.

H. O'Shea *A Guide to Spain* (1865)

Having reached Boca de Huérgano and burst out of the Picos, it was time
for another look at my notes and a brief history lesson. These always make
more sense on the ground, and this is especially true in Spain where,
thanks to that multiplicity of kings and kingdoms, history tends to be
confusing. León was once a kingdom, and is now a province of the region
of Castilla la Vieja, Old Castile. The kingdom of León began at the start
of the Reconquista, some time in the 10th century, when the Christians
of the Asturias broke out of the mountains onto the edge of the plains and
adopted León as their capital. The kingdom of León then spread steadily
south from the Asturias to the frontier along the Río Duero, a path which
we shall presently follow. This frontier region had to be first conquered
and then held. To do this the Christians studded the land with castles,
castillos, which eventually gave this land the name of Castile. Castile
first became a county, held from the king by a *conde*, or count, as did
most newly-conquered lands at the time. In the early years of the 11th
century, the three kingdoms of Asturias, León and Castile, were briefly
combined under Fernando I, who scored great victories against the Moors
and pushed the Christian frontier from the Duero valley as far south as
Madrid. One of Fernando's captains was a legendary knight, Rodrigo Díaz
de Vivar better known to history as El Cid, but Spanish history is nothing if
not complicated, so we will leave El Cid and what happened to these three
Christian kingdoms after the death of Fernando I for another part of this
journey. Like the Asturian kings, I had made my way out of the mountains

to the plains, and like them, I was glad to be here. This is the place to look at the kingdom of León.

To do this we must first go back to Pelayo and his heirs. León itself, a very fine city with a splendid cathedral and a famous hotel, the *San Marcos*, lies away to the south-west, a far cry indeed from this frontier village at the foot of the Picos. The kings of the Asturias did not reign for long and it is said that the later ones bought their freedom from Muslim domination by paying a yearly tribute of a hundred virgins to the emir in Córdoba, then the capital of Umayyad Spain. The Asturian kings established their capital in Oviedo, where they received a steady stream of refugees from the Muslim south, the ancestors of the Mozarabs, and these settled on the frontiers of the Asturias. During the 9th century, Christian Spain received a great moral boost when the relics of the apostle St James were discovered at Santiago de Compostela, and the saint himself appeared to rally the Christian forces at the battle of Clavijo in 846, scattering the Muslim army with the aid of the Heavenly Host and his great war cry '*Santiago . . . y cierra España*', 'St James . . . and close up Spain'. This became the war cry of the Christian armies from that time on. By the end of the first decade of the 10th century the Christians had reoccupied about a fifth of the Peninsula.

During this period, between say AD 750 and 950, the plain of the Duero, which lies south of Guardo and León, was a ravaged, desolate area, but having shorter lines of communication, the Christians gradually gained the upper hand and had occupied much of the Duero valley by about 875. The great leader of the Christians during this period was Alfonso II of León, who appointed three of his sons to rule over his three subject kingdoms of León, Galicia and the Asturias. As happened to King Lear, this dividing of Alfonso's realm proved unwise. In 910 the three brothers dethroned and exiled their father, and then fell to quarrelling among themselves. The victor and the new overlord was García I of León, who became King of León, Navarra and the Asturias. This so-called Empire of León endured until the middle of the 12th century.

Alfonso II had adopted a policy his son was to continue. García I also endowed each of his sons with their own kingdom and gave them the lordship of Muslim territory beyond the frontier, so long as they could wrest it from the Muslim occupiers. This policy brought fire and sword to the Christian–Muslim frontier along the Duero. In this the Christian lords prospered and consolidated their conquests by building castles along the banks of the river to control any ford or bridge. The Muslim emirs were by no means subdued, however, and they, too, continued raiding in the north, burning Burgos in 924 and pushing García's successor, Ramiro II, back to within the confines of his León kingdom. Abd al-Rahman, then the caliph of Córdoba, raised a great army in 939, but the hastily gathered armies of León and Navarra routed him on the field of Simancas. When the caliph's officers retired in defeat to Córdoba, they found the banks of the Guadalquivir lined with crucifixes, to which they were presently nailed. Flushed with success, the León army marched south across the Central Cordillera to ravage Talavera. Meanwhile, a fresh kingdom was being carved out in the north, between the Duero and the Ebro. Centred on the rebuilt town of Burgos and surrounded by magnificent castles, this became the heartland of Castile. The first man of note to arise in Castile was the warlike Fernando Gonzalez, the Count of Lara. Fernando warred against the King of León, Sancho the Fat, and eventually became his equal, ruling undisturbed in his kingdom of Castile, and all was going well with these several Christian kingdoms, León, Castile, Navarra, until a new star arose in Andalucía, and put the Peninsula back into turmoil. This was the terrible Al-Mansur, and we shall hear more about him later.

This little tale does set the pattern for most of the Reconquista. The Christian states spawned others in an almost amoeba-like fashion as counts became, in effect, sub-kings and then rulers in their own right. There was strength in this because, mighty as the caliphs of Córdoba were, they could never quite overcome all the Christian kingdoms in one fell swoop. The Christian states nibbled away at Muslim territory, gaining ground until a caliph ruled in Córdoba who could drive them back, or a fresh wave of fanatical Muslims arrived from Africa to put steel into the languid Muslims of Andalucía. Let us leave it there for the moment and walk on towards the next landmark on my travels, the Río Carrión.

*   *   *

One of the particular blessings I was counting on this trip was the fact that I had already slipped into a routine. There are those who think that routines are boring, but I see a routine as a way of getting things done in the most efficient and painless way. When I was in the Royal Marines all those years ago, our great aim in life, apart from skiving and scrounging and hanging out in bars, was to get a good routine going. If we could do that, we were happy little Commandos. If not, long faces sprang up on every side.

For the long-distance walker, a good routine is essential, simply to get the miles done while keeping body and soul together. The first element in a good routine is an early start. I like to get the feet on the floor at the first peep of daylight and be on the trail as soon as it is light enough to read a map. The next element is to find a steady pace you can maintain all day and get into it as soon as possible. I prefer to start a little slowly, and then swing into my stride gradually, over the first hour, after which I keep going until I have either reached a point of interest or gained a significant distance. During this period the great thing to avoid is boredom. In some books the walker is forever stopping to sniff flowers or pat a passing caterpillar, but

I never have time for that. I enjoy the view if there is one, and otherwise let my mind drift into what John Hillaby used to call the 'skull cinema', where the brain takes over and you forget your feet. This is really daydreaming, and if you can get into a good, exciting daydream, where you make a million or win the VC, the miles spurt past unnoticed beneath your dusty boots. On this walk, and in particular on the plains of Castile which now shimmered somewhere ahead, my great problem was boredom, almost to the point of *cafard*. Here in the hills, where I had to pick my way from point to point, this was never a problem for I had plenty to keep my mind occupied in simply finding my way. I had never before been on a journey with antique maps, and since they were virtually useless, I found my way across country by a combination of compass bearings and heading towards the south without too much concentration on individual points along the way. As long as my face pointed south, that was sufficient, and by about four or five in the afternoon, if I had covered enough ground, it was time to seek shelter for the night.

Come the end of the day, and the routine continues. It is never a good idea to flop, groaning, on the bed, for there is work to be done. I would dump the rucksack, strip off and shower, using the shower to wash my clothes and socks, for these had to be hung out while there was still warmth in the air to get them dry. It usually took two days to dry a pair of socks, which were suspended from the rucksack straps during the day, and sometimes I had a damp shirt to put on in the morning, but if all went well I usually had cleanish clothes and a pair of dry socks to put on each morning.

Washing hung out, there was still work to be done, sights to be seen, bars to be explored, food to be purchased and, if possible, locals to be engaged in conversation. All this took place during what I came to refer to as the evening limp when, in my trainers and carrying my walking stick, I would seek out the main square and join in the evening *paseo*. Boca was too small for a plaza or *paseo*, so I just sat on in the sunshine outside the bar. I was tired, but tired or not, there were still things to do. Every day I had to translate the scribbled lines in my notebook into some form of coherent text in my big exercise book. This was often a considerable chore at the end of a dusty day, but it had to be done. I am glad I did it because, especially on the flat *campo*, the days soon became a blur. Besides, it gave me something to do in that waiting time between arrival and dinner – when I could get dinner.

All in all, I felt pretty content with my first few days on the trail. I had stormed out of the Picos like Pelayo, pushed my way across these beautiful gold and green foothills between the mountains and the *meseta*, and Old Castile, with all its romance and history, now lay just ahead. It would be two or three weeks before I saw mountains again.

*   *   *

My luck ran out a little that night when I failed to realise that the clocks had gone back. I awoke in a panic to find the hotel as quiet as death, at eight-thirty in the morning. This will not do; on a walk like this, early starts are essential. Tumbling down the stairs and out to find another freezing morning, my racket roused the señora, who was understandably somewhat put out to have me demanding *café con leche* far too early in the morning on the only Sunday in the week. However, she obliged, while I hurriedly packed, and thus organised I set off about nine. A hard frost was still freezing the road above the bridge as I headed out towards Guardo, which lay a long day's march to the south. Even so, and in spite of some large blisters on both heels, I was starting to enjoy myself. I was doing twenty miles a day or more, and my left arm had ceased to give those alarming tingles. So far, so good.

So far, also, nothing much had happened. I can report that in spite of Paco's doubts it is perfectly possible to walk south, across the Picos from Arenas de Cabrales to Guardo in about five days. There is no need to camp or carry weighty packs, for you can stop at *fondas* and have a great time. All would-be trans-Spain walkers should be grateful for this information, which is more than months of effort had provided me with before the start of my journey. I also felt good on this crisp autumn morning because the walk was already giving me what I needed most: the chance to do nothing, or rather, think of nothing but what I was about. Certainly, I had to walk a definite number of miles each day, come hell or hard weather, and I had to write notes for this book (and think about the plot of the next novel in my spare time), but the real pressure was off. They couldn't get at me here because, to within fifty miles, nobody even knew where I was. It was blessing-counting time as I strode along, swinging my stick.

Early starts are in general a good thing on this kind of caper, and I felt in fine form. My boots were comfortable, I had had a good night's sleep, and a big cup of coffee and half-a-dozen biscuits had set me up for the eighteen-mile slog to Guardo. This was also a good thing, because snacks are not easy to come by on the minor roads of Spain.

*   *   *

The countryside hereabouts, between Boca and Guardo, is still mountainous, but much more green and far less stark than the Picos. There is a good mix of bare mountain, open river valley and rolling foothills, these last

given over to beech trees and conifer afforestation. Hills bar the direct road
south, forcing the road to wind about along their sides, but I had already
learned to avoid this and the hard surface by walking directly from bend to
bend along the valley floor, hopping over the cropped frost-glinting grass,
slipping across stepping-stones when the river was shallow, and finding
the shallow parts by following cow-tracks. There were no cows but plenty
of cow-tracks. It may be simple, but it works, and it saves the feet from
too much wear and tear. You have to think of these things.

This method brought me, after an hour or so, just about coffee-stop
time in fact, to Siero de la Reina, another small, manure-splattered
hamlet. Here, even the older houses have abandoned their red-tiled
roofs for more utilitarian, if less attractive, corrugated iron or asbestos
sheeting. The main excitement on this Sunday morning was two men
who were dragging a reluctant cow down the high street, to great yells
of encouragement from the locals and a deal of barking from half-a-dozen
lurking hounds. One of the more popular delusions foisted on the world by
travel writers is that the Spanish are reserved. 'He was a typical Castilian,
tall, dark . . . dignified,' writes one very distinguished but obviously deaf
travel writer. All the Spaniards I have ever met, Castilians, Aragonese
or Andalucians, are small, pale and incredibly noisy. The Spanish are
fully-paid-up members of the Friends of Noise, an organisation that
contains Greeks, Italians and Chinese mah-jong players. The motto of
the Friends of Noise is 'Never speak when you can shout'. Members of
the FON all speak at the same time, never listen to replies and pit their
lungs against flamenco music and television sets. The effect on the passing
stranger can be wearing, and I shall deliver myself of a few thoughts about
the Spanish and television sets later on. Meanwhile, I will have my coffee
and crack my head on the door of the *servicios* on the way out. I am just six
feet tall, which is no great height these days, but I crossed most of Spain at
the crouch, smashing my head into door lintels at regular intervals, almost
kneeling to peer into every shaving mirror.

It was here in Siero that I had that long, fascinating conversation on
the merits of manure. I did notice that in spite of the general squalor,
the local girls, like most young Spanish women – I intend to generalise
– still managed to keep themselves neat and tidy, their hair brushed to
a high gloss and arranged in a glamorous coif, all ready for the evening
paseo. I remarked on this to my manure-obsessed companion, hoping to
change the subject, but what with the usual bar-room clamour and the
television set, I don't think he can have heard me. In Siero even the dogs
can do nothing quietly. As I left the village they skulked about my heels,
barking so hard that one of them fell over.

Past Siero the hills crowd in from either side and the road climbs steeply
to the first of two cols. This is the Puerto de Monteviejo, at 1,437 metres
(4,714 feet), but before I got there I saw a track leading off up the valley

to my right, round the humped *montaña* of Monteviejo, the Old Man's Mountain. Ever seeking the soft option, I thought that this might be an easier route. This proved to be a mistake. I shall try not to labour the point, but using antique, forty-year-old maps is a real trial. The excuse for even attempting to do so is that, with any luck, the way-finding situation will have improved since the map was drawn. In theory there should be more roads, more houses, more people to ask the way, but in the remoter parts of Spain the reverse is true. People have left the land and half the tracks on my map were either overgrown or had completely vanished.

The track here soon petered out in a swampy meadow and I was about to turn back for the road when I met señor Isidro. To be exact, I met his dog, a remarkably friendly Alsatian, which came lolloping up to play. The dog led me back to señor Isidro, who was sitting high up on the edge of the meadow, drinking something evil from a *porrón*. This he offered me, and I squirted the strong liquor into my mouth, forced it down my throat and declared it excellent. We then sat about in the sun to discuss our lives. I soon learned that señor Isidro was seventy-two, had worked in Madrid for Iberia, the Spanish airline, loved the countryside, and had never been to Britain.

'I will go when I am older,' he said cheerfully, 'and when I have more time. Now you, señor, where are you going?' When I told him I was walking to Tarifa, he blinked with amazement and looked at me almost nervously.

'In Andalucía . . . *no es posible*. Why don't you take a train? Are you Dutch . . . or German?'

'No . . . *yo soy inglés*.'

'Ah . . .! *Inglés*. . . .'

That seemed to explain everything. I was getting quite partial to the contents of señor Isidro's *porrón*, but time was yet again pressing and I was lost. When señor Isidro offered to show me the way out of this blind valley I had wandered into, I was very grateful. The way out led up the mountainside, no easy route for a heavily laden walker.

'What is the English for *arriba*?' he asked.

'Up,' I said.

'*¡Arriba, arriba!*' We climbed. In fact, we kept on climbing for nearly an hour, he like a mountain goat, me like an elephant. I had come this way around the Puerto de Monteviejo to avoid climbing, but we climbed, first up the bed of a stream, then up on a vertical earth bank cut in the forest as a fire break, then through a quantity of fallen trees. Señor Isidro, despite his age, climbed like a youngster, leaving me labouring behind under the dead weight of my rucksack, grateful when he stopped to listen to the distant roaring of the stags. Eventually, and none too soon, we emerged onto an open escarpment, and there, far before us, but definitely to the south, lay the silver ribbon of the road. I collapsed onto the grass groaning, while señor Isidro pointed out the way down to the valley.

'Go down there. Just by the bend you will find a spring, with good water . . . and then there is Besande and another col, not so high as Monteviejo. You must hurry if you want to reach Guardo tonight.'

We parted on the mountainside, and I ploughed down the slope, crashing through the bracken and the purple heather, out to the road and so to the spring by the river. Ah, blessed stuff, water. Why do I ever drink anything else? Then on across the meadows for a few miles, and when I finally got to Besande, everything was shut. Everything included the only bar, so I gulped more water from the fountain in the village centre and set off again along the river and up the hillside to the next col, the 1,275 metre (4,183 feet) high Alto de las Portillas. On the way there the countryside changed yet again, becoming rather more arid, with stony slopes falling directly onto the road from the encroaching mountains. The river ran out just below the col by the side of a dam, forcing me back onto the road and over the col. The view was again superb, a green and gold ripple of hill and valley falling to the distant plain.

Up here, by the col at Las Portillas, I left León behind and entered the next province to the south, Palencia. That made four provinces, Asturias, Cantabria, León and now Palencia, reached in as many days, so this at least felt like progress. As I descended the far side of the mountain in that warm afternoon sunshine, I felt like singing.

The sun was actually quite hot, really too hot for fast walking, but the views south and north were stupendous, and I soon managed to return to the valley, scrambling down to the grassy meadows far below the road. Then I followed the faint outline of a track down to Velilla del Río Carrión, which is a small, rather industrial place with a power station by the river, but on the whole a rather pleasant spot, especially in the bar which I found on the way in and stayed at for quite some time.

It was here, and not at Boca de Huérgano, that I finally realised my watch was an hour fast and I therefore had an hour in hand. This was welcome news. I was pretty tired by now, so I had a beer. Then I had another beer. While I was sitting in the gloom of La Cantina drinking my beer, the bar slowly filled up. It was quite a while before I realised that I was the focus of all attention, but the Spanish are like that. 'Hey, there's a strange fellow sitting in the bar down the road . . . come and look.' They all had a look, peeping over their shoulders from the bar, but nobody said a word to me. Well, I suppose it filled an otherwise empty Sunday afternoon.

I reeled out of La Cantina at about four and struck out fast for the last few miles, across the Río Carrión, for my night-stop in Guardo. I could happily have stayed in Velilla, which has a couple of likely-looking hotels. The one I inspected (and had another beer in) seemed full of friendly people, but I have this thing that if you have to do a day's stint, then you must do it, and not fall behind schedule. What you do not do today is a burden on tomorrow.

Guardo is a curious place. It owes its existence to the local anthracite mines, which are also responsible for the layer of black dust that coats the town, but clearly the coal mines are running out and there is an air of desolation about the place. Weeds are growing between the railway tracks, and many warehouses are empty. The town is busy enough and there are a number of bars and a couple of hotels, so I found a room without much trouble, but to my consternation, there was nowhere to eat on a Sunday evening. All I had had to eat that day were a few biscuits, taken twenty miles away and twelve hours before, so I found this information alarming. I prowled the town hungrily and dined at last on an egg *bocadillo*, served with great reluctance by a girl in a noisy bar, and crept off to bed still hungry, and desperate for something to read. One of my problems is that I am a very fast reader, so even a fat book would not have lasted me for long. I might have bought something in Spanish, but this was Sunday and the town was like a tomb, so to break the uneasy silence in my room and hear the sound of a human voice, I got out my copy of *Poetry, Please* and did some declaiming. Arthur Hugh Clough's *Say not the Struggle*, one of my favourite poems, went down very well. Then, into my stride and fuller voice, I attempted Rupert Brooke's *The Old Vicarage, Grantchester*. If you are ever stuck on a Sunday in a small hotel in a place like Guardo, the appeal of this archetypal English verse will become obvious. But at:

> God! I will pack, and take a train,
> And get me to England once again!
> For England's the one land, I know,
> Where men with Splendid Hearts may go . . .

there came a pounding and a shouting at the door. I opened it to reveal the landlord worried not about the din – what Spaniard ever worried about that? – but that I had smuggled someone in and we were quarrelling. I had to show him the bathroom and the book before he believed me, but when I offered to regale him with a snatch of English verse, he declined. 'Please don't make a noise,' he said. 'Some of my guests are sleeping.' Then, smiling at the wonder of it all, he departed. On the way downstairs he slammed every door so hard that the very windows shook. Only when I was writing up the incident later did it occur to me that it cannot be every day that a Spanish hotelier finds an Englishman declaiming Rupert Brooke in one of his bedrooms. It probably sounded just like noise.

CHAPTER FIVE

THE ROAD TO OLD CASTILE

*John Bull, like the snail, loves to
carry his native shell with him,
irrespective of changes of climate or
habits of different conditions and
necessities.*

Richard Ford *A Handbook for Travellers in Spain* (1855)

After Guardo it was soon clear that the nature of the country had
changed. To the north all is mountainous and wild, but south of here
the country has been tamed. The mountains were still clearly visible,
but heading south from Guardo, ambling along beside the Río Carrión
or trudging across the country south of Saldaña, it became more obvious
by the mile that I had left the mountains behind for a while and was
heading, like a lone yachtsman on the wide ocean, out into the almost
equally wide *meseta*, the great tableland that occupies the heartland of
Old Castile. That great plateau lay some days ahead, for this was not
yet the true *meseta*, but the *tierra de campos*, a place of farms, but still
significantly different from the land at my back. I had left behind the
country of the cow and moved into the country of the sheep.

I spent that day, a fairly long hike of some twenty miles, walking
between the main road and the Río Carrión, crossing ever flatter country
at a steady five kilometres an hour, through fields of maize and wheat
stubble, split up by great concrete irrigation channels. Some of these
I walked in, for they were quite empty, fairly wide, and kept me away
from those packs of dogs that came hurtling out yelping from every
farmyard. In between times, I sat in what shade I could find, drinking

from my water bottle and filling in the diary. There was not really a lot to write about but that hardly mattered. The important thing is to write something, for if you fail to write it down as you go, you will surely forget the manner of your passing. So I scribbled a bit and walked a bit, and in this fashion came at last to Saldaña late in the afternoon. The streets were a texture of bright sun and dark shadow, and here I finally got something to eat in a small restaurant where a sad little scene was being played out at an adjoining table. Grandmother had just spent the weekend with her children and grandchildren and now she was leaving and waiting for the bus, weeping silently while her family and the other café patrons sat about helplessly. 'Are you sad, *abuela*?' asked the smallest granddaughter. '*Sí*, very sad,' said the *abuela*. We all felt wretched, and watched them trail away towards the bus stop almost with relief. Poor lady.

I also discovered that I had developed sunburn, which was a cause for alarm. One of the reasons for choosing the autumn months to walk across Spain was that by the end of September the weather should be fairly cool and getting cooler, so that as I marched south, cool air would come with me, making the walking pleasant. In fact it was scorching, and hot weather and hard walking do not mix.

* * *

Saldaña lies, or rather crumbles away, around a small hill topped by a ruined castle, the whole encircled by the Río Carrión. I found another *fonda* here, scrubbed a little of the *campo* off my Rohan trousers and had yet another meal, before settling down for the night, a practice I was to follow where possible from now on. The snag in Spain is that everyone dines so late. You could fire a machine-gun in a Spanish restaurant between six and nine in the evening and never hit a waiter, so, when in *España*. . . . I arrived when I arrived, found my *fonda*, washed my socks and slept for a little if I could manage to ignore the noise. Then, after another splash or shower, I went out for a beer, a limp round the sights or a share of the evening *paseo*. That is a good routine, but I would prefer to dine about seven-thirty and be in bed by ten.

Spain really hasn't changed so much. In spite of outward appearances, it still moves to the rhythm of the sun. During the day, wise people stay in the shade, or under shady hats, coming out in the cool of the evening, much as they have always done, to meet friends, join a *tertulia* for a good, noisy argument, or just stroll up and down the Plaza Mayor, nodding to the passers-by. You can soon get used to a life like this. After dinner, drugged with weariness and wine, I would sleep like a log, get up at dawn or sooner and attempt to be away by first light. From Saldaña this was easy. I had my coffee with a crowd of workers in a bar, all of whom were spiking their coffee with gin or whisky, and after crossing the bridge over the Carrión, soon found a path through the fields running across country to the misty south again. It was going to be another scorching day.

*   *   *

Spain must be one of the few countries in Western Europe where shepherds still follow their flocks about, day by day, as they graze across the *meseta*. To be exact, they do not drive or follow their sheep but lead them, as shepherds were said to do in the Bible, and you will find these shepherds with their flocks everywhere on the *campo* of Castile. I met one of these flocks, complete with shepherd and dogs, a little south of Saldaña and, never having met a real Spanish shepherd before, I stopped for a chat. Shepherds lead a rather solitary life (it goes with the job) and Jesús, like everyone else I had met so far, had never met an Englishman, so we started even. I began, as is wise, by admiring his sheep. This was easy, because his sheep were beautiful. Their fleeces a pure white, shading to a rich, silky cream, they moved across the cropped wheat like a shimmering blanket, with hardly a bleat to mark their passing, though the air jangled to their bells. I was impressed, and I said so.

'*Gracias, señor*,' said Jesús, speaking proudly for his sheep. 'They are beautiful, but they have to be. We breed them only for their wool. A few months ago they would have been magnificent, but we shear them in July, before the real hot weather comes, so they are not at their best now. I have about 200 to 220 sheep here . . . it's enough for one man. We move only about four kilometres each day, and I live over there,' he pointed, 'in that village. Further south, in the *meseta*, they have to go a long way to feed each day, but here, with the rain and a good harvest to help as well, we can do well and not have to travel too much.'

Even so, it looked like hard, lonely work, out there on the sun-baked *campo*, and Jesús' dogs were little help. These were not true sheepdogs like our Border collies, but a collection of mongrel curs who slunk about the edge of the flock, some trying to get behind me for a quick bite. All seemed unresponsive to any command. There were, in fact, no whistles or signs to command them. Jesús got them to do his bidding by hurling a stone at them or across the front or sides of the flock. The dogs promptly dived after the stone and the sheep duly scattered in the right direction. It was hardly out of *Lassie*, but it seemed to work. We shared some hard cheese and a mouthful of wine from

Jesús' bottle. Then, with another handshake, we went our separate ways.

*   *   *

It took me two days to walk across the flat country from Guardo to Carrión de los Condes, and I have to say that it was something of a trial. Something was seriously wrong with my left foot. To come straight to the point, when I finally removed boot, sock and moleskin in Saldaña, my heel bore the largest, fattest blister I have ever seen, and I have squeezed blood from my socks before this. Every walker worth his salt has done that, so I won't complain, but a big blister can be a considerable nuisance. Limping along with a vague sense of disquiet about your feet is one thing; knowing that you have this great big blister is quite another. My speed, which at best varies from slow to slower, quickly dropped to a limp. My walk must come to a halt until I could dry this blister out, and I decided that the best place to do this was at Carrión de los Condes, a full day's walk south of Saldaña. This lies on the Pilgrim Road to Compostela, a fine old town, and one of my favourite places anywhere on the *Camino Francés*. This decided, I limped on from Saldaña, thinking that the quicker I got to Carrión, the sooner my blister would heal.

The Río Carrión is a pleasant stream in summer days, but it must be wild in winter, for all the bridges over it were much wider than seemed necessary for the late summer flow. At Guardo the river is a foul, polluted stream, but the Carrión picks up a little as it moves south. Though I started out from necessity on the main road, as soon as I had cleared the various factories which mark the outskirts of Guardo, I moved down into the valley. Thereafter, I kept to those concrete channels over the ploughland, or just walked straight across the fields, which were still unploughed after the wheat harvest.

I wrote the first draft of this book each day as I moved along, trying to get about a thousand words scribbled down by evening, while the events of the previous twenty miles or so were still fresh or even, as happened quite often, a total sun-blasted blank. It is a fact that while most of Spain does not have footpaths in the familiar British or French fashion, with fingerposts and waymarks and 'Beware of the Bull' signs, you can get along perfectly well off the roads by using your wits, following tracks and using your compass to maintain direction. Here, in the valley of the Carrión, it was even easier. I always had the high escarpment of the *campo* to my left, and the river valley, across which the stream wandered, led me down directly to Saldaña and beyond. As long as I kept the river on my left it was easy. All I had to do was keep walking or, as time went by, limping, and slowly the little dusty villages went by. I broke this up from time to time by following a rough stone and chipped earth track which seemed to run south all the way to Carrión de los Condes, once perhaps the main road, now a route for high-wheeled tractors.

*   *   *

September is a good month for crossing the *campo*, for after the wheat has been cut you can walk almost anywhere, if you don't mind hard and often stony ground. Even so, it is tough going across the open fields, though rather better when stuck among the shady plantations by the river. When I ventured out onto the open plain, the sun hammered down on my head, thumping like a mallet on a nail. It is really a question of pressing on, making the happy discovery that I had reeled off another twelve kilometres from Saldaña by eleven in the morning. I had only managed another five by one o'clock when I arrived at the dusty village of Villanueva de los Nabos, which had no bar – a minor tragedy at that hour of a scorching day. Fortunately, it did have a tap in the main street, against which I sat to slake my thirst and fill my water bottle. Even better, from the road junction just outside the village, I could see the towers of Carrión de los Condes, now just three miles away. My way in led past the *Abadía de Benevivere*, the Abbey of Good Living, a strange name for a monastic institution. Benevivere is a splendid place on the banks of the Carrión, the great abbey riding the flat, cropped, golden plain like a stone ship. According to Richard Ford, it was built in 1161 by a local lord, Dujo de Martinez, who served several Spanish kings before giving away all his wealth and becoming a monk at Benevivere, where he died in 1176. In the afternoon heat, it took nearly two hours to get into Carrión, but apart from my feet, I felt fine and in no particular hurry. I had passed through Carrión de los Condes when riding my bicycle to Santiago de Compostela in 1982, and when I got there I felt instantly at home.

Those who have never heard of Carrión de los Condes should know that it is a famous place, and famous for at least four reasons. It lies in the very centre of the *tierra de campos*, which I was currently crossing. It is a main staging point on the *Camino Francés*, the ancient Pilgrim Road to Compostela. It was the scene of a great quarrel between El Cid and the sons of the counts, or *condes*, of Carrión. Last but not least, it is famous in its own right for the Shrine of San Zoilo.

The story of the Road to Compostela is closely linked to that of Pelayo and the start of the Reconquista, so we might begin with that. Pelayo's grandson, Alfonso II, was still ruling precariously in 842, more than a hundred years after the Moorish invasion, when away to the west, in Galicia, a peasant called Pelagro discovered the body of the apostle James the Great, one of the sons of Zebedee. This was great news for the beleaguered Christian kingdom, so King Alfonso built a shrine on the spot of the *Campo Stellae*, the Field of Stars, at St James – *Santiago de Compostela* – and by 846 St James, now the Patron Saint of Spain, was lending a hand in the battle against the Moorish invader. In his new role of *Matamoros*, Moor-Slayer, he appeared with the Heavenly Host at the battle of Clavijo near Najera in 846, and by the year 1000, the pilgrimage to the Shrine of St James at Compostela was the third most important pilgrimage in Christendom after Jerusalem and Rome. For those who completed it, the long and arduous pilgrimage of a thousand miles or more offered the remission of half the time in Purgatory. This alone was a considerable inducement in a wicked world. All manner of people make the pilgrimage to St James, most recently Pope John-Paul II, most memorably, Chaucer's Wife of Bath, who was forever going on pilgrimages, and before setting out for Canterbury had been 'In Galice at Seint-Jame'. The world's first guide book, written in the 12th century by a monk from Poitier, Ameri Picaud, was about the pilgrimage to Santiago.

The pilgrimage to Compostela, like many medieval pilgrimages, was rather more than a religious mission. Organised by the Cluniacs of Burgundy, who established official starting points in Paris, Le Puy, Vézelay and Arles, the routes passed by various Cluniac abbeys, many with their own shrines, like that of Ste Foy at Conques, and the pilgrims therefore brought much useful revenue for the Order in the shape of alms for the shrines and payments for lodgings. The Holy Church also used the pilgrimage to direct devout soldiers to the aid of the beleaguered Christians of the Peninsula. Spanish knights were forbidden to join the Crusades to the Holy Land, but knights from other lands could gain great merit by joining them in campaigns against the infidel Moors of Andalucía. All this traffic was naturally watched with great interest and concern by the Moors. In 996, one of their spies wrote to the emir of Córdoba, describing Santiago as 'the great and holy city of the Christians, to which they flock from all points, and in great numbers'.

The curious fact is that they still do. When I rode my bicycle to Compostela during the Holy Year of 1982 (any year when the Feast of St James, 25 July, falls on a Sunday is a Holy Year), I was joined on my journey by some two million others and while hundreds of thousands went the easy way, by coach, car or aeroplane, many thousands walked or rode horses or bicycles. All the 'true pilgrims of St James' passed through Carrión de los Condes, which, apart from various pilgrim inns and hostels, contains the relic of its own saint, San Zoilo.

Fernando, the Count of Carrión, acquired the relics of San Zoilo in 1047, as tribute from a Moorish emir, 'Gold and silver I have enough,' declared the count. 'Give me the relics of San Zoilo.' Given the alms that pilgrims would leave at the shrine, and the money they would spend in his town, this act was not entirely motivated by Christian zeal, but the relics duly arrived in Carrión, where they remain to this day. It was partly because of these relics, and partly for the wealth they created, that Rodrigo Díaz de Vivar decided to marry his twin daughters to the Count of Carrión's two sons. The count was pleased to have his sons linked with the powerful Cid, and – a man with an eye for money – he anticipated and received rich dowries with each bride. Doña Elvira and Doña Sol were duly married to the sons of Carrión, and the Cid returned to his castle of Valencia.

Unfortunately, the heirs of Carrión, Dons Diego and Fernando (it seems that half the men in Spain were called Fernando), proved to be brutes. Jealous of the Cid's success and prowess, they vented their rancour on their young wives whom they beat and stripped naked and abandoned beside the road outside the town. Unfortunately for the heirs of Carrión, the Cid had put a spy in their court, to keep an eye on the welfare of his children. When these details were reported, the Cid's rage was awesome to behold.

The Cid rode at once to the king's court in Burgos to denounce his sons-in-law. Then he took his knights to Carrión, where he rescued his daughters and retrieved their dowries, before two of the Cid's knights challenged the heirs to a joust and overthrew them. Why Rodrigo did not simply kill them out of hand is never revealed. This story, of the Cid and his daughters, makes up the main part of that medieval epic poem, *Poema de Mio Cid*, one of the classic tales of medieval Spain. It may or may not be true, either entirely or in part, but here, in the narrow streets of Carrión, the medieval world seems very close at hand and El Cid himself certainly existed. His martial image still bestrides the legends of Spain like a Colossus.

*   *   *

Rodrigo Díaz de Vivar, known to history as El Cid, from the Moorish words *sidi* or *cadi* meaning lord, was born in the dusty little village of Vivar, a few miles north of Burgos, around 1045. As we have already learned, this was about the time when Fernando I was ruling over Castile, León and the Asturias. On his death in 1064, Fernando unwisely divided the united kingdom between his three sons. Sancho, Alfonso and García were respectively endowed with Castile, León and Galicia, while his two daughters, Urraca and Elvira, were given the rents and revenues from all the abbeys in Christian Spain. Fernando also directed that should his children fall out they should listen to the judgement of his champion, Rodrigo Díaz de Vivar. The children fell out before the old king was firmly in his grave. The two elder brothers took up arms against García and he was confined in the *castillo* of Burgos for seventeen years until he died, while his brothers first divided his lands and then quarrelled among themselves.

This quarrel between the brothers put El Cid in a difficult position, but since Sancho was the eldest, El Cid gave him his support. The brothers met in battle at Golpejerra, where Alfonso was defeated and, like García, confined to prison. After some months their sister Urraca persuaded Sancho to release him on the promise that Alfonso would return to his town of Toledo and busy himself against the Moors. Instead, he fled with Urraca to the strong castle of Zamora, and began to raise another army.

Sancho promptly followed and laid siege to the castle, but in early October 1072, a spy came from the castle and, on the pretext of revealing how it might be captured, saw King Sancho and stabbed him to death. These were violent times. Alfonso VI now seized the thrones of Castile, León and Galicia, and installed his sister Urraca in Burgos, some said as his paramour. When the king came to be crowned in public outside the Church of Santa Gadea in Burgos, El Cid came to give his homage and stunned the king and his court by producing a Bible and insisting that Alfonso swear he had played no part in his brother's murder. It must have been a spell-binding scene. Subjects do not usually seize their sovereign's hand and clamp it on the Bible.

'Do you swear you did not order King Sancho's death?'
'I so swear.'
'Do you swear you did not wish King Sancho's death?'
'I swear it.'
'If you are forsworn may you die as your brother did, murdered by a traitor.'
'You press me too far, Rodrigo.'
'Swear it!'

The king had little choice under the circumstances, but it all ended in tears, for if the king's oath were true, this pointed the finger of blame at his sister Doña Urraca. Alfonso afterwards refused to accept Rodrigo's homage and banished him. This caused El Cid little hardship. He left his wife Ximene and his daughters in the care of the Benedictines at San Pedro de Cardena, and made a good living for the rest of his life as a mercenary soldier, fighting with equal enthusiasm for both Christian and Moorish paymasters. He always hankered for Castile, however, and made several attempts to pay homage to Alfonso, an act made even more necessary by the arrival of a new flood of Moorish invaders from Africa, the fanatical Almoravids.

These were invited into Spain in 1086 by the emir of Córdoba, Ali Mu-Tamid, and with the kings of Badajoz and Seville, the Moors met Alfonso's army on the field of Sagrajas, and totally defeated it, cutting off Christian heads by the thousand and sending the wounded Alfonso fleeing for safety across the wastes of Extremadura. Relations between El Cid and his lord were not improved by this disaster for, although summoned to join the king's muster before the battle, El Cid refused, advising the king to avoid battle but seize instead the city of Valencia, which the African Moors were anxious to obtain as a stepping stone for a further advance north.

The complexities of the Moorish invasions are worthy of another chapter, so we can look at them in more detail when we get to Córdoba. For the moment we can leave El Cid hurrying to the conquest of Valencia, where he lived until his death in 1099.

The life of El Cid is full of colourful tales. He was 'nourished' as a page at the court of King Fernando the Great and the sinister Doña Urraca strapped on his spurs when he was knighted in 1058. Then he killed the king's champion, the lord of Gomez, and later married the champion's daughter, the beautiful Ximene. Legend relates how he raised money to pay his army by pledging a chest full of sand to the Jews of Burgos, swearing it was full of gold treasure and, lo and behold, when the Jews opened it, the sand had indeed turned to gold. He united Christian and Moor and fought off the invading Almoravids at Valencia, where, dead from an arrow wound, he was strapped to the saddle of his warhorse and sent out at the head of his army to scatter the besieging Arabs. It is all great stuff. The story of El Cid has provided the basis for an opera, a ballet, several books and an epic film, although most of it is pure fantasy. However, we do know that Rodrigo was a great knight. In reality he was also something of a robber baron, but we know that he pledged his treasure chest to the Jews of Burgos because the chest is still there in the cathedral, where Rodrigo himself now lies, near his wife Ximene. Better than that as proof of his existence, back in 1099 a monk of Cluny wrote an epitaph in the diary of his Order: 'We hear that, far away in Spain, Don Rodrigo has died, to the grief of Christendom and the great joy of the pagans'. English readers may care to note that after the Black Prince won the battle at Najera in 1366, he gave the lordship of Carrión de los Condes to a mercenary English captain, Hugh Calveley, but that is the only English connection I can discover in the town of Carrión.

*   *   *

I like these old tales, which is why I put them here. If it were not for stories like these and a few fine buildings, Carrión de los Condes would be little more than a dusty town on the northern *meseta*. Instead, it is a place of legend, and in its own quiet way, well worth a visit on any journey to Santiago de Compostela or across the *campo* of Castile. The town stands on a hill and is a main staging post on the Road to Compostela. This old Road has now become the first of the Trans-European Cultural Routes established by the Council of Europe as a common link across the Continent, and as a result Carrión is in some danger of becoming a tourist trap – but perhaps not quite yet.

On the way into town, I decided to stop at the roadside Red Cross centre and let the gallant lads of the *Cruza Roja*, the Spanish Red Cross First-Aid team, have a go at my blister. Their red and white painted aid post lies off the road junction just outside the town. They all gave admiring whistles when my blister was finally revealed, and though I preferred not to watch, they let the water out, swabbed it down, gave me some plasters and advised me to let the air get to it. All this proved sound advice. I limped on into the town and by that evening my feet felt much better.

True pilgrims, who make their way to St James by foot, horse or bicycle, have their own network of places on the route, places where pilgrims have been staying for years and can rely on a good welcome. Since part of my purpose was to make a pilgrimage to Guadalupe, I headed for the *Mesón Pissarosas*, where señor Pablo Payo, a member of the Spanish pilgrim fraternity, *Los Amigos de Santiago*, welcomes travellers with open arms, and offers both good food and cheap rooms. Unfortunately, when I got there the *Mesón Pissarosas* was shut.

Other places for pilgrims to stay in Carrión include the Casa de Huéspedes, near the Church of Santa María del Camino (St Mary of the Road). This too was shut. If all else fails, the priest of Santa María will offer a mattress and blankets on the floor. I felt in need of something rather more comfortable and, besides, the priest was conducting a funeral service when I came to his church. So casting about I found a hotel, not a *fonda* but the *Mesón Cortes*, just before it closed for the annual holidays. There I had the best meal I have had in Spain for many a year. I washed my socks, made a few phone calls, and just after eight that evening, went wearily to bed. Crossing the *campo* can be quite hard work. Thinking of my feet, I put off the evening limp, but the next day, before I set off again, I had to explore the town.

*   *   *

Thanks to the policy – I might almost say the intervention – of the
Council of Europe, little Carrión de los Condes now boasts a tourist
office. This is largely devoted to peddling the attractions of the Road
to Compostela, but since I prefer to make my own way about the streets,
the lack of information on Carrión was no problem. The Monastery of San
Zoilo was said to have been one of the finest Benedictine monasteries in
Spain until it was sacked by the French during the Peninsular War, but
it is still very attractive and has been partly restored. Fine cloisters are
embellished with a superabundance of saints, and enclose a pleasant
garden. The pilgrimage is recorded in the Church of Santa María del
Camino, just opposite my hotel, which is also called *La Victoria* because,
according to Richard Ford, it was built to commemorate the victory over
the infidel emir who came to Carrión to collect his annual tribute of a
hundred virgins. The facade of Santa María has a frieze which shows
bulls chasing away the Moors, an event which, with the intervention of
St James, became the battle of Clavijo.

Carrión has been a frequent witness to battles for it was near here, in
1037, that Fernando I of Castile defeated his rival Bermundo III of León.
Fernando then married Bermundo's sister, Sancha, and so united the two
kingdoms. You will see the blazonry of the two kingdoms everywhere in
this part of Spain: the lion of León and the towers of Castile, in stained
glass and faded hangings. Here, to mark the union, the rampant lion of
León is often quartered with the castles of Castile, and you will find some
good examples near the other worthwhile sight in Carrión, the Church
of Santiago. This has a Romanesque facade and a pilgrim frieze, but a
good deal of Gothic in the interior. North of Carrión, certainly in the
Picos and the remoter part of the Asturias, it is the Romanesque style
which prevails among the churches, but Gothic came into Spain down
the Pilgrim Road about 1200 and many of the great cathedrals along
the Way, especially those at Burgos and León, are triumphs of classical
Gothic architecture.

*   *   *

We are not going to follow the Road on this occasion. My feet had cooled
down considerably in the last twelve hours, and I now felt like another
long but gentle stroll in the direction of my next stop, Palencia. I was
now on the northern *meseta*, the great tableland of Castile, but on the part
known locally as the *tierra de campos*, literally the 'land of the plains',

and very flat it is, devoted to the growing of grain, and it was time to move across it at speed for the city of Valladolid. I was quite sorry to say goodbye to Carrión, 'a town full of wine, bread, meat and all good things,' as Ameri Picaud put it after his own pilgrimage to Santiago back in the 12th century. Perhaps I shall go to Compostela again myself, and so gain that full remission of all my time in Purgatory.

Carrión seemed a good place to take stock and review the walk so far. I had now been walking for a week and covered about a hundred and fifty miles, a third of it through mountains, the rest across foothills and across the *campo*. Apart from a few blisters, which were now healing, I was going well and starting to enjoy myself. This is a process that tends to take time, for it is not easy to shake off the trappings and habits of civilisation and settle to a walker's rhythm. Well, that would come. All I had to do was keep walking.

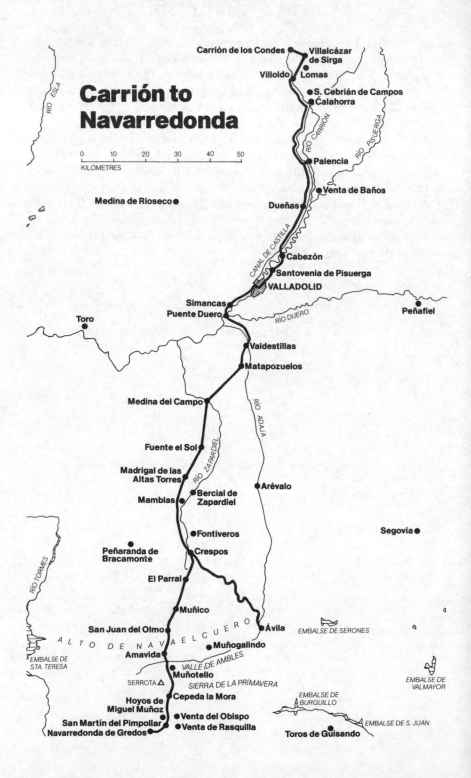

Carrión to Navarredonda

KILOMETRES
0 10 20 30 40 50

Carrión de los Condes
Villalcázar de Sirga
Villoldo
Lomas
S. Cebrián de Campos
Calahorra
RÍO CARRIÓN
RÍO PISUERGA
RÍO ESLA
Palencia
Venta de Baños
Medina de Rioseco
Dueñas
CANAL DE CASTILLA
Cabezón
Santovenia de Pisuerga
VALLADOLID
Simancas
Puente Duero
Toro
RÍO DUERO
Peñafiel
Valdestillas
Matapozuelos
RÍO ADAJA
Medina del Campo
Fuente el Sol
RÍO ZAPARDIEL
Madrigal de las Altas Torres
Bercial de Zapardiel
Mamblas
Arévalo
Fontiveros
Peñaranda de Bracamonte
Crespos
Segovia
El Parral
RÍO TORMES
Muñico
San Juan del Olmo
ALTO DE NAVAELCUERO
Ávila
EMBALSE DE SERONES
Amavida
Muñogalindo
VALLE DE AMBLES
EMBALSE DE STA. TERESA
Muñotello
SERROTA △
SIERRA DE LA PRIMAVERA
EMBALSE DE VALMAYOR
Hoyos de Miguel Muñoz
Cepeda la Mora
EMBALSE DE BURGUILLO
San Martín del Pimpollar
Venta del Obispo
Venta de Rasquilla
Navarredonda de Gredos
EMBALSE DE S. JUAN
Toros de Guisando

CHAPTER SIX

CROSSING
THE CAMPO

*The inhabitants [of Valladolid] are genuine old Castilians,
grave, honourable, and first-class bores.*

Richard Ford *A Handbook for Travellers in Spain* (1855)

I left Carrión at a smart pace, heading east for the village of Villalcázar
de Sirga. This was, in fact, a little off my route but it gave me a better
angle of advance for a long day's stage to Palencia. Anyway, as a firm
friend of St James, I really could not cross his Camino de Santiago
without walking at least a little of it. Besides, Villalcázar contains the
hermitage of Nuestra Señora del Río, and that Church of Santa María la
Blanca that is said to have led the poet king of Castile and León, Alfonso
X (Alfonso the Wise), to produce some of his more inspired work. I
actually prefer Gothic and find that a little Romanesque architecture
can go a long way, but there is more to a walker's life than boots and
blisters and walking across the *campo*. There must be things to see and
think about. The real glory of this parish church at Villalcázar which
was built by the English arm of the Knights Templar, is the huge,
elaborately-carved tombs, one to a knight of the Order of Santiago, the
other to the Infante Felipe and his wife Leonora. Felipe was murdered
by Alfonso X in 1271. In Old Castile, even kings and poets were not
above a little fratricide. These tombs still retain much of their original
polychrome decoration and are quite outstanding.

These seen, and the morning air still chilly, I took a hurried coffee
at the nearby bar, and concentrated on my map. On leaving Carrión
I had seen a track leading out into the *campo* in the direction of the
obvious aiming point for this day's walk: the village of Lomas. This track
actually appeared on my map and led south to San Cebrián de Campos
and Calahorra. This would be a good route, but would leave me on the

wrong bank of the river. I therefore marched at speed across country
for Villoldo, which is easy to spot from miles away, as the rooftops are
overlooked by the tower of the new, or new-looking, church. Villoldo
is a rather nice town, and was playing host to a travelling theatre,
who performed their works in a large tent set up in the Plaza Mayor.
I crossed the Carrión and Pisuerga rivers near here and turned south,
directly across the fields, keeping as far as possible to the shade of the
poplar trees and plantations that line the banks of the river. I stopped
for a drink at a garage on the road and finally arrived on the towpath of
the Canal de Castilla. This great canal, built to connect Reinosa with the
still distant city of Segovia, on the far side of the *meseta*, was begun in
1753, and although now abandoned for commercial use, it is still both
a beautiful waterway, a source of irrigation water for the *campo*, and a
convenient route to follow south along the towpath.

One has to be careful of modern Spanish canals because some are
little more than irrigation channels, or concrete troughs, but the Canal
de Castilla was built in an age when beauty was no barrier to utility. I had
ridden some way along it years before, on my way to Compostela. Now I
turned right along the towpath and followed the canal to the outskirts of
Palencia, through a countryside where flat *campo* gradually gave way to
farms and farms gave way in turn to urban sprawl, all overlooked by the
great statue of the Christ of Otero, high on a hill to the north-east of the
town. It was a fast marching day, and by the late afternoon, in the fading
light of day, I had already found a small *fonda* on the Calle Mayor and
washed my socks. Then I went out to see the sights and enjoy a good
dinner.

*   *   *

Palencia, once the Roman *Pallantia*, is a pleasant riverside town on
the Río Carrión, a city full of squares and shady streets, and busy
people, a merciful release after the empty arid wastes of the *campo*.
It is the capital of the modern province of Palencia, and was once a
famous place. Alfonso VIII of Castile established the first University
of Spain here in 1208, although this has now gone and that pride of
premier place goes to the University of Salamanca, founded in 1218.
Most of the great cathedral of Palencia went up in the 14th century, a
three-naved Gothic building, gloomy, cool and empty of people. Parts
of the cathedral date from the 11th century, when Sancho of Navarra
built a chapel here, and even that rests on the site of a Visigothic
church. Most of the present building is pure Gothic, with marvellous
ceiling bosses and an intricately carved altarpiece and retable, with,

as a special attraction, the tomb of Doña Urraca, Queen of Navarra, who died in the castle at Saldaña in 1189. Other treasures include a painting of San Sebastián by El Greco, an interesting clock with a knight and a lion to strike the hours, and some fine tapestries. All in all, the cathedral in Palencia is well worth seeing.

Like Carrión, Palencia is full of religious buildings, of which the little 13th century Church of St Francis, near the Plaza Mayor, looked most inviting, but was unfortunately closed. So, too, was the old Hospital of St Lazarus, which is where El Cid married Ximene. Fortunately, I have only a limited interest in old buildings and was quite ready to use this pleasant evening to rest, croon happily over my feet which were healing fast, and write down the events and places of the previous few days before I forgot them. This proved wise, because if I had simply stuck to my notes, very little would have been remembered. One day follows another on the *campo*, each a golden blur. Tomorrow I must press on, out of town, down the Canal de Castilla again, and south to my next stop, the city Geoff cannot pronounce: Valladolid. In the meantime, I could scribble a little, and drink a little, and look out of my window at the life surging up and down the Calle Mayor, as the yellow street lights come on and cast romantic shadows around the colonnades.

My room in the *fonda* in the centre of Palencia was the archetypal garret. I had the sagging bed, the unshaded light-bulb, the green louvre blind which was half-rolled up with the gap largely obscured by my wet laundry. There was lino on the floor, a table without a chair and a huge wardrobe. It would have been perilous to swing a cat. Palencia has several good hotels, but it is now the home of the Spanish branch of Renault, and Renault were presenting their new range of cars to the local dealers. Modern commerce has a way of swamping cities, so every hotel room in the town was taken. Anyway, this room was clean, the bathroom was just down the hall, and a little touch of *La Bohème* never hurt anyone. I have, in fact, become very fond of the country *fondas*, and if the town version was perhaps a little lacking in charm, it was still better than sleeping in my tent. That, still untouched, rested in my rucksack. Crossing Spain without using it had now become one of my private ambitions. Nice as Palencia is though, this was the first city I had been in since leaving London, and I didn't really like it. After a week I was getting used to the small villages and empty countryside of Spain. My Spanish had already improved, for I had spoken no English, and if I had a complaint it could only be that crossing Spain on one's own can be a little lonely. I must find something to read. Meanwhile, I could think about another Spanish monarch, Carlos I, the Holy Roman Emperor Charles V.

We make our first encounter with Carlos in Palencia, but to explain how he got there we must go back a little to the days of *Los Reyes*

Católicos, Fernando and Isabel, the first sovereigns of a united Spain. They drove the Moors from Granada and sent Columbus to the New World. Their daughter and heiress, Juana, married Felipe I (Philip the Fair), son of the Holy Roman Emperor Maximilian, and had a son. Then Felipe died and Juana went mad. Queen Isabel was now dying, and so Spain was ruled for his grandson by the old king, Fernando. The story of Juana la Loca is so terrible and so Spanish that it must be known in more detail, but with Juana mad, the throne passed to Fernando's grandson Charles, on the old king's death. Charles had been born in Ghent and brought up at the court of Maximilian. He arrived in Spain in 1517 and in 1519 Maximilian died. Charles was then elected Holy Roman Emperor, heir to the Spanish colonies in the New World and to the old Burgundian lands in the Low Countries, Franche-Comté, Austria, Germany and, of course, to Spain, a union that was to bring the Religious Wars to Holland later in the century. He was, therefore, variously known as the Emperor Charles V, or Carlos I of Spain.

When Carlos arrived in Santander in 1517 to claim his inheritance, he brought with him a number of Flemish and Austrian nobles and his mistress, Barbara Blomberg, mother of his illegitimate son who became the great Don Juan of Austria, the victor of Lepanto. Carlos' first mistake was to grant the great offices of state to his Flemish followers, at which the ever-insular Spanish rose in the Communeros Revolt. The aims of the Communeros were that Carlos should be King of Spain first and only then Holy Roman Emperor; that he should therefore reside permanently in the Peninsula; that Spanish gold should not be used to fund foreign wars and, most of all, that offices of state should go to native Spaniards. Carlos crushed the Communeros with great ferocity, executing scores of them in Palencia, and did not shift his Imperial Court to Spain until 1523.

Most of Carlos' life was spent in war. He fought five campaigns against the French, seeking to quell their ambitions in Italy where Spanish claims to the kingdom of Naples had been outstanding for a century; captured François I at Pavia; repulsed the armies of Henri II and overran the Duchy of Milan. All this, while ruling ever-turbulent Spain and coping with his mad mother. In 1556, tired and worn out, Carlos abdicated in favour of his son Felipe II – of Armada fame – and retired to the monastery at Yuste in the western foothills of the Sierra de Gredos, where he died two years later, on 21 September 1558.

*   *   *

Getting to Valladolid from Palencia is quite easy, even on foot. You just follow the Canal de Castilla, which is both the shortest and the best way, if a little short of drama, because the main road is a race-track. The Río Pisuerga, which links the two cities and flows into the Duero at Valladolid, might provide a route, but it takes a winding course to the union. The Canal de Castilla, on the other hand, is lined with trees, is very shady and straight as an arrow. Neither do you miss much *en route*, for the canal runs directly to the first worthwhile spot, the town of Dueñas, and although there is no towpath in the accepted sense, there is always a path of sorts. In a way, this route between Palencia and Valladolid displays the full range of land transport. There is the railway line, which is still fairly busy, although not all the trains stop at every station. There is the canal; already a relic of a bygone age and devoid of craft. The new giant of transportation, the modern motorway, the *autovía*, parallels both the others for part of the way and is already a deathtrap. Finally, dodging about from track to towpath comes the solitary walker, another relic of the past, or perhaps a warning figure of that future time when all the fuel runs out and the horse, bicycle or Shanks' Pony come, once again, into their own.

It was a cool, rather than a cold morning, and as usual I left early, getting out of town by just after seven, determined to make as much time as possible before the sun got up. I had definitely got Peter's damned cold and my path echoed with explosive sneezes. A good tramp – Doctor Footpath – should soon sort that out, and besides, I had an inducement to press on to Valladolid. When, if, I reached Valladolid, I would be past the first fold in the map. For the serious walker that is a greater moment than any landmark. In addition, if I could yomp the distance today, I could have my first full day off.

On an average day I was already marching further than Geoff's plan envisaged, or I would normally wish to do, but the reason was simple. Spain is a very empty land. There is usually damn-all between one point of interest and the next, except miles and miles of empty countryside. This commits the walker to either camping in the middle of nowhere or pushing on as fast as the feet will carry him or her to the next stopping place. There is very little in between and, as I was about to discover, a distinct shortage of water, which makes camping less than enjoyable. Stopping overnight by a tinkling stream is one thing, a thirsty night on the dusty Spanish plain quite another. Neither was it possible to do a good walking stint and then hop on a bus to the next town, as any sensible walker might do. I usually avoided roads, there are few buses anyway, and so far no one had even offered me a lift. Therefore, *faute de mieux*, I shrugged my shoulders into the rucksack straps, swung my stick to warn off the dogs, and really put my foot down. The walker through Spain must be prepared for long daily stages.

The countryside is very flat along the valley of the Pisuerga, and at last I managed to leave the Río Carrión, which had kept me company for the last few days. The countryside here is hedged in with small escarpments a few hundred feet high. The *campo* lurks up there, but down here I had trees, irrigated fields and small farms, though one farm was huge, surrounded by a wall with turrets, rather like a castle. There are also, alas, a lot of factories and warehouses. It looks as though 'ribbon development' is taking over on either side of the *autovía* between Palencia and Valladolid. Venta de Baños, though a railway centre, still looked rather pleasant from the canal side, and Dueñas, where I stopped for a beer, is a little gem.

Dueñas is pretty. I could live in Dueñas, and I can say that of very few other places I had passed so far, though I gathered in the bar that the town's prosperity had waxed and waned with the canal. Dueñas was once an inland port, shipping out the wines and wheat of the *meseta* to the cities of the north, but the railway and the motorway have put a stop to all that, and the purpose of Dueñas has gone. Still, there are a couple of pleasant *fondas* and one of those castles on the hill. From up there, you get great views over the *campo*. Dueñas is a place to linger in, if you have the time, but I had to get on.

Pressing on was hard work. It was getting warm, as the sun hauled itself higher, so the Rohan jacket went in the rucksack and my knees started to creak. I passed a hotel: *Camas y Comidas* it said invitingly. I was going well now and surely that haze ahead *must* conceal Valladolid, a very large city of the plains? I came to Cabezón and decided to leave the canal path for the far side of the Pisuerga, crossing the river by a mighty bridge that must be medieval. I then walked through the quiet deserted streets of this little *pueblo* and up a long, straight road to Santovenia de Pisuerga. This took an hour or so and put me on the outskirts of Valladolid by early evening. Here a friendly farmer gave me two very welcome apples and directed me to the bus stop by the chemical works. 'It is just chemical factories from now on,' he said. 'They want to buy my farm to build more and fill the air with their dirt . . . wash these apples first, before you eat them.' With a cloud of bright yellow smoke pouring out of the factory chimneys ahead, this seemed good advice, and when the bus finally arrived, I needed no encouragement to get on and collapse. It was getting dark and I had walked quite far enough for one day.

*   *   *

I have always wanted to visit Valladolid, probably because of the name. It is a large city, with over three hundred thousand inhabitants, a successful industrial, commercial and university centre and capital of the central *meseta*. The great northern plain of Old Castile runs south, flat as a board, from here to the foot of the Sierra de Guadarrama, extended north by the *tierra de campos* to the foothills of the Picos. Half of this desert I had now traversed by arriving in Valladolid. I spent the next day here, resting up at noon in the great central park, the only municipal gardens I have ever seen where peacocks strut about unrestricted. I strolled about, like any other tourist, before enjoying a leisurely lunch in a pavement café. Then, after a siesta, I returned to the Plaza Mayor as the evening was just beginning. By then I had a grasp of the city and a very fine city it is.

If you can ignore the ghastly industrial suburbs, Valladolid is a splendid city, usefully compact, full of history, ideal for exploring on foot. It is a capital city in more ways than one, because this was the centre of the court and kingdom of Spain for much of the Middle Ages. That notorious monarch, Pedro the Cruel of Castile, moved here in the 14th century, after shifting the capital from Burgos as the Moors were forced ever further to the south. The capital was shifted to Madrid in 1560, but Felipe II preferred to live and rule from El Escorial, the great palace he was building in the Guadarramas, and Felipe III moved the capital back to Valladolid in 1601. The capital finally settled in Madrid only in 1621, when Felipe IV declared Madrid the only Royal Court in Spain. *Los Reyes Católicos*, the Catholic monarchs, Fernando of Aragón and Isabel of Castile and León, were married in Valladolid in 1469, an act that united Christian Spain into one mighty whole. Felipe II was born in Valladolid on 21 May 1521, as were other kings, and the Princess Anne of Austria, mother of the Sun King, Louis XIV of France. There is a lot of history in Valladolid. The one place worth seeing, though, is the Colegio de San Gregorio, now a museum of sculpture. Though I am no great lover of sculpture, this building which dates from the 15th century is quite marvellous; the riot of stone tracery and carvings are quite outstanding. The other places to see are, as always, simply stopping points on a walk around the city. The cathedral is quite late; only started in 1580, it took two centuries to complete. The San Gregorio and the streets and squares about it are beautiful and you may be as lucky as I was and see people pushing the famous polychromatic tableaux, the *pasos*, about the streets, though at other times they can be seen in the museum. The final attraction is the great arcaded Plaza Mayor in the centre of the city.

*   *   *

Like many Spanish cities, Valladolid has Roman roots, though it is deep in the country once overrun by the Moors who called this city *Belad-Walid*, the Land of Walid, which they held until 980. Valladolid is a corruption of this Moorish name. The great days of the city came in the 15th century and early 16th century when it became the capital of all Christian Spain until the central position of Madrid made the latter city more suitable. As for famous inhabitants, Valladolid can lay claim to plenty, and not just royalty. Columbus died here on 20 May 1506, worn out with poverty and disappointment, and Miguel de Cervantes, author of that classic of Spanish literature, *Don Quixote*, lived here during the last years of his life. His ivy-draped house in the city centre is still much as he left it. The city even survived the ravages of Kellerman, Napoleon's fiercest general, who occupied the city in 1809 and 'spared neither church nor cottage, age nor sex, man nor beast'. This area was much fought over in the War of Liberation, a campaign known to the British as the Peninsular War, when the French troops, forced to live off the country, devastated every city they took. However, Valladolid was no stranger to such bloody doings, as it had been for centuries the home of the Spanish Inquisition.

*   *   *

Together with the Armada of 1588 the Spanish Inquisition is the one institution of Spain that most foreigners have heard about. Perhaps this is because of its terrible reputation, perhaps because the Inquisition lasted until the early years of the last century and was only extinguished by Napoleon. The Inquisition did not begin in Spain. It can be traced directly to that fanatical friar, St Dominic, who used the fire and the rack to root out the Albigensian heretics of Languedoc in the early years of the 13th century. The Inquisition took root in Spain because here the two rival religions, Christian and Muslim, confronted each other face to face, and heretics were seen as traitors as well as blasphemers, enemies of the State as well as the Church. It may also have something to do with that deep strain of intolerance that runs just below the cheerful facade of Spanish life. The rooting out of heresy abroad became the great mission of the Spanish kings and their weapon against heresy, at home and abroad, was the Inquisition, which gained fresh strength after the Reformation swept across Europe in the 1540s and 1550s.

The Catholic Kings invited the Inquisition to Spain, and Felipe II even began his reign in 1556 by attending a great *auto-da-fé* (literally, an 'act of faith') in the Plaza Mayor here in Valladolid. An otherwise tolerant and humane man, he remained an enemy of the Protestants and a supporter of the grim familiars of the Church. What followed thereafter, and endured for centuries, has been duplicated by other tyrannies in later times. Denunciations, false testimony, accusations of son against father, sister against brother, followed by torture and terrible death. A man or woman might be kept for years in some dark cell, brought out for torture and questioning, yet never know the names of the accusers or the reasons for arrest. Once condemned, a man's property was seized by the Church, so that before long the Holy Office grew rich on the wealth of the condemned. Their special enmity was reserved for those 'heretics' who had once known the Catholic faith and then renounced it for the Protestant religion. The outlook for any English or Dutch sailor cast up on the shores of a Spanish dominion was bleak. He would be handed over to the Holy Office, questioned, racked, condemned and sentenced, a process leading inevitably to the *auto-da-fé* and the stake.

At an *auto-da-fé* the prisoners, blinking in the daylight after months or years in prison, were brought out to hear their sentences, each clad in a yellow shirt called a *sanbenito*, with a halter round their necks and a heavy candle in their hands. Some were sentenced to long terms of imprisonment, others to a scourging through the streets, followed by incarceration. Others, the final group, the recalcitrant heretics, were 'surrendered to the secular power' and burned. The Church may not shed blood, so this burning both kept to the principles of the Church and gave the living victim a taste of hellfire. This grisly process of sentence and punishment went on all day, as it was not until evening that the victims were led to the *quemedero*, the place of burning somewhere outside the city, and put to the fire.

*   *   *

Here in Valladolid we are in the heart of Old Castile, the great pulsing heart of Spain, the arid, demanding country from which present Spain evolved, and the fact that Fernando and Isabel married here can be taken as a symbol of Spanish unity, fragile though that unity has often been. In fact, although Madrid is the central capital of Spain, a glance at the map reveals how central Valladolid is to the land of Castile. To the north-west lies León, to the north-east Burgos. To the south-west lies Salamanca and, my target for the week ahead, Ávila de los Caballeros, Avila of the Knights, lies due south at the junction of the Gredos and the Guadarramas. This is a land of high, blue sky, blazing sun, endless plain, rocky sierras and mighty castles. I could not hope to see even a small amount of it on this walk, but at least it would be to me what it has been in turn to Moors and Christians: a real challenge. I braced myself for this with another good meal, for I could feel my ribs again after only ten days on the trail. That done, I returned about ten o'clock to the Plaza Mayor.

*   *   *

Spanish days ebb and flow rather like the tides. The ebb comes between three and five, when the shops are shut and the city slows to a crawl. This is the time for lunch, love or siesta. Then at five, almost as if some magician has waved a wand, the city springs into sudden life, with all the shops and cafés doing a roaring trade till nine, ten or even later. Centrepiece to all this in Valladolid is the *Café del Norte* in the Plaza Mayor, the square where Felipe II held that great *auto-da-fé*. The *Café del Norte* first opened for business in 1861 and has changed very little in the century since. On the outside, under the colonnade, there are the usual battered metal tables and chairs, served by a trio of frantic waiters, but inside is the place to sit later in the evening. Along the walls or at the bar, all is deep, lamp-lit gloom. The noise is tremendous, the air thick with cigar and cigarette smoke, the talk is of *toros*, football, women. Male talk. The bar walls are plastered with the curious things you find in Spanish bars – a bull's head, a vast treasury of bank notes, old photos, posters, stuffed birds, newspaper cuttings. Each table has a fat, glass-stoppered carafe of water to mix with your glass of wine or *Ciento y Tres* brandy – if you can ever get one delivered. You could die of thirst trying to get served in the *Café del Norte*, but I hung on till midnight before going to bed, lapping up the company. I would need memories like this in the days ahead.

CHAPTER SEVEN

THE ROAD TO MEDINA

*The Castilians have no perception of landscape
and a singular antipathy to trees.*

Richard Ford *A Handbook for Travellers in Spain* (1855)

Valladolid was the largest town I had encountered on my journey so far, so this seemed the right place to apply some new-found common sense and take a bus out to the outer suburbs at the start of the next day's walk. At half-past six in the morning this proved harder to do than I had hoped. I was already halfway out of town before the first bus came along. This was already jammed with workmen, so getting on with a rucksack took our united efforts, and the bus transported me only to the factory suburbs. This at least gave me the chance to see a Spanish city early in the morning, before the tourists are about. If there is really any truth in the theory that you only have one chance to get a first impression, early morning is the time to do it in a foreign city. Morning is the time when the air is clear of fumes and everything seems fresh, new and almost delightful.

There is a perception, and I will put it no higher, that the Spanish are a scruffy people, much given to throwing litter about and quite indifferent to squalor. This is not a point on which any Englishman can take a position, given the present state of British cities, but the thought is there. Up to a point, this may indeed be true, for if you stand at the counter in any Spanish café or bar you will usually be ankle-deep in torn sugar packets and cigarette ends. What you may not see is the daily clean-up. As I trudged out of Valladolid and across the Plaza Mayor and headed south early in the morning, the cleaners were already at work on every side, tidying their city for the new day. Bars were being swept, tables wiped, windows cleaned. Carts trundled past spraying water to

damp down the dust, and old men with brooms were busy sweeping up
the debris and litter of the last twenty-four hours. Every day sees a new
beginning and the city is just about tidy when the townspeople rush out
of their houses and litter it all up again. You can't win.

Leaving a city where cafés and hotel desks open early does mean that
you can actually depart before daylight, so with that and the bus ride, I
was walking into Simancas by half-past eight, just in time for another
breakfast. Wise walkers through Spain will eat and drink whenever they
can. I had a coffee and a small sweet cake, a *magdalena*. Everyone else
in the bar drank beer or whisky. How they do it at that time of the day
beats me, but the Spanish are serious drinkers and the tippling never
stops.

I visited Simancas, which is about five miles south of the city, partly
because it lies on my way, partly because it has a splendid castle. I like
castles. You cannot, in fact, visit the castle of Simancas because it is a
repository for the National Archives of Spain, and has been since 1545,
but it was built in 1480 and, as a royal castle, has been wonderfully
well preserved. This was also the site of a great battle in 939, when the
King of León, Raimondo II, beat the Moors back across the Duero – for
a while. I duly admired it from below the moat, and then sped off for the
Duero, wishing I could have gone west a little to Tordesillas, which has
another castle and two relevant tales.

The first concerns that sad queen, Juana la Loca, Joan the Mad.
Medieval kings and queens were prone to insanity, the inevitable result
of marrying their cousins, which may have expanded their dominions but
played havoc with their genes. Juana's brother, the Infante of Castile,
son of Fernando and Isabel, died, and as heir to the kingdom, Juana
married Felipe I, Philip the Fair of Austria. There is no way of judging
whether Philip was as handsome as his nickname implies, but Juana
was already unstable and her love for him went beyond reason. When
he died, she collapsed into insanity. For years she roamed the kingdom
with a small party of retainers, bearing her husband's body from place
to place in an open coffin, tearing off the shroud to cover his decayed
face with kisses. Some say she slept with the body. Finally, her father,
Fernando, came with his guard and carried the body away for burial
at Burgos, before escorting Juana to the castle of Tordesillas, where
she was kept confined for the next fifty years, living in total darkness
in a windowless cell.

The other tale of Tordesillas is as interesting and less ghastly, for
it was at Tordesillas in 1494 that Papal legates met with the kings of
Spain and Portugal and concluded a treaty which divided up the New
World. This was the decision which gave most of the Americas to the
Spanish and Brazil to the Portuguese, with effects that the people of Latin
America live with to this day. The Pope at the time was the infamous

Alexander VI, father of Cesare Borgia, and we will meet Cesare soon, at Medina del Campo.

* * *

It was now a brisk morning, with a keen north wind sweeping in from the *tierra de campos*, pushing me down to my first landmark, Puente Duero, about seven miles south from Valladolid. The Duero, which rises in the Sierra de Urbión, is one of Spain's more significant rivers, but it lacks size hereabouts, not being reinforced by the Pisuerga for another few miles. On the other hand, even here, the Duero is interesting. The poet Southey said that the murky waters of the Duero made the Roman soldiers melancholy. I certainly wouldn't drink it and I will drink almost anything if I'm thirsty enough. Once across the Duero, I could have set 205° on the compass and, with a little assistance from the church towers marking the villages on either hand, marched cross-country directly for Medina del Campo, which now lay about twenty miles away. Unfortunately, there was yet another river in the way, the Adaja, so I put the compass away and marched south to cross this stream near Valdestillas. The dry weather had left the Adaja as a rather insignificant torrent and I could probably have splashed across anywhere, but this was at the end of a dry summer and it might be a different proposition at other times. Once across the Adaja I followed the railway line to the village of Matapozuelos, finding plenty of tracks across the Castilian *meseta*, as it now was, with only periodic patches of shade available from clumps of trees or small plantations of umbrella pines. This was still good walking, for the weather was crisp and the countryside varied. This part of the *meseta* is certainly flat, but it was not the ironing-board smooth plain I had been warned about, or gathered from previous crossings by car. Rather it rippled, with low ridges and small smooth hills. While much of it was golden with short wheat stubble, there were plenty of patches of green, some created by the potato crop, others by vines. In one of the small vineyards I met two old gentlemen from Pozaldez, out for a walk with their dog and taking the chance to gather a few bags of grapes for some wine-making later in the day. Company is rare on the *meseta*, and I was still hoping to meet that homespun philosopher, so I slowed for a chat and we strolled along together.

'*Sí*, it is beautiful, the *meseta*,' said one, 'but you have to get used to it. How long have you been here, *señor*? Only a week? Ten days? That is not enough. I'm seventy and my friend,' indicating his companion, who was being pulled along by a small terrier, 'is seventy-three. We have lived here all our lives. It's the wine and the weather that keep us going – and work, *señor*, work. Young people don't know how to work. They sit in offices and get fat. *Tan gordos, todos*. Work, work, work . . . that is what you want.' I, at once, began to feel rather tired.

'As for the wine . . . ,' he continued. It was sweet and strong, about 12° proof, and far from appetising. They went up and gathered a few bags of grapes *de vez en cuando*, from time to time, whenever stocks ran low, and did a little pressing. I strolled along with them for a mile or so, until I found their slow pace tiring. Then they sent me off with a slap on the back, and a '*buena suerte*' to see me on my way.

You can save miles on a walk like this if you can head directly for your destination, avoiding the swings of the road. Hence the compass. I only needed to use the compass to maintain a general line, for anywhere south would do. Incidentally, this book is not intended to provide a navigation aid to crossing Spain, or a list of stiles and footpaths. Other than at the beginning or end of the day, I rarely knew where I was to within five miles. This did not matter on the plains where you can see for miles anyway.

Topping a low rise, I saw, far ahead on the plain, the towers of a castle that could only be that of Medina, my destination for the day and a place I had long wished to see. It looked a rather small and disappointing castle, not the fortress I had read about, but it was still a fair way off across the open *meseta*. The plain between was marked only by two large plantations of umbrella pines. I took a bearing on the tower, then came down off the ridge and hopped across the railway line before setting off towards Medina at a smart pace. It was only five in the afternoon when I arrived, but I had been ten hours on the trail. Early evening is a good time to look around, for the sun was already starting down the sky and casting interesting shadows, and the day was finally cooling off.

I found a small hostel just across the main level-crossing in Medina, which is a great rail centre, changed quickly into comfortable trainers and went out to explore the castle on the hill behind, which seemed to be just a tower among the trees. When I got there, I had a shock.

The castle of La Mota in Medina del Campo is vast – huge. You can't see that until you are close to it because about fifty feet of the walls, and the drum-towers of the inner bastion, are sunk into a deep ditch. It cannot be a moat or, if so only a shallow one, for there are arrow slits and cannon ports only a few feet above the present surface of the ground. Besides, a moat on a hilltop is impractical. The castle of La Mota was built about 1440 in the Mudejar style, one of the two mixed styles of Christian and Muslim Spain. Mudejar art and architecture is that work carried out by Muslims in their own style and materials, while under Christian rule or direction. The Mozarabic work was that executed by Christian workmen serving the Moors. Mudejar work tends to be delicate, with narrow bricks, pointed or curved arches, almost filigree tracery. The Mozarabic style owes more to the Visigothic, but the Moorish influence is seen in the horseshoe arches and again in the delicacy of the work. In Spain, for most of the Reconquista, it was the Moors and not the Christians who lived a cultured, artistic life, preferring airy courtyards with tiles and flowers and fountains, places open to poets and musicians, while the Christians lived in great draughty castles, lit by torches, echoing to the tread of armoured men.

The Mudejar castle of La Mota is built in thin, pink bricks, which glow beautifully in the evening sunlight. Huge as it still is, La Mota must once have been much larger, for the remains of the outer walls litter the hilltop. Even so, what remains is a stunning and beautiful sight, almost worth walking across Spain for.

The sheer walls of La Mota are graced at the corners with drum-towers for all-round observation, with slender, cone-like turrets resting on the central tower, the one where the important prisoners, like Cesare Borgia, must have been confined. Our word dungeon, which is used in English to describe a dark, dank cell underground, is simply a corruption of the French word *donjon* meaning tower. Prisoners like Cesare were valuable. Their health was important and they were usually kept in fresh, airy towers, rather than rat-infested underground cells. From his tower Cesare would have seen the stark open beauty of the *meseta* and ached to be out there. Any prisoner must have felt even more confined than usual when held at Medina del Campo. The castle interior is not open to visitors, which is a pity because I would have liked to see Cesare's cell and the window through which he staged his spectacular escape for, in a way, Cesare is a hero of mine. The man depicted in Machiavelli's *The Prince* is not a fair portrait of the real Cesare Borgia.

Cesare was the illegitimate son of Pope Alexander VI, one of the most corrupt pontiffs ever to have occupied the Throne of St Peter. Cesare, the second son, was born in 1476, while his father was still a cardinal, but while Alexander only wished to be Pope, Cesare grew up to have greater ambitions. His aim was to restore the temporal power of the Papacy, recapture the Papal lands in the Romagna and Umbria, and then unite all Italy; but for the accidents of fate he might well have succeeded.

The Borgias were Spaniards, lords of the castle of Borja near Zaragoza. Eight Borja, or Borgia, lords marched to the conquest of Valencia in 1238, but as was usual, the younger sons were often dedicated to the Church. In 1456, the first Borgia, Calixtus III, was elevated to the Papal throne. Calixtus III was Cesare's great-uncle, and Rodrigo Borgia, Cesare's father, achieved the same elevation in 1492. One of his first acts was to appoint the young Cesare, then aged about fourteen, as the Cardinal of Valencia. Cesare stayed in the Church for only a few years, but they were the years when Charles VIII of France invaded Italy, humiliated the Papacy and almost overran the kingdom of Naples. Then Charles VIII died and his successor, Louis XII, had a problem. To keep France united he needed to divorce his present wife and marry Charles' widow, Anne of Brittany, and to obtain a divorce he required the help of the Pope. He asked for a Papal dispensation and Cesare was sent to deliver it.

As Cesare saw it, the snag with Papal power was that it lacked secular roots; the exercise of Church authority conferred only temporary benefits on the Papacy. Louis could get his divorce from the Pope only, but could offer nothing tangible in return. There had already been a classic example of this use of Papal influence in 1494, when the Spanish and Portuguese kings invited Pope Alexander VI (Rodrigo Borgia) to arbitrate in their dispute over the division of the lands then being discovered in the New World. Pope Alexander, whose knowledge of geography was minimal, duly sent legates to meet the kings at the castle of Tordesillas and at the Treaty of Tordesillas they accepted his decision. Only the Pope could award lands in this fashion, but if he attempted to impose his rule in Italy – his own backyard – even dukes and counts refused to obey him. What the Papacy lacked was temporal power.

Pope Alexander sent Cesare to deliver the divorce papers to King Louis, but Cesare refused to hand them over until the king agreed to exchange his divorce for an army. With this French army Cesare proceeded to reconquer the Papal lands in the Romagna. Castle after castle fell to his French cannon and Swiss infantry, and all seemed to be going very well for Cesare until 1503 when his father died. What was worse, when his father fell sick, Cesare was also ill, probably with syphilis. As he himself said later to Machiavelli, he had thought of every eventuality in the event of his father's death, *except* that he might also be sick and unable to execute his plans. Into the vacuum swept the Borgias' great enemy, Guiliano della Rovere, who became Pope Julius II.

Cesare anticipated a swift visit from the Papal stranglers, but Pope Julius allowed Cesare to escape to Naples, where he was quickly imprisoned by the Gran Capitán of the Catholic Kings, Gonzalo de Córdoba, whom we shall meet later. Gonzalo sent Cesare in chains to Spain, where he was imprisoned first at Chinchilla and then in this great castle of La Mota at Medina del Campo. Here he stayed for three years, while the Catholic Kings wondered what to do with him. Then, somehow, he obtained a rope and escaped from his cell down the walls at night. The alarm was given and the rope was cut, so that he fell into the dry moat and broke both arms and a leg. Even so, he somehow got to a waiting horse and rode north to take shelter with his brother-in-law, the King of Navarra. Here, being entirely without friends or money, he was given the meanest of welcomes and employed as a mercenary captain.

In the following year, 1513, the King of Navarra sent Cesare to lay siege to his city of Viana, which was then in rebellion. Cesare duly invested the city but, some weeks into the siege, the Lord Louis of Beaumont came by night with a convoy of provisions and Cesare rode out to meet him. The end of Cesare is told in the Chronicles:

> Then this Borgia, ever lusting for blood, hurried on his armour and galloped out, cursing and blaspheming against the Lord of Beaumont, whose men drew him into a fold in the ground and set on him and killed him, four men giving up their lives to destroy this bloody dog. For all that this Duke and his father the Pope had made and done, and caused to have done, there was nothing left save a name to frighten children, and he whose motto had been 'Aut Cesare, aut nihil', was become nothing indeed.

I had seen Cesare's grave when making my way to Compostela. His body was carried into Viana, which lies on the Compostela road east of Logroño, and buried in the chancel of the church. In the 18th century the Bishop of Viana declared that he would not have even the body of this notorious murderer within the walls, so they disinterred Cesare's bones and placed them under a stone at the entrance to the church, where everyone going in and out is forced to step on him. I have always thought that cheap. You can see the gravestone inscription: 'Cesare Borgia, Captain General of Navarra and Gonfalonier of Holy Church', and a poor memorial it is. Whatever Cesare's faults, most of his contemporaries were little better and he had his admirers, even during his lifetime. He was an autocrat and the hero of Machiavelli's *The Prince*. This may be no particular recommendation, but Fleuranges, his French companion during the Romagna campaigns, declared him to be 'A kind companion and a very brave man'. I wandered about his prison at Medina and could have wished Cesare a better end. La Mota is a splendid castle, but I fancy it looks better from the outside.

*   *   *

Apart from the whisps of smoke from the factories on the outskirts and the steady rattle of trains, Medina del Campo is a rather pleasant town. Seeking the way out of town that night, in order to make my departure easier in the morning, I met señor Alonzo Justina, who had once owned a jewellery shop in the vast Plaza Mayor, and, being very proud of his town, was most eager to show me around. This warmth was rare, though not unknown, during my journey through Spain, for although the Castilians are not sociable they can be quite friendly if you touch on a subject they care about. In one corner of the Plaza is the site of the Royal Palace, long since destroyed, where Queen Isabel the Catholic died on 26 November 1504. The site is now marked by a plaque which, apart from her other titles, awards Isabel with the accolade, *Madre de la Hispanidad*.

This matter of the *Hispanidad* has bothered me ever since I started visiting Spain and learning Spanish more than thirty years ago, because I have never quite been able to make out exactly what *Hispanidad* is. I asked half a dozen Spaniards about it on this trip alone, but they could not enlighten me. Put simply, it seems to be a sense of Spanishness, expressed artistically – if that is the term – by the cultural and linguistic unity of the Spanish-speaking countries, with Spain, quite correctly, as the mother of all the 'new' nations of Spanish America. Even though most of these countries threw off the Spanish yoke nearly two hundred years ago, Spain still tries to execute a kind of Mother-knows-best attitude to Latin America, under the mantle of the *Hispanidad*. South American nationals do not need visas to visit Spain, for example, which is marvellous if you happen to be a revolutionary or a Colombian drug dealer, and there is a constant interchange of students, priests, politicians and intellectuals. The Spanish-American nature seems to accept this somewhat patronising attitude with equanimity. Indeed, when I was in Mexico, there used to be a joke: Question: Why is there no such thing as a rich Mexican? Answer: Because the second a Mexican becomes rich, he becomes a Spaniard.

True *Hispanidad* seems to go even deeper than this. My first Spanish teacher attempted to illustrate *Hispanidad* by telling the class a story about four learned European philosophers who were asked to write a treatise on the elephant, which must also demonstrate some common national characteristic. The English professor wrote a slim volume entitled *Our Friend the Elephant – and How to Shoot Him*. This demonstrated English hypocrisy. The French intellectual wrote *The Sexual Life of the Elephant – with Intimate Illustrations*. What this demonstrates, I leave to your imagination. The German wrote a fat tome entitled *The Elephant – Does he Exist?*. This illustrates Germanic confusion. The Spaniard laboured for years and finally produced a ten-volume encyclopaedia entitled *Elephantidad*. At this point our teacher fell about and the class looked blank. I still don't understand *Hispanidad*.

*   *   *

Isabel the Catholic, the female half of *Los Reyes Católicos*, is even harder to understand. Her reputation as a warlike queen, implacable against the Moors, and supporter of the Inquisition, which she personally invited into Spain, tends to obscure her as a woman. Her life cannot have been happy. Her daughter went mad, her husband was unfaithful; no wonder she devoted her time to Spain.

Isabel was born not far from Medina del Campo, in the little town of Madrigal de las Altas Torres. Her father was Juan II of Castile, who built the castle of La Mota. Her mother, Queen María, was already showing signs of mental instability, and soon after Isabel was born in 1451, she was put aside and the king married Isabel of Portugal, who had no great love for her step-children. Then Isabel's older brother died and the little Princess of Castile was very much alone. When the king died, the queen tried to foist her own illegitimate daughter on the Castilians, but they would have none of it, and in 1474 Isabel became Queen of Castile, and after a great deal of conniving, the wife of Fernando of Aragón.

Together they united Spain and overran the kingdom of Granada, but her personal life was still unhappy. The madness which affected her mother, which often seems to skip a generation, broke out in her daughter Juana. After that great sadness, the queen retired to Medina, where she lived alone until her death in 1504.

*   *   *

Richard Ford does not seem to like Medina, which he describes as 'The city of the plain, the capital of the level district' which is brief enough, before adding the comments of the Bishop of Mondonedo in 1502. 'This towne has neither grounde or heaven, for the one is covered with clouds and the other with dirt. Some call it Medina of the Plain but we courtiers do call it Medina of the Dirt. It has a river so little deep that geese in summer do cross it dry footed.' They can still do that after a long dry summer, but Medina was clean enough and there was not a cloud in the sky.

I spent an hour or so ambling around the Plaza de España in Medina, with señor Alonzo, who seemed glad of some company. He showed me his shop and the terrace bar of the *Café Gloria*, the great spot for evening *tertulias* if the din from the customers was anything to go by. Across the Plaza lies the great Church of St Antolin, built in the Mudejar style like the castle. The central arena in the Plaza is crowded with plaques sent from Central Banks over many centuries, recording the fact that it was at the great fair of Medina del Campo that *libros de cambio*, bills of exchange, were first issued. The fairs of Medina were preceded by an open-air Mass conducted from the pulpit on the exterior of the Church of San Antolin, and no deals struck before the completion of Mass were binding in law, which seems a very sensible arrangement. They still have a great market in Medina del Campo, which occupies the whole of this vast Plaza every Sunday. Sunday is therefore a working day in Medina, which takes Thursday as its day of rest. A little rest now seemed about right, after a long and busy day, so I said goodbye to señor Alonzo, who raised his hat gravely and said 'I have enjoyed this walk . . . perhaps we can meet again tomorrow'. Tomorrow, alas, I must walk on to somewhere else, and right now I needed to eat, having eaten nothing since that sweet cake in Simancas, many hours before.

Medina is a fair-sized town, with a number of good bars and restaurants. I found one in a quiet street off the Plaza Mayor and dined very well indeed on a full bottle of Sangre de Toro, Bull's Blood, with *sopa castellana* and a new dish to me, *magras de cerdo en cazuela*, slices of pork in tomato sauce and wine. That, plus some *manchega* cheese from La Mancha and several cups of coffee, sent me heavily off to bed, but another spot of advice: eat well when you can on a journey through Castile. Out on the *meseta*, meals are not easy to find.

CHAPTER EIGHT

THE ROAD TO ÁVILA

Above all things beware of walking or riding in summer.
The calcifying heat will bake the mortal clay until it
becomes more combustible than a cigar. Those 'rayes'
that do not warm you in England will half roast you
here. These beams that irradiate your honeysuckle
fields do here parch and scorch the gaping soil.
Then will an Englishman discover that he is made of
dust, only drier, and learn to estimate water.

Richard Ford *A Handbook for Travellers in Spain* (1855)

Crossing the Castilian *meseta* demands an early start, and south of Medina lies the true *meseta*. By daylight next morning I was trudging out of Medina, leaving the hostel just after seven, heading for my next stop, the town of Madrigal de las Altas Torres, about seventeen miles to the south. I went to Madrigal simply because I like the name.

Madrigal lay off my direct route, which would have taken me like an arrow across the plain to Ávila, but there is no point in travelling on foot if you travel too fast. If you are in a hurry, take a car. If you want a challenge, just getting through the day and getting across Spain must be challenge enough. Walking is, or should be, a gentle occupation, and since I was on schedule, fairly fit, losing weight and not feeling half as poorly as I had done at the start, I decided to indulge myself and go to Madrigal.

This intention provided rather a long day's walk. I found nowhere open in Medina for breakfast and ran into a distinct shortage of water out on the plain as the sun came up about ten. That apart, the road to Madrigal is too straight. The great castle of Medina del Campo looks much more impressive from the south than from the north, but it also looks right down the road to Madrigal. Try as I might, I could not shake it off. Every time I looked back, for mile after mile, there it was, as big as ever and seemingly just as close. I eventually took to the wide *meseta* and began to lurk in the scattered pine clumps, partly for the shade, partly to get something between me and my departure point.

People had told me that I would find the flat *meseta* a trial, and this was from people who had only read about it or driven across it by coach or car. The *meseta* is not actually flat. I had already noticed that it ripples. It has patches of green, there are little hamlets and the occasional farm and in autumn you will find great patches of small purple flowers, rather like gentians, which do provide a little contrast and brighten up a landscape which is otherwise just corn stubble, brown ploughlands, blue sky and green pine trees. What does become apparent as you walk across the *meseta* is the space. You can stride out how you will but you hardly seem to be moving across this golden carpet. You can see for miles ahead, miles behind and miles out to either side, and there is nothing anywhere but more of the same. MMBS: miles and miles of bloody Spain.

*　　*　　*

I am not going to go on and on about the difficulties of walking across the *meseta*. As we used to say in the Royal Marines, 'If you can't take a joke, you shouldn't have joined'. I will say that walking across the *meseta* in hot weather is not something one should undertake lightly although it is rather easier than walking across Extremadura. Lack of water is the real snag. I was now carrying two one-litre water bottles which I filled up every morning and as often thereafter as possible, but even so I was thirsty for most of the day and I sucked up beer and water like a camel from any bar, tap or water trough. The only snag is that bars, taps and water troughs are somewhat rare on the high *meseta* of Castile.

I stress the point here because were I to walk in Africa, a shortage of water might be accepted as normal and hardly worth mentioning. This, on the other hand, is Spain, the plains of Spain, where, according to the famous saying, 'the rains mainly fall'. Don't you believe it. If you set out to walk or cycle across any part of Spain, but in particular the flat *meseta*, take heed and carry plenty of water. Out there, the latter half of the 20th century has had very little impact. The other useful items would be sunglasses and a shady hat. I had my old Commando beret and although I pulled it round and forward over my eyes, it did not provide sufficient shade. Trees are rare, but when you are under them, what bliss: the temperature drops perceptibly within seconds. Then you are out of the shade again and the sun comes and clubs you over the head.

By reaching the *meseta*, we have taken another step forward in the Reconquista, and moved on a century in time. The Christians broke out of the Duero valley in 1085, with the capture of the Moorish stronghold of Toledo, which in one round shifted the frontier across the central sierras of Gredos and Guadarrama, which were outflanked, and down to the Sierra Morena. Beyond that lay Córdoba, and the fertile Andalucía. This was a region the Moors had to retain and defend. Their efforts to do so turned the *meseta* into a wilderness of scorched earth and burned villages studded with walled towns.

The Almoravids, who arrived from Africa in 1086, besieged Toledo on several occasions, most notably in 1114, and cut the roads leading to it every summer. In 1109 the Almoravian emir, Yusuf, arrived with an army from Africa and brought fire and sword up the Tajo valley, capturing Talavera and burning the suburbs of Toledo, before storming Madrid and Canales. In all these places, the Muslims could overrun the city but failed to capture the citadels where the garrison and townspeople held out until the Moors marched away. Siege warfare never came easily to these Berber people. Christian resistance was led by Alfonso VII of Castile and León, who held on to his conquests with defended towns and a policy of resettling the countryside with land-hungry peasants, who were willing to take the risk of Muslim raids in return for land tenure. So, between 1085 and 1140, the Christians gradually expanded their territory and drove the Almoravids back. By 1130 the Christians had even managed to seize a number of towns in Andalucía.

It is not hard to understand why the Christians coveted Andalucía after seeing this land of Castile, not from the comfort of a car but as their infantry must have seen it: on foot. It is a harsh place, short of water, trees and any form of gentle greenery. Throw in marauding Muslim bands and dark thoughts of decapitation and slavery, and living on the *meseta* must have been a trial indeed.

*　　　*　　　*

Accepting this and with nothing to detain me, I marched on fast. The kilometres went rolling past at one every ten minutes or so for the first fifteen miles. Then the sun got to me and I began to tire. I did come to a roadside restaurant at the scattered hamlet of Fuente el Sol, but it was closed – curses! Then far ahead on the plain I saw what had to be that day's destination, Madrigal de las Altas Torres, waiting at a distance. When you walk across the *meseta* in the heat of the day, it takes a lot of effort to keep moving. You crawl, dogged by your shadow, counting each patch of shade as a landmark, keeping your head down to avoid the glare and the evidence that your pace is so slow, while the rucksack digs into your shoulders and sweat drips steadily from your nose and runs into your eyes. I had to carry a handkerchief to wipe it away, but I was soon coated with a paste of sweat and dust. I finally crawled past the walls of Madrigal, or what is left of the walls, at about one-thirty in the afternoon, more than ready for a spot of deep shade and a cold beer in the first bar I could find. This bar turned out to be full of locals, all watching a video of their exploits at the recent town bullfight. During the daily *encierro*, when the bulls are run from the holding pens to the arena, all the young bloods of the town and some of those old enough to know better, try their hand at a little cape work. The bulls are mostly too confused by the noise, the glare, and hosts of dashing figures to single out anyone for a serious charge. Dicing with Miura bulls is still a risky and rather cruel affair, although the locals loved it, cheering on anyone they recognised in the rather wobbly picture. I don't like bullfights and my sympathies lie firmly on the side of the bulls. I watched the film, half hoping to see someone flattened by a charge. The whole bloody business might not have seemed so funny after that.

Madrigal de las Altas Torres is a pretty name – Madrigal of the High Towers – for a pretty place, though I gather that the word Madrigal in this sense does not mean a song but a copse or thicket. Anyway, most of the towers which once studded the curtain wall of Madrigal have long gone. There are two guarding the gate on the eastern side, but most of the rest, like the wall itself, now lie in ruins. Once the walls are entered, Madrigal is a clean and cheerful town, especially in the central cobbled Plaza Mayor, which lies about the huge Mudejar Church of San Nicolás of Bari. This, unlike most Spanish churches, is light and airy and full of fine glass and statuary. Most Spanish churches are either too ornate or very gloomy. This church seen, I bought an ice cream and settled in a sunny corner of the Plaza. There, boots off, I began to rest my feet and write these notes, before finding a *fonda* up on the main road and taking my usual evening *paseo* round the town. Madrigal is famous in Spain as the birthplace of Isabel the Catholic, who was born in the Palacio de Juan II. This is now a convent but Isabel lived here until she married Fernando of Aragón. The town walls went up in the 13th century as part of the grand plan for resettling this part of Castile and guarding against the Moors, and the three great churches of the town, San Nicolás of Bari, Santa María and Santa Augusta, went up in the 12th, 13th and 14th centuries respectively. Madrigal is a very agreeable town, built in golden stone and red tiles, and well worth the effort it took to get there.

*   *   *

Having veered a little west of my route to visit Madrigal, I had presented myself with a problem. I wanted to visit Ávila de los Caballeros, which now lay to the south-east, off my direct route. I also wanted to travel due south, off the *meseta* and directly into the Sierra de Gredos, which although still out of sight in the heat haze could lie no great distance ahead. Once there I would be almost halfway across Spain, and over another fold in the map.

Madrigal was not on my original list of stopping places. Geoff's plan had me stopping at Arévalo, another town of the *meseta*, with a large castle, which lies over to the east, due north of Ávila. If I headed south now, giving up Ávila, I would swiftly enter the foothills of the Gredos and perhaps complete this bound across the *meseta* with a day off in the *parador* at Navarredonda. On the other hand, there was a *parador* in Ávila and I could have a day off there. Decisions, decisions. I got out the map and began to brood over it.

Ávila was a place I had to visit. I have been there several times, and I even went there once when walking in the Sierra de Guadarrama, but I had never seen it in good weather and the weather at the moment was beautiful. Too hot but beautiful. I had only ever seen Ávila in the winter and in winter Ávila is freezing. Besides, to cross the province of Ávila without visiting the capital would be a crime. Then, after studying the map for a while, I saw a solution. A hard day's march to the south of Madrigal lay the village of Crespos on the railway line between Ávila and Salamanca. I could march to Crespos, take a train into Ávila, spend a night there and return to Crespos next day to resume my southern march with a short stage to Muñico. Please note that the word march has replaced the word walk. You may walk, stroll or ramble over green countryside, but in the *meseta* you march to get off the scorching plain as soon as possible. The road distance from Madrigal to Crespos was about twenty miles, but I could shorten this a little by compass marching directly across the *meseta*. So, after another early start I set 185° on my compass, which is just about due south with the local magnetic variation, and set off across the plain. It was on this section of the journey that I had that encounter with the bees.

Much to the obvious disappointment of the villagers, the sudden gush of water did not upset the bees, and once full on, the standpipe ceased to hammer against the post. Indeed, the bees, who may have been as thirsty as I was, came crawling back to paddle in the wet. I filled my bottle, drank, topped it up and strode out of the village in a rage. It was miles before I calmed down again, and the troubles of the day were not over.

*   *   *

I was running out of *meseta* at last. Leaving Madrigal in the cold light of morning around seven-thirty, I could already see the foothills of the Gredos quite clearly, though far ahead. By noon they had disappeared in the haze but the *meseta* had begun to ripple slightly and become much more stony. My main points of reference were the church towers to the east, first Bercial then Mamblas, then the dry bed of the Río Zapardiel, the river I had crossed the day before on leaving Medina del Campo. I crossed a main road a little to the west of Fontiveros, which is quite a large town, and by mid-afternoon I was sitting in the railway station at Crespos, waiting for an evening train and gulping down more water drawn from a tap behind the waiting room.

Were I ever to do this walk again (which God forbid), I would make more use of trains, especially for crossing empty, even desolate, parts of Spain, like this endless *meseta*. I had been on it for a week, fool that I was, and while towns are fine, the villages are half empty and the inhabitants surly. My spirits were somewhat low and they had not been improved by my encounter with the Castilian villagers and the bees. However, I had to wait a while at Crespos for my train and in the interval I cheered up. I am rarely depressed for long, and I had Ávila to look forward to in the evening and the green Gredos after that. Life was not so bad. All I had to do now was sit in the shade and wait.

Spanish trains are cheap, clean and reliable, but not very frequent, at least outside the commuter hours. Unfortunately, there are not many tracks where you need them – running through tiny places and across the wide, flat, empty bits of Spain – probably because there are so few passengers. I sat on in the shade and ate a ham *bocadillo*, purchased from a nearby bar. Eventually my train arrived. I heaved the rucksack on board, found a seat and off we went to Ávila, clanking across the plain, through little San Pedro and one or two other places. By early evening I was trudging up the hill into Ávila, looking forward to a fresh look at one of the finest cities in Spain.

*   *   *

Ávila is one of the great fortress cities of Europe, a place to rival Carcassonne in Southern France or Tuscany's famed Siena. The Spanish say Ávila was founded by Hercules, who came this way seeking the Golden Apples (or oranges) of the Hesperides. In fact, Ávila is one of a series of fortress towns built by Alfonso VI after the fall of Toledo in 1085. The others are Segovia and Salamanca and, peopled with Christians from the Asturias, they were designed to be places of refuge and strongpoints on the new frontier. Hence those marvellous walls.

Coming in from any direction it is the walls of Ávila which catch the eye. A completely circling *enceinte*, set on a hill above the Río Adaja, they are two and a half kilometres long, twelve metres high, up to three metres thick, crowned with over 2,500 merlons, and studded with no less than eighty-eight towers, all in a splendid state of preservation. There are nine gates into the interior of the city, which contains a huge cathedral and two vast plazas. All this is largely due to that roving princess of Castile, Doña Urraca, and her French husband, Raimundo de Borgoña, which I suddenly realised is the Spanish version of Raymond of Burgundy. According to Ford, Raimundo rebuilt Ávila about 1088, and the fortifications he erected still stand. They knew how to build in those days.

This Doña Urraca is not the daughter of Fernando I, but his niece. Raimundo, the son-in-law of Alfonso VI (and he was only given this city after taking it from the Moors), began work on the walls in 1090, and has now bequeathed his name to the attractive *parador* near the north wall. At this *parador* I met yet another small setback of the Castilian kind, when the receptionist flatly refused to accept my pre-booked hotel voucher. In itself this didn't bother me, for I am quite indifferent to where I sleep, but I am not too keen on insolence. I quickly found a small room in a comfortable *fonda* just up the hill for 1,000 pesetas, but they could have been more polite about it. Heads will roll when I get to a telephone. I found this thought a comfort as I proceeded, teeth grinding, up the hill to my new lodging, but I am not alone in finding the Avilese a little short on charm. Listen to Richard Ford: 'The Avilese, physically and morally, are of a low standard. The clumsy, uncourteous boors gape with ignorant wonder at the interest taken by travellers in objects to which they are stupidly indifferent.' I wouldn't go that far, in spite of what happened later.

*   *   *

It could take several days to explore Ávila, but I did what I could in two hours the following morning. Most people will begin with the cathedral, which was started in the Late Romanesque style in the 12th century and slowly changed to the present, rather ponderous Gothic, when that style came to Spain down the *Camino Francés*. In fact, with the cathedral at Sigüenza, Ávila's cathedral, parts of which date from 1107, was the first Gothic church in Spain. Once you have got past the beggars lurking in the gloom of the porch, the interior of the present cathedral is a bright and airy place, with good stained glass and some interesting carvings and effigies, as well as works by El Greco in the museum.

Ávila is a real fortress town, a place where it is quite easy to get lost, even with the aid of a street map from the tourist office. Having only a little time, I ticked off the places I wanted to see and since I hold the All-Comers record for a tour of the Louvre – eighteen minutes including the Mona Lisa – I got around all the sights of the old city in fairly short order. The Deanery was still shut, but I had a look at the Valderrabaños Palace, which is now a hotel. In fact, I had coffee there. This being Sunday, San Vicente's basilica was open, so I saw the tomb which depicts the saint's martyrdom, and to complete my contact with the Catholic Kings, I stopped by Santo Tomás to see the tomb of their only son, the Infante Juan. Incidentally, Spanish princes – *infantes* – were always given foot guards, the mounted escorts being reserved for the kings, and this has given us the common word for foot soldiers: infantry. You can easily spend a couple of days prowling the cobbled streets of Ávila, but one place which must be visited, and opens early, is the convent of La Encarnación, which also houses a museum dedicated to the great local personality, Santa Teresa of Ávila.

Santa Teresa was born in Ávila on 28 March 1515, and took the veil in 1535. She devoted much of her later life to reforming the Carmelite Order, founded seventeen convents of barefoot nuns, and wrote numerous works of faith, an important task during the tormented years of the Counter-Reformation, assisted in this latter task by another eminent Spanish divine, San Juan de la Cruz. Santa Teresa is now buried in the Church of the Carmelites at Alba de Tormes, some distance to the north-west. It is said that ten thousand martyrs assembled at her deathbed, and her body still lies under the High Altar. The story goes that when she was dying and the Sisters asked her if she wished to return to Ávila, she whispered, 'Have you no place for me here?'

Santa Teresa sounds an interesting and rather jolly lady, as many nuns are. I have spent a certain amount of time with monks and nuns over the years, and the one thing about them that sticks in my mind is how cheerful they are. One of Santa Teresa's problems was that when she started to pray, she tended to levitate. She could float up to ten feet into the air, calling loudly on God to put her down. She is also credited with the creation of a local cake, a sweet, sticky confection of flour and egg-yolk called the *yemas de Santa Teresa*. It is worth mentioning that Ávila is full of good restaurants and they can boast some excellent chefs, which is by no means always the case in Spain. Just for the record, my dinner here consisted of yet more *sopa castellana*, roast sucking pig, a speciality of Segovia, some cheese, and rather too much red Rioja.

My visit to Ávila was rather brief, and even briefer than I had intended, as I shall presently reveal. I am still glad I went there, for in early October the great tourist crowds have gone and on this occasion at least, the weather was glorious and the evening sunlight picked out all the detail of the great walls and towers. If you have the time, Ávila is a great centre for excursions to Segovia and the palace of El Escorial, or for great walks along the Gredos, which lie to the south-west, or the Sierra de Guadarrama, which runs way to the east, or even across the range to Madrid itself. The only snag is that Ávila can be perishingly cold in winter and was not all that warm after dark even in October. On that first evening, an hour after arriving, I had my shower and dressed, then pulled on my Rohan jacket but reflected that I was probably not smart enough to even dine at the *parador*. Therefore, taking my stick, I set off for the restaurants and cafés around the central square, the Plaza de la Victoria. A few minutes later I got mugged. All in all, it was not my day.

*   *   *

When you consider that I am no longer in the first flush of youth, and wander around the world on my own a lot, I might have been mugged before. We were, in fact, attacked by thugs in Jordan, while riding our cycles to Jerusalem. A group of Arabs stopped us at the top of a long hill outside Amman and demanded money. Fortunately they stopped us just on the *downhill* side of the hill, so we were able to push them away, leap back into the saddle and pedal off into the dark, pursued by shouts and stones. Any fool knows that you always mug cyclists on the *uphill* side of the mountain.

Now I come to think of it, most of my friends have been mugged or assaulted in recent years. Geoff was hit over the head with a spanner some years ago at a village fête, and Keith was beaten up by South African louts on a train outside London. A few months before I left on this walk, Toby Oliver and his lady were attacked in Madrid and Christine's bag was slashed from her shoulder and stolen . . . now it was my turn.

I was still brooding over the *parador* incident and the bee incident, and not paying much attention to my surroundings. Then three youths came past from behind, much closer than even the narrow street justified and bumped into me. What happened then went something like this: once in front, they turned across my path, standing shoulder to shoulder, and this brought me to a sudden halt. Then, the one in the middle asked for money.

'*¿Eh, señor . . . tiene dinero?*'

I was totally surprised. Why were my finances any of their concern? '*Sí, gracias,*' I said, stupidly. I still didn't realise what was going on.

'Give it to me' he said, grabbing the strap of my shoulder bag. Only then did the penny drop.

On the face of it I was a fair enough target. A middle-aged gent, grey hair glinting in the dim street-light, limping along with a stick, and all alone. Perfect. They were lurking outside the *parador* for just such a target as this and I must have looked a real prize. Fortunately for me, these were amateur muggers. Unfortunately for them, I was in a very bad mood. Besides, they didn't know their business. Two of them should have grabbed my arms and hustled me against the wall while the third ripped the bag from my neck. Then they could have had the fun of kicking my brains loose. As it was, we gazed at each other for a split second, gaping. Then I raised my stick and cracked the one in the middle across the bridge of his nose with the handle. I don't recall it as a hard blow, but the effect was dramatic. He put his hands to his face and began to bleed; copiously.

I then hit the one on my right. This was a real blow, a hard, full-bodied and most satisfying crack, right across the ear. It must have hurt. Suddenly there was a lot of yelling. Then we all ran off, the three of them back down the street, me as fast as possible up to the comfort of light and people in the main square. It was all over in much less time than it takes to tell. I can only admit that my present feelings – and I wrote this account in the first bar, my hands still shaking – are firstly elation and secondly regret that I didn't score a hat-trick by belting the third one. It is also curious that before this trip, when people asked me if it would be dangerous, they were probably thinking of the barren *meseta* or the mountains, or nasty rough peasants in small villages. Out there, I will happily leave my rucksack alone for hours, propped against a church wall, or enter a crowded bar to sit with the locals, and think nothing of it. Then I arrive in this popular, civilised, tourist city of Spain, where I get set upon within the first hour. It's not fair.

Years ago, anyone visiting New York was advised to carry 'Mugger's Money'. Then, when you were stopped by the guy with the knife and he said, 'Stick 'em up', you handed over your $20 or $50 bill. The mugger then said, 'Gee, thanks mister', ran off, and life went on as before. Then the muggers decided that just getting the money wasn't enough fun. They started stabbing and beating and even killing their victims into the bargain, and if that is going to be the way of it, you might as well fight back. This was just a small incident of travel, hardly worth mentioning. I have a thought though. My salvation was due to my heavy, horn-handled walking stick. Maybe one answer to street crime by juveniles is to bring back walking sticks. Spain already has National Service.

Anyway, that is my first mugging, and although it ended well, I don't recommend the experience. It could easily have ended in tears, and this little fracas rather put me off Ávila. In spite of several brandies and a good meal, I didn't enjoy the rest of my stay. Early next morning I took the train back to Crespos, ate breakfast there in one of those small and grimy but safe and civilised bars, and set off again towards the foothills of the Gredos. It might be hot in the day and cold at night, there may be little water and a lack of *haute cuisine*, but there are advantages. In spite of everything I've mentioned, it is really much safer out there.

CHAPTER NINE

THE ROAD TO
THE GREDOS

He who would really see Spain must be prepared to rough it;
must be unembarrassed by a guide, content with humble
inns, coarse fare, and lay aside all expectations of
what one might find. Spain is not a beautiful country,
and those who wish to find beauty must look for beauty
only of a special kind . . . without refinement.

A.J.C. Hare *Wanderings in Spain* (1873)

The Central Cordillera of Spain, which divides the wide *meseta* into two
rather unequal parts, runs north-east to south-west across the Peninsula
for a distance of about two hundred miles. If you are walking north to
south there is no way to avoid crossing the crest, other than by taking
one of the roads across the range. These are few and far between. This
Central Cordillera divides the *meseta* into two parts. To the north lies Old
Castile and the *tierra de campos*. To the south lies New Castile – Castilla
la Nueva – and the plains of La Mancha. To the north lies the Río Duero,
to the south the Tajo. The entire Cordillera straddles Central Spain, and
here, between the *meseta* to the north and the southern foot of the range
at Candeleda it is about forty kilometres wide – as the crow flies. As a
man walks, it's further. Scenically, the Gredos are most attractive, very
green, covered with trees and seamed with lush valleys, interspersed with
steep sierras and smooth, rising plateaux or *parameras*. The summits are
usually covered in snow from October until the end of June, but in this
year of great heat, the summits were bare, covered now with rich heath,
bracken and patches of burnt matt-weed.

My route from Llanes led me unerringly to the central Gredos, which
lie south-west of Ávila and past or close to some of the highest peaks: La
Serrota (2,294 metres, 7,526 feet), La Mira (2,243 metres, 7,359 feet)

and Almanzor (2,592 metres, 8,503 feet). That was the bad news, but there were compensations. With these three peaks to aim for, I could hardly get lost. For much of the year they are snow-covered with fresh falls common in October, but this year's long, dry summer had left even these high peaks bare. I saw no snow at all. Finally, my route led across the mountains by one of the few established footpaths, first from the *parador* at Navarredonda, up to the Plataforma – and this part of the route is now a metalled road – then over the Candeleda Pass, which lies at about 2,018 metres (6,620 feet) and so down and down to the town of Candeleda. As the crow flies this distance, from the C500 road at the *parador* over to Candeleda, was about thirty kilometres. Even with a mountain in the way, I could hope to do it in one full day. However, as I got off the train at Crespos, the Candeleda Pass lay a long way ahead. First, I had to cross the northern foothills, skirt the La Serrota peak and come out on the C500 road, somewhere near the little town of Hoyos del Espino. This road lay directly across my path and if I kept more or less south, I could not miss it. When crossing unfamiliar mountain country with maps which are known to be inaccurate, pin-point map-marching is hardly possible, and can be time-wasting. I therefore picked out something I could not miss and bush-bashed across country until I got there. It may sound primitive, but it works.

*　　*　　*

According to Geoff's original plan, I should have gone directly south from Medina, through Arévalo and into Ávila, and had a day there out of the boots. Then I could have taken a bus west to the little *pueblo* of Amavida, and picked up the southern trail once again. As it was, walking south from Crespos, I still had two days over the Gredos foothills before I reached Amavida. Ah well, after the recent alarms and excursions in Ávila, I was very glad to be back on the trail and off the *meseta*, and a very fine two days they were.

Although it hung on for a while, even after Crespos, I had now left the *meseta* behind. Truth to tell, I was glad to see the back of it. The *meseta* of Castile is no country for walkers, and although hill terrain may be harder, I travelled across it with a far greater sense of enjoyment. Once I was across the main N501 road south of Crespos and heading higher into the hills, the scenery got better all the time. This part of Castile is rather like parts of south-west Ireland or Dartmoor, granite country, full of rocks but grey and gold rather than lush, rain-washed green. There are stone walls and tumbled rocks to clamber over, many of them bright green with lichen, while a host of beautiful amber butterflies came out to dance about my feet.

There is much wildlife here, somehow surviving in this golden desolation. Great eagles wheel lazily overhead and every church tower is crowned, rather than graced, with a huge bonfire-shaped pile of untidy sticks and branches which have been gathered up over the years by nesting storks. Spanish hunters will shoot anything that moves, but storks are supposed to be lucky, so in spite of pollution and natural predation, the storks survive and come gliding in from Africa at the start of every summer. I saw several large hares, which leapt from almost beneath my feet in a heart-stopping fashion, to go jinking wildly across the plain, and then there were russet butterflies and a variety of thrushes and singing birds, heard more often than seen.

The warm sun makes a difference. I trudged up the road to El Parral, and there found a well-trodden track which took me over the top of the first foothills with a large hill to my right just glimpsed from about the 1,300 metre mark. Then I found another track and then a road and then the village of Muñico. I liked Muñico; a pretty little place dozing in the sun, with not a soul about in the heat of the afternoon. But for the usual semi-crazed dogs which came out yelping from every side street, I would have dumped the pack and had a rest, but I still had some way to go, and yet another ridge to cross that day. So, on up the Alto de Navaelcuero and up to San Juan del Olmo at about 1,500 metres, a fair climb at the end of the day, and then down to Amavida to stay there, or somewhere in the Valle de Ambles. This valley divides the northern foothills from the next sierra to the south, the Sierra de la Primavera, after which one finally comes to the Sierra de Gredos proper. It is all up and down, but quite well wooded with plenty of water – wonderful!

Some way to the east, at Muñogalindo, lies an area of grain fields and tumbled stone walls, known as the Desierto de Ulaca, the wilderness of Ulaca, which is laid out around an Iron Age settlement and contains a village of *pallozas*, houses and barns thatched with brushwood, and the castle of Viciosa. There are lots of small castles hereabouts, many of them the country seats of the Knights of Ávila, the Military Order that gave Ávila de los Caballeros that romantic suffix. This Alto de Navaelcuero is really rather pleasant; open walking country, with plenty of tracks through the rocks, scrub oaks and great swathes of springy matt-weed in the undergrowth. Most of the tracks run east–west along the tops of the main ridge, linking little hamlets at the ends of other tracks or mule trails, generally pushing up from the valley below. If you want to go south, you can either go cross-country on a compass bearing, or follow one of these rough little roads down into the valley.

This is the sort of walking one might find among the tors of Dartmoor in a dry summer, though the views are better. Hills ripple off in all directions, presenting a far more interesting prospect than the interminable vistas of the *meseta*. Hill-walking like this is definitely much less tiring than crossing the flatlands, perhaps because there is more to engage your attention and so distract you from the heat and distance and the weight of the pack. I put this down because I noticed it at the time. The sheer monotony of the plains induces a kind of depression, a general lowering of the spirits. Once in the hills, the heart rises with the landscape. I pressed on across these beautiful, if lonely, hills, looking across the deep valley to the next sierra, and reached the road as the sun flared down to the west. This done, I walked into Amavida and rested there, having done quite enough for one day.

I also managed to eat well here, in a very shabby little restaurant just off the main road past Amavida. Spanish food seems to depend very much on the state of the diner. I don't think Spanish chefs care too much about it either way, probably because the Spaniards are largely indifferent to what they eat, provided there is plenty of it. A Spanish gastronome is a contradiction in terms. I actually ate very well on this walk across Spain. Not very often, but very well, and if there is nowhere I liked enough to recommend, except perhaps the lunch buffet in the *parador* at Córdoba, I had some very adequate meals. Good local dishes hereabouts include *judías del barrio de Ávila*, white beans and pork in a paprika sauce; good *tortillas*, with peas and potatoes chopped up with yellow-yolked eggs, quite unlike the flat, greasy *tortillas* that pass muster as *tortilla española* in Britain and even out here; and Santa Teresa's *yemas*, which seem to be formed from sugar and egg yolk. Eggs, potatoes and beans are the staple ingredients of the Spanish peasant, but he, or more often she, can make some marvellous meals from them. I felt quite fat and twice the man I was before as I polished off a good bottle of the local Cebreros wine and went to bed. Tomorrow I would storm across the Sierra de la Primavera, and up the north face of the Gredos to spend a night, if all went well, at the first and most famous of all the Spanish *paradores*, the *Parador Nacional de Gredos*.

The word *parador* originally meant an inn, or simply a stopping place. A *posada*, which is now the word used for *parador*-style hotels in Portugal, is an inn with stabling for animals, and pallets for mule drivers. More respectable travellers stayed in *ventas*, *fondas* or *paradores*. In 1926, the Marquis de Vegan-Indan, who was then the Royal Commissioner for Tourism, put the idea of establishing State-run *paradores* to his sovereign, Alfonso XIII, and the one in the Gredos was the first to be opened. The *paradores* which followed, at Oropesa and Mérida, were a distance apart directly related to the then state of roads and the range of motor cars. The idea then, and now, was to build hotels in areas where there was no profitable incentive for private hotel owners to do so, but the idea has gone much further and now plays a major role in the preservation of old buildings, castles, monasteries and stately homes.

*   *   *

One of the things I ought to have learned about this walking business is that good beginnings do not necessarily make good endings. Lord knows, I've done enough walking over the years to learn that. I was up early, as usual, downed the by now traditional cup, or rather glass, of *café con leche*, with a sweet cake to serve me in lieu of sugar, and was soon trudging up the road towards Muñotello. By now I could see the pattern of the Gredos. They came curving in from the north-east, a wide series of hills rather than one high crest, but reaching ever higher as they moved south, separated by lush valleys full of fields and farms and clumps of olive trees. Under these same olive trees now lurked black cattle, some of which were clearly *vacas*, cows, some of which were probably bulls – a problem perhaps? The question remaining in my mind was, were these *toros bravos* destined for a brief half-hour of glory in the bullring, or stud bulls which, by and large, lead rather pleasant lives? Whichever they were, they were the famous black cattle of Ávila and I was to see many more of them in the days ahead.

Muñotello I never saw. According to the map and an aged crone in black whom I accosted on the highway, a track leads up from near the cemetery of Muñotello through a deep valley into the hills, a little north-east of the great mountain of La Serrota (2,294 metres, 7,526 feet), which now loomed up clearly ahead. I marched up this track, passing a house where several people were sensibly splashing in a cool blue swimming pool, and climbed up into the hills. Before long I had left the modern world behind, down in that green misty valley, and was again very much on my own.

The clear track soon petered out, leaving me with a wide choice of footpaths which were, in fact, cow-paths. There was no clear indication as to which one I should follow and my map was, as usual, useless. The Spanish are not great walkers and waymarking is a largely unknown art here. Cows, being sensible creatures, contour round the hillsides as they move about to graze and so create decent foot-wide paths. The only snag is that the cows may not necessarily go in the right direction. However, I had 185° on my compass to keep me heading south to the C500 road, and another road lay even closer. The blind end of the valley lay higher up ahead, and I had the great Serrota to my right. I could hardly get lost.

The first snag came halfway up the valley, when I encountered my first herd of black cattle. They were huge beasts, roaming all over the hillside and cropping the grass right beside the path ahead. I am not afraid of cows, but several of these were clearly bulls. I took to the hillside, climbed higher and drifted past, above the main herd while all the cattle stopped grazing and gazed up at me silently. This I found somewhat unnerving. These are splendid cattle, black as pitch, with shining coats and wide, glittering horns, beautiful to look at but not to be trifled with. I kept to the hillside and passed on.

The valley climbed in a series of steps beside the stream, each step marked with a low waterfall, one col after another, each delivering me to yet another false crest. Getting to the top took time. The ground was covered with thick brown bracken, interspersed with burnt patches of matt-weed, gorse and juniper. Brushing through this I was filthy before long and, even worse, losing valuable time. I eventually came out onto the hilltop, high above the hamlet of Cepeda la Mora, and after skirting another vast herd I arrived there, fairly tired, at about three in the afternoon. Fortunately, there was a bar, fortunately it was open and, even better, the inhabitants were friendly. They were the last friendly Castilians I was to meet that day.

I have relieved my mind on the subject of Spanish attitudes to the passing stranger. My opinion has not changed much since I rode through Spain on my bicycle years ago, heading for Compostela. The Aragonese were totally indifferent, and ignored me if they could. It was quite hard to get served or find a room. The Basques of Navarra were jolly, friendly and usually drunk, but this was the San Fermín time in Pamplona, so being drunk was almost respectable. The Castilians were reserved and polite enough, but you had to make all the running. The Galicians were the friendliest of all and rushed out to offer the passing pilgrim water and wine. Mind you, being friendly is part of the stock-in-trade of Galicia. The great export of Galicia is waiters; ask the waiter in any restaurant where he comes from and I would give long odds that he comes from Galicia. On this occasion, my main contacts were with Castilians, and Castilians can be damned hard work. It is so easy to lump the Spaniards together and assume that if you know one you know the lot, but Spaniards are as different from each other as the Irish and the Scots are from the English, and their temperaments vary from the dour to the gleeful. Also, it would be a brave man who could look at a nation of thirty-eight million people and use one or two sweeping phrases to describe the lot. Spaniards are (and you discover this easily on foot) a nation of nations; Basques, Aragonese, Castilians, and half a dozen more. Perhaps the 'true Spaniard' is the only one who doesn't exist.

*   *   *

However, back in the cool depths of the bar at Cepeda la Mora, we were all friends while consulting my map. One cheerful Castilian soul, after buying me a beer (wonder of wonders) even offered me a lift (wonder of wonders of wonders) which he strongly advised me to take, but I thought that the country looked flatter now, and I was able to refuse. Besides, if I angled myself a little west I should strike the road for Hoyos de Miguel Muñoz. From there a road would lead me to San Martín del Pimpollar, close to the *parador*, which was, say, ten miles away, or about four hours' march. I should be there after dark, but still in good time for dinner. This decided, I ate a huge *bocadillo* of mountain ham, drank another large beer and set off again.

The Gredos countryside, between Crespos and Cepeda is some of the most beautiful I crossed in my walk across Spain, but the section south from Cepeda to San Martín del Pimpollar was, if anything, even more beautiful, and perhaps the best of the lot. On leaving the village I followed a clear track across a green, lush valley. From here, low hills crept up to the mountains, which lay ahead and swept up on either side. Directly ahead lay yet another vast herd of black cattle, but I was getting used to free-range cattle by now. I simply skirted the thickest part of the herd, chasing odd cows from my path with flourishes of my stick. This stick, apart from its use as an anti-mugging tool, is a marvellously useful implement against aggressive animals. You don't have to use it, you just point your stick at dog or cow and they wisely steer away.

Remembering my time herding cattle in Montana, I attempted to soothe the savage beasts with a little singing. I was well into bellowing *The Yellow Rose of Texas*, when I looked up, directly into the eyes of a *vaquero* staring down at me from the top of a flat rock. On balance, I think he was the more surprised. It is not every day that a Spanish cowherd finds an Englishman singing to his cows. Being covered with embarrassment, we conversed. He was looking after all the village cows; apparently the farmers took it in turns. Sometimes he did it on horseback, sometimes, as now, on foot. There was very little grass after the long hot summer, so the *vacas* stayed down here, close to the river, but, *por Dios*, even the river was low and there was still no sign of the autumn rains. This lack of water was causing everyone problems and was to plague me further in the week ahead, and this thought clearly occurred to my companion who spends all his time in the hot heartland of Spain.

The idea of anyone *walking* across Spain left my new acquaintance almost dumbfounded, not least because there was a perfectly good train service from Ávila or Talavera. If I did it for fun, as I claimed, well, he just wished he had the money for fun like that. He told me to watch out for small penned herds of bulls. These would most likely be fighting bulls, although the best fighting bulls, the Miuras, came from further south, in

Andalucía. My new best friend was a great expert on Miuras. Miuras are
famous and ferocious. A Miura bull killed the great Manolete, the most
famous and graceful of *toreros*, and indeed some Miura herds produce
such ferocious bulls that some *toreros* refuse to fight them. Miura bulls,
he told me, are naturally cunning and can learn. The young bloods from
the villages think it great sport to try a little cape work with a young Miura,
but when this bull gets older and into the ring it remembers that the cape
is nothing and goes for the man. I vowed to keep an eye open for Miura
bulls and refrain from teaching them cape work.

We spent the best part of half an hour sitting on the rocks in the
bright afternoon sunshine, surrounded by the black Ávila cattle, before
I realised that time was passing and I had to get on. Stopping like this is
not always a good idea; you tend to creak as you get under way again.

Somewhere after leaving the herd I lost the track. From that moment
on nothing went well for me during the rest of the day. Still bearing east,
I plunged into more matted undergrowth, and eventually made my way
down a steep hillside to a road. I was now well off my compass track
for the *parador*, I could not find little Hoyos de Miguel Muñoz, and
was well behind time. Even worse, I was now very tired. I decided to
put back my anticipated arrival at the *parador*, which was now dancing
in my imagination like some impossibly comfortable and desirable
caravanserai, and stopped to ring ahead and warn them at Venta del
Obispo. Halfway through the call I decided to stop the night in Venta,
so I moved my booking at the *parador* back a night, only to be informed,
quite gleefully, by the (Castilian) señora at Venta del Obispo that she had
no accommodation. Nor did she know where I might find a room anywhere
else. Her smirk was . . . well, irritating. I therefore marched wearily on
up the road, with two further villages ahead as backstops. At Venta de
Rasquilla, where the C500 road turns west for the *parador*, there is a small
hostel but the lady here, clearly a relative of the crone at Venta, told me
equally gleefully that she too was full. It was now dark. I don't mind bad
news too much, but their obvious delight in telling a tired, loaded walker
to push off into the night did take a little getting used to. Neither was there
a phone which I could use to call the *parador* and rebook my room. So,
hitching up my pack yet again, I trudged on up the hill to San Martín del
Pimpollar which, according to my small guidebook had a hostel. For the
record there is no hostel at San Martín del Pimpollar.

It was now nine at night and very dark. I had been marching for some
fourteen hours that day, mostly over mountains, on just one ham *bocadillo*
and two beers. I was quite worn out, fed up and far from home. There is a
rough little bar called *El Cortijo* in San Martín, run by a pleasant old soul
and his wife. This was full of archetypal, gnarled peasants, who gazed at
me as at a visiting Martian, but then became quite chatty. They fed me
beer and sympathy and the old man suggested I try the nearby camp site

and come back for coffee in the morning. It was now too late to crawl about in the dark and pitch the tent, so I simply found a low wall and did the next best thing. I flung down the inner tent, put my sleeping bag on top of that and covered everything, bag, boots and rucksack, with the tent outer, to guard against the night dew. I then pulled off my socks – ah, the relief of it – and turned in. Stony ground notwithstanding, it was the best sleep I'd had in days. I lay back, watched shooting stars blaze out across the sky and listened to the rushing sound of a mountain torrent. Then I closed my eyes and went out like a light.

*   *   *

I woke up just as the sky was turning grey, but warm and snug in my sleeping bag I was in no great hurry to get up. I was also as stiff as a board. Sleeping on the ground is something that takes a little getting used to. Years ago in the Commandos we used to sleep on the ground quite a lot, an art we developed to the point where I can distinctly remember my Section sleeping quite blissfully on the tumbled stones of a stream bed. The trick is to relax and let your body mould to the ground. This is rather easier if you can sleep on your back, for bony hips and elbows otherwise make sleeping difficult. The snag is that people sleeping on their backs tend to snore. You could hear my Section sleeping from a mile away on a good, still night. Anyway, I had to try to work out how to get my over-used body moving again, and thought I might as well stay where I was until I had done so.

I lay on in my bag until it got light, thinking that my main requirements now were a good wash, a good meal, and a general clean-up. If the state of my clothing was anything to go by, stained with sweat and the black ash of the burnt gorse and matt-weed, I must look like the Wrath of God. I almost felt some sympathy for the two hostile crones of the previous evening. I cannot have looked the most inviting guest. Well, a rinse in the nearby stream might work wonders so, rather stiffly, I crawled out and began to splash about in it, groaning happily to myself as my limbs began to work.

The stream was icy, ideal for getting the eyes open and sluicing sweaty grime from my face and hands. Then I cleaned my teeth and even shaved before hiding my rucksack in the bracken and walking back down into San Martín for that long-anticipated coffee at *El Cortijo*. I had eaten only one ham roll since the previous morning, but all I wanted now was a hot, milky coffee. After that, I collected my rucksack and walked on up the road, climbing higher into the Gredos. After about an hour I arrived at the *parador* at Navarredonda, checked in and met yet another snag.

*   *   *

The path across the Gredos from the *parador*, up through the Puerto de Candeleda, begins with an eighteen kilometre uphill trudge along a winding tarmac road to the start of the footpath. There seemed no virtue in a road-walk, so I decided to do what any sensible walker would do and take a taxi to the start of the trans-Gredos footpath at the northern *Plataforma*. The usual surly receptionist greeted my request for a taxi with the news that there was only one taxi hereabouts, and could not contain his smile when, on being forced to ring and book it, he was able to tell me that the taxi was not available. I therefore had to start my crossing of the main Sierra de Gredos range with an eighteen kilometre approach march. I was not at all pleased.

It was not my original intention to be a purist about walking every step of the way across Spain. I intended to walk the walks, but after I had done enough for one day, I would take a bus or train or a lift from the hospitable motorist, and so be wafted gently to my next warm bed. None of this happened. I walked because I had no choice but to walk, and if I wanted to cross the Gredos to Candeleda next day, I would have to walk every step of the way. Damn it! Neither would the receptionist change any money. Having scrubbed everything I owned other than what I needed to wear, I walked down into the village of Navarredonda de Gredos and found a bank. I also found the *Mesón de Almanzor*, a very pleasant little hotel beside the road where the cook took my order and served my lunch with a smile. This was the first smile I had seen in days, and it hit me like a sunbeam. When I asked this charmer where she came from, she said, 'From Andalucía'. Ah, that accounts for it.

*   *   *

I was getting noticeably slimmer. I realised this when I stripped off at the *parador* that afternoon and had yet another shower. Bones were now sticking through my skin here and there. The shower completed, I crawled into bed for a siesta, and then got up for another shower and an evening stroll about the *parador* to work up an appetite for dinner. Here, at least, the *parador* did me well, for the food was very good. I had a decent red Rioja with the meal, half a bottle of white Cebreros to get the juices flowing, and the *especialidad de la casa* – *tocino del cielo* or pork from Heaven.

This *parador* of the Gredos at Navarredonda was the first ever *parador*. The doors opened as long ago as 1928, on a site chosen by the then King of Spain, Alfonso XIII. It is fairly modern, not a castle, and is surrounded by a thick belt of pine trees, standing at 1,800 metres. It is built around a former hunting lodge, but many of the *paradores* opened since have been constructed from the ruins or remains of old castles and monasteries; a marvellous way of restoring these often beautiful buildings and returning them to useful life.

Travel a little west from here, for example to the *parador* at Jarandilla de la Vera, and you can stay in the room where the Holy Roman Emperor Charles V slept while he was waiting for his cell to be prepared in the nearby monastery at Yuste. This monastery is well worth visiting, and you can get there quite easily from Madrid or Salamanca. The monastery at Yuste was founded in 1408, and parts of it are decorated with colourful Mudejar azulejos, tiles from Talavera, which is famous for such articles, though they look rather odd in the sombre setting of a monastery. The room where Charles V died in 1558 is still kept draped with black, and even the sheets in which he died have been preserved. (I sometimes think that the Spanish have a love of death. During the Civil War the Spanish Legion's war cry was *Viva la muerte*, Long live death, and their monuments seem to make great play of skulls and bones, a dark shadow on this sunny land.) The *parador* at Jarandilla occupies the 14th century castle built by the counts of Oropesa, and is among the finest castles in the entire *parador* network and therefore one of my favourites.

Over the years I have become a devoted *parador*-bagger, and rarely miss the chance to stay in one if it lies anywhere on my path. Since I also like castles, I prefer the *paradores* at Viana, Carmona, Sigüenza and Jarandilla to modern ones like the one at Fuente Dé in the Picos. I was now looking forward to staying in the *paradores* at Oropesa and Guadalupe, which lay somewhere ahead. All I had to do was get there.

The immediate section of the walk, over the spine of the Gredos, looked tough but interesting. I comforted myself with the thought that this part of the Gredos is famous for walking and riding holidays. There must be well-trodden paths, maybe waymarks, perhaps even people to talk to. Either way, just hacking over to Candeleda would be a challenge. Beyond Candeleda, the bloody *meseta* would begin again for a while, certainly as far as Oropesa, but I could live with that, and two days ought to see me over the mountains and out of Castile, with another leg of my walk completed. I hung the breakfast order leaflet outside my door – breakfast in bed, what bliss – and went to bed.

One of the other things I have noticed on my walking or cycling trips over the years is that, plan them how you will, sooner or later something will go wrong. The trick then is to push on and get over the difficulty whatever the cost, then pick yourself up and start again, as problems are inevitable. On the way to Jerusalem we had traumas crossing the Syrian–Jordanian frontier, with footpads and stone-throwing children. On the way to Compostela, the north face of the Pyrenees, steep and infested with horseflies, proved a memorable barrier, while walking across France I can recall various difficulties on the snow-covered slopes of the Plomb du Cantal. I anticipated no such problems when crossing the well-trodden slopes of the Sierra de Gredos, but I was wrong. Seriously wrong.

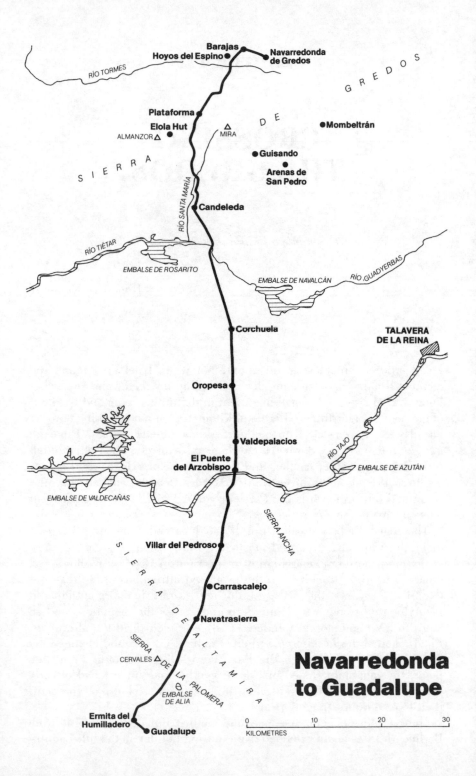

RÍO TORMES

Barajas
Hoyos del Espino
Navarredonda
de Gredos

GREDOS

DE

Plataforma
Mombeltrán
Elola Hut
ALMANZOR
MIRA

SIERRA

Guisando

Arenas de
San Pedro

RÍO SANTA MARÍA

Candeleda

RÍO TIÉTAR

EMBALSE DE ROSARITO

EMBALSE DE NAVALCÁN

RÍO GUADYERBAS

Corchuela

TALAVERA
DE LA REINA

Oropesa

Valdepalacios

El Puente
del Arzobispo

RÍO TAJO

EMBALSE DE AZUTÁN

EMBALSE DE VALDECAÑAS

SIERRA ANCHA

Villar del Pedroso

SIERRA

Carrascalejo

DE

Navatrasierra

ALTAMIRA

SIERRA DE LA PALOMERA

CERVALES

EMBALSE
DE ALIA

Ermita del
Humilladero

Guadalupe

Navarredonda
to Guadalupe

0   10   20   30

KILOMETRES

CHAPTER TEN

CROSSING
THE GREDOS

First, you bite off more than you can chew;
then you chew it.

Robert F. Kennedy

I had ordered breakfast in my room, but when I got up I found the menu still hanging outside my door. Grinding my teeth, and somewhat hung-over, I snatched something to eat in the dining room and sped out of the door at eight-fifteen. Eighteen kilometres of road-walking now lay ahead before I even started up the Puerto de Candeleda footpath. From the *parador* the road leads down to the village of Navarredonda, then through little Barajas, another hamlet, and then, just before Hoyos del Espino, a side road leads south, over the Río Tormes, a wide, cool stream, and so on and on, up towards the *Plataforma*. All in all, it was a pleasant enough start to the day.

The road climbed steadily uphill, so I gained some useful height along the way, and it carried me to the *Plataforma*, a great car park at the main northern access point to the Central Gredos. Walkers and climbers head up from here to the promised attractions of the region – the hills, the views, the birds, the flowers – and I therefore anticipated plenty of well-trodden trails up, into and across the mountain, and so down to my night-stop at Candeleda. By one o'clock in the afternoon, I had reached the *Plataforma*, where I bathed my feet and changed my socks and prepared for the Big Push across the mountain. From this point, the mountain sloped up, quite gently, and since I had already gained a fair amount of height, and the footpath was shown on the map, it all looked quite straightforward.

Here I met Jochem, a somewhat mature university student from Berlin, who was on an extended cycletouring holiday in the hill-country around Madrid. Jochem was having a great time. He had an eighteen-speed mountain bike, a small tent and a girlfriend in Madrid who came out to meet him at weekends. Some people really know how to organise travel. We had in fact already met on the way up to the *Plataforma*, when we were both too puffed to do more than exchange nods. After a chat here, Jochem decided to chain his bike to a nearby post and walk up to the *puerto* with me before walking round to spend the night at the Elola hut, which is the only fully-equipped mountain hut in the Gredos. This hut is usually open in high summer only, say from June to September, but a group of Spanish walkers resting at the *Plataforma* told us that owing to the extended summer the hut was still open and could be reached from the *Plataforma* in about three hours with no great difficulty. This seemed a good thing, as Jochem only had sandals, which are far from ideal footwear for mountain-walking, and it was shatteringly hot. I was very glad of his company, and it was nice to speak English again after weeks of speaking Spanish. I was even beginning to dream in Spanish.

The path up to the col, or *puerto*, is delightful, but the trick is to stay close to the stream at the start. Do not follow the more obvious winding cobbled footpath. We made the obvious mistake, of course, but corrected ourselves after half a mile or so, and plodded back down to rejoin the stream. From there a very faint footpath, helped out with small cairns here and there, could be seen weaving its way across the grassy valley ahead, and so towards the distant skyline.

According to my map the footpath rises some 1,000 metres between the *Plataforma* and the col, which lies at about 2,000 metres, but it didn't seem like it. We walked on slowly across the cow-cropped grass, among more of those black Ávila cattle. There were hundreds of them, dotted all across the plain, but by following the cairns and the ever-narrowing stream, we soon drew near the foot of the final ascent to the col, with the Elola mountain hut now in sight high on the upper parts of the mountain to our right. On the way there we put up clouds of beautiful blue-winged grasshoppers, which spurted out from under our feet and joined the regular dancing passage of copper-winged butterflies. This is one of those soaring mountain walks across springy grass. The stream chuckled over the stones at our side and it was all quite delightful. Further on, near the foot of the final ridge, we met a herd of *cabras montañesas*, the Gredos mountain goats. These are small brown friendly creatures who let us get very close indeed before scampering away for a short distance over the rocks. Then they stopped to pose, silhouetting themselves romantically on the very top of small crags, a habit which must shorten their life-span dramatically when the shooting season comes around. Before long there were little brown goats leaping about everywhere. Kites and great eagles swung overhead, riding the afternoon thermals, the sun shone down and trout finned lazily in the deeper pools of the stream. It was all quite idyllic. Then we reached the col.

This route, running directly north to south over the crest of the Gredos from the *Plataforma* to Candeleda, is the main footpath route through the mountains. According to the guidebook, wise people like me usually approached the Gredos from the north where, as I had already seen and experienced, the land rises gradually in a series of open, grassy plateaux, each reaching a false crest, which in turn pulls you ever higher to the final ridge. This can be achieved without apparent effort if you just keep plodding on and take your time. It is also possible to trek along the crest of the ridge from centres like Arenas de San Pedro, a small town on the south side of the Pico Pass at 1,352 metres, 4,436 feet, through which the main C502 road runs between Talavera de la Reina and Ávila.

The Gredos is a great area, full of birds and flowers, a natural paradise for botanists, birdwatchers and lovers of the great outdoors, especially backpackers, hill-walkers and pony-trekkers. There are a number of riding stables in the Gredos and long horse-back trails are possible along the spine of the mountains. Those who like to take in the outdoors at a more gentle pace can tour around the base of the hills by car, to see the castle at Mombeltrán, the 14th-century seat of the dukes of Alburquerque, or the famous carved stone bulls at Guisando, which are said to date back to pre-Roman times. The great centre for walking tours is the little town of Arenas de San Pedro at the southern end of the main Pico Pass. Arenas also has a castle, known as *El Castillo de la Triste Condesa*, the Castle of the Sad Countess. The countess in question was the widow of Alvaro de Luna, chief minister to King Juan II of Castile. Alvaro got too big for his boots and the king had his head cut off.

With the possible exceptions of the Ordesa Park in the Pyrenees and the central Picos de Europa, this area of the Gredos offers the best hill-trekking area in Spain. What followed after the col was probably my own fault.

The Puerto de Candeleda is marked by a large cairn set on a small platform just below the crest. Here we paused to take photographs. One of the snags of the solitary journey is that your photos are restricted to those you can take yourself, and so the walker remains out of shot for most of the journey. I have never found anyone passing by who can successfully master the complexities of speed and aperture while operating the zoom lens. Fortunately, Jochem knew all about cameras. Then, our photo session concluded, we moved up to the crest – and gasped. We stood on the lip of a void, the ground dropping away at our feet into a great blue misty chasm, reaching far out into space and down into the valley below. 'Great God!' I cried.

'This is the Pulpit of the World . . . but how am I going to get down?'

* * *

Note the brief bit of Bunyan before the abrupt return to practicality. Even so, the view south from the Gredos crest is quite stunning. On a clear day the view from the 2,200-metre peak of the Puerto de Candeleda must be almost limitless. On that hot and hazy afternoon, the view was still superb. We could see for miles across the farmland far below, even to the glinting waters of the dam near El Puente del Arzobispo. Far below, between that distant point and where we now stood, lay the little town of Candeleda, my destination for the day. First, I had to descend this mountain, and no obvious way down presented itself. The mountainside seemed almost sheer, give or take a few ridges, and it looked like wild country to my weary eyes.

Jochem and I sat down to admire the view and consult the map. The map certainly indicated a track but I could see no clear route that in any way resembled the one shown. However, there had to be one somewhere, and eventually, searching about along the crest, we found a cairn, and then another one beyond that, further down the ridge. I shook hands with Jochem, thanked him for his company, hitched my rucksack up on to my shoulders for the umpteenth time that day, and set off down the mountain.

* * *

Like most Spanish footpaths, this path down the southern side of the Sierra de Gredos is not a footpath in the accepted sense. At the start it is easy enough to follow most of the time, as you move from cairn to cairn, but that means stepping over huge rocks, or easing nervously across open and very exposed rock faces. It is no easy route for a loaded walker more than halfway through an already long day. The constant need to watch where you are stepping and pick out the way ahead can be wearing, but it is important. If you don't watch your step you can fall or stumble and do yourself no good. On the other hand, you have to keep looking ahead for the next cairn. If you miss a single cairn and wander off-track, it is difficult to find the path again. Many of these 'cairns' were just a single small rock placed on top of a boulder, and only obvious if you were looking for one ahead and knew it when you saw it.

Having no other choice, on and on I went. Eventually, about halfway down the mountain, I met a broader track leading directly downhill, more obvious perhaps but no easier to walk on. The snag now was that it followed steep stone runs, full of loose rocks, large and small, a route plentifully studded with sharp stones jutting up from the rock-hard, dusty soil. Imagine the almost sheer bed of a dry mountain stream and you will have some idea of the terrain. Sitting down for a brief rest and a cup of my rapidly diminishing supply of water, I contemplated one of the longer stone runs below and thought it resembled nothing so much as the scaly back of some gigantic crocodile, waiting to swallow me up. It is terrible stuff to walk on.

Paths like these are really no joke. On steep slopes your toes are thrown forward painfully into the front of the boots. The constant stumbling over shifting rocks also puts a great strain on the legs and ankles and is very tiring. I had no real idea where I was going, except downhill. There were no waymarks, no splashes of paint, and the cairns had stopped or disappeared. After an hour or so of this I was drenched in sweat, crushed by the weight of the rucksack and nearly exhausted. Then I lost the path completely.

I had been slowly and painfully descending yet another stone run when I met — oh joy! — a road; an earth-surfaced logging road admittedly, but a road nevertheless, an undeniable smooth road. The snag was that it seemed to run uphill in both directions. Only a Spanish road can do this. There were no signs on the ground to indicate the way, and the road was not marked on the map. There was nothing to show the route I should follow, left or right, so I hunted about thinking 'Give me a sign, oh Lord', but still no path appeared. I could now see the river in the valley far below, which had to be the Río Santa María. That was shown on the map and flowed out to Candeleda, but it was still a long way down, and how could I get there? Then I found what I thought *might* be a path, leading off the road and down through the woods. I decided to follow it, and this was a mistake.

If you have followed my travels attentively, you may have noticed by now that many of these Spanish 'footpaths' are made by animals, not walkers. So it was here. Perhaps a deer or a goat had made this near-vertical descent through the fallen trees and thick bracken of the increasingly steep slope. There was certainly little space under the low trees for a fully-grown Englishman with a rucksack. I bashed on down, plagued now by flies, disgusting creatures, which came buzzing in hordes to swarm upon me, drinking my sweat and crawling into my mouth and nose, even into my eyes. Lacking the strength to climb back up again, the only way I could descend now was to let myself slide down the slope from level to level, cascading through the bracken and great ropes of thorns in a cloud of dry dust, crashing from foothold to foothold, from ledge to ledge.

This had an inevitable outcome. I slid down one sheer slope and hit the ground hard. My knees buckled, the rucksack shot up onto my shoulders and hurled me headlong over the next drop. Crashing and rolling through the undergrowth — this drop too was practically vertical — only the undergrowth stopped my going into free-fall. I fell for fifty feet, and maybe more, before I was finally stopped by a tangled network of thorny liana-like branches. There I swung, gently to and fro, suspended over the drop like a climber in a tangle of ropes, while the flies swarmed back in to feast on the bloody scratches, the rubbed-raw skin and the drenching sweat that poured into my eyes. Life became difficult.

About this time, I began to realise that I could be in serious trouble. Night was coming on fast. There was no one else on the mountain, I had no water left and I was stuck. I was also exhausted, and being eaten alive by beasties. I began to feel very sorry for myself, but there is some comfort in knowing that it's all your own fault. After racking my brains for someone to blame for it all, I decided that I had better do something and move before I either died up here or was carried off by the flies, or both. It did not seem too funny at the time.

I was now hanging upside down in the thorn branches, more or less resting on my shoulders. Fortunately, my camera bag, complete with buck-knife, had swung round onto my chest. Moving carefully, I got out the knife and began to saw away at the tangle of thorn branches which were holding me in suspense. One, two, three parted without much difficulty. It did occur to me that this was rather like sitting high in a tree, sawing through the branch you are sitting on. But what else was there to do? I cut through the next liana, and fell. Away I went, ripping and rending through the undergrowth to land with a terrible crash on some rocks about ten feet below. The knife, God bless it, came clattering down after me.

I don't recommend this sort of behaviour, and I must make that clear. I have to be careful what I write because, if not, I will get more of those letters, written on recycled paper in green ink, accusing me of luring walkers from the leafy lanes of Surrey to a lonely death in the Sierra de Gredos. Had I broken a leg or sprained an ankle, I might be up there yet, but if it is no good crying over spilt milk, it is even less use weeping over that which remains in the bottle. I had got away with it, minus some skin, some blood and with a bent frame on the rucksack, but otherwise I was fine. The flies were having a marvellous time feasting on my flesh and blood and driving me crazy, but I could hear the river clearly now. Once the moon came up I would be able to move again and get down there. God, I was thirsty.

I lay on a slight but definite path and, after about two hours in growing darkness but with no more falls, I finally found the main footpath. This led down to a concrete footbridge over the river. It all looked most promising, so I limped down the bank, flung off the rucksack and plunged my head into the river. I could have drunk it dry. Taking stock, I had lost my hat, a map, a compass and several straps off my rucksack. My glasses had snapped in two, but this was no problem because I had a spare pair of glasses and a spare compass. I'm not entirely stupid. My clothes were filthy again from the burnt bracken and torn in several places, and my neckerchief, which I used to polish the spectacles and mop the brow, had been ripped to rags. I was covered in dirt, sweat and blood, and was still under serious attack from crawling, biting flies, but after stripping off my shirt and washing away most of the mess, I decided that, on the whole, I was lucky. I would live. All I needed to do now was walk out of the valley, get off this accursed mountain and have a long, cold glass of beer. I hauled the rucksack on again, which now seemed to weigh a ton in my exhausted state, and set off down the gorge, picking my way along the path in the clear moonlight. After a mile or so the path vanished . . . I could have wept.

Weeping or whingeing does no good in this kind of situation. Perhaps the sensible thing would have been to stop and rest, but there was still no level ground, and I was still being ravaged by the flies. I scrambled down to the river and waded across to the flatter left bank. There I was considerably cheered by meeting a herd of donkeys. All I could see were their great long furry ears, sticking up out of the bracken, and they scrambled up as I came closer and clattered off before me down the path, but this was a sign of civilisation. Where there were donkeys there would be people, tracks, a road, a suburb, a bar!

I did my best to get out of the valley before the light finally faded, splashing to and fro across the river several times in my attempt to find a route out, but eventually I gave up. I could go no further in the dark and I had to wait for daylight, sleeping on a patch of grass, the rocks around me draped with wet clothes. Fortunately it was a warm night, and once I had my clothes off, it seemed only sensible to hop across to the river on bare feet and have a bath. This nearly proved my undoing, for I stepped in where it was both deep and fast and was yards downstream before I came up spouting, banged into a rock, ran aground on gravel, stubbed my toes and crawled damply up the bank. It took quite a while to find my sleeping bag and I had to hop up and down on it to get dry and warm, but I was beyond caring. I crawled into the bag, watched the shooting stars for a few minutes and woke at dawn. Then came the grisly business of putting on wet clothes; those in the rucksack were dry, but they were clean, so I saved them and put on the wet, dirty ones, and set off swiftly downstream. Trying to get

warm, I walked waist-deep in a thick white mist that hung about the
river, going as fast as I could.

I now found the footpath without difficulty and followed it up and up,
finally to reach a metalled road. By eight in the morning I was sitting
in a café in Candeleda, being stared at by the other patrons, and who
can blame them. I had a large coffee and that large glass of beer I had
promised myself the night before. Then I had another one. I don't usually
drink beer at eight in the morning but I felt I had earned it.

*   *   *

There is a point to make about all this. After I wrote my book about
France, one or two people complained that I made too much of the
difficulties of the journey and went on and on about my feet. Well,
they were *my* feet. Lacking encounters with the great and the good
on my travels, I fill in the pages by telling it like it is, sore feet,
steep mountains, warts and all. Maybe those who find this hard to
take have never really tried it. The fact remains that if you set out
to cover a certain distance in a certain amount of time, you have to
expect difficulties, and I do. I don't even mind them. Life would be
terribly dull if it all went according to plan, and walks like this rather
match the classic description of life in a Commando – a pleasant sort of
pain in the neck. I scribbled that thought in my notebook and ordered
another glass of beer.

CHAPTER ELEVEN

CROSSING
LA MANCHA

The traveller is sickened by the wide expanse
of monotonous steppes, over which naught but the
genius of Cervantes could have thrown any charm.

Richard Ford *A Handbook for Travellers in Spain* (1855)

I was not a pretty sight when I crawled into that bar in Candeleda. The flip side of the general Spanish indifference to the welfare of others is that you get left alone most of the time. On this occasion my entrance drew a general intake of breath. Even the usual bellow-level of bar conversation dropped for a moment as heads turned to view this sudden apparition. I have to say that my response to all this was a mental 'To hell with the lot of you', though I am in the main a bashful soul. I flung the pack into the corner, elbowed my way through the crowd of the bar, and ordered a beer and a coffee. Since everyone else was flinging down whisky or anis or *Ciento y Tres* as fast as they could manage, I might as well have ordered milk.

This done, I hauled my wash-bag from my rucksack and marched to the *servicios*, where the sight of my face in the mirror made me feel rather sorry for the clientèle. Matted hair, wild eyes, a face scratched and blackened with cinders, filthy clothes, bloodstains here and there. I looked like an axe-murderer. It took a lot of scrubbing to transfer most of the grime from my hands and face to the porcelain of the sink, but after that and a scrubbing of the teeth, I looked and felt practically human. I had another beer at the bar to celebrate this fact. I could easily have spent the day like that, getting quietly wrecked, but it was still only nine-thirty in the morning, and I might as well walk on. Besides, I had had more than enough of the surly citizens of Castile. If I could push on hard across the flat land ahead, below the now towering southern slopes of the Gredos, there was a fair chance I could spend that night in the castle of Oropesa, eighteen miles to the south. I would not actually have minded spending twenty-four hours in Candeleda, which was becoming more pleasant by the glass, but since I had time in hand and was feeling no pain, I thought I might as well press on.

*   *   *

South of Candeleda the *meseta* begins again, but this *meseta* rocks and rolls and is no longer flat and boring. There are great olive and oak tree plantations. Even the occasional deer could be seen flitting away through the trees and, with a breeze from the mountains to push me south, I almost enjoyed myself. Considering the rigours of the previous day, I felt in surprisingly good form as I headed out of Candeleda, but the mood did not last. One of the things you have to get used to as the years whirl by is that you don't bounce as high, or back as quickly, as you used to do in the golden days of youth. Before an hour had passed, I was moving very slowly and was only saved from stopping completely by the fact that the country I was crossing was relatively flat, but at least not boring. I followed the road for about five miles, then cut off through a chain-link fence and onto a compass bearing for Oropesa.

The snag here, and it was to be a snag for much of the next week, was that my direct route to the south was barred not so much by rivers as by a series of *embalses*, dams. On the map these appeared as wide and formidable obstacles, though in fact most of them were empty. That was another snag. The Spanish make great use of dams on all their rivers both for irrigation and for hydroelectric power, which is quite right and sensible, but the result is to create a series of lakes some of which are as large as inland seas. These dams spread wide across Central Spain, there is a general shortage of roads and a subsequent lack of bridges. This limits the number of potential crossing points. *Embalses* therefore have to be skirted, and skirting a dam takes time. Where is 617 Squadron when you need them?

The first of these dams, the Embalse de Rosarito, lay across my path a few miles south of Candeleda where the road eased itself carefully between two great misty lakes. The Embalse de Rosarito and the Embalse de Navalcán are the results of dams on the Río Tiétar and the Río Guadyerbas, which run across the southern foot of the Gredos. The latter *embalse* was a surprise, for it was not shown on my map. Looking on the bright side, crossing the eastern end of the Rosarito took me at last out of the province of Ávila, scene of so many traumas. I stopped to celebrate the fact by washing the dust of that inhospitable province off

my boots in a trickle of water by the road. This is the first time I have
done this and I was watched patiently by a peasant with a small flock of
sheep, who came up to ask what I was doing.

'I'm just glad, *muy, muy contento*, to be out of Castile,' I told him. 'I
can't wait to leave Castile behind.'

'But this is still Castile,' he said, shaking his head. 'This is *Nueva
Castilla — Castilla-La Mancha.*'

Damn!

*   *   *

The La Mancha written about by Cervantes actually lies further to the
east of my present route, in a rough triangle drawn between Madrid,
Ciudad Real and Albacete. Those who think the *meseta* flat should try
the plain of La Mancha. La Mancha is like an ironing-board planted with
orange groves and olive trees. In La Mancha, it is the colours and not the
terrain which give life to the countryside, and those who have read *Don
Quixote* will be particularly miffed by the distinct shortage of windmills.
There are a few on a ridge at Consuegra, south of Aranjuez, and a
photogenic collection at La Criptana, but that is about it. El Toboso,
where Don Quixote met his fair Dulcinea, hovers between being a scruffy
village with unpaved streets and a tourist centre for the Don Quixote
industry. La Mancha gets away with this lack of attraction thanks to the
usual Spanish indifference to the interest of others, and by continuing
echoes of Cervantes and his unforgettable creation, Don Quixote.

Miguel de Cervantes was born in 1547, the son of a doctor. At the age
of twenty-one he became a soldier serving in the Italian Wars and at the
Battle of Lepanto, when Don Juan of Austria defeated the Turkish Fleet.
Fortunate on this occasion, Cervantes continued to serve at sea until he
was captured by the Barbary corsairs in 1575 and sold into slavery in
Algiers. His master was a Greek who kept him about the house, so he
was spared the usual fate of poor prisoners who rowed out their short lives
at the oars of the galleys. After five years in captivity, Cervantes was
finally ransomed and returned to Spain. He was now thirty-three and was
to spend the rest of his life in poverty, interspersed with several terms
in prison for debt. He was now writing all the time, but it was another
quarter of a century before he finally made his name with *Don Quixote*.
Fame perhaps, but no money, for the book was swiftly pirated. Three
unauthorised editions were on the streets within weeks, and Cervantes
was still a poor man when he died in 1616: 'an old man, a soldier, a
gentleman, and poor'. Had he enjoyed the benefits of fame today, he
would have seen that *Don Quixote* has never been out of print, is now

available in more than thirty languages, and has been made into an opera, a ballet, a stage play and a film. The money he might have made is incalculable.

The Penguin paperback edition of *Don Quixote* runs to nearly a thousand closely-printed pages, and I have to say I found it heavy going when I decided to read it for this trip – and I am a very fast reader. You have to take it in digestible amounts and trace the story of this half-crazed gentleman, Don Quixote, his head spinning with knight-erranting and his down-to-earth squire Sancho Panza, as an allegory for both 16th-century Spanish society and the Spanish temperament; if there is such a thing as Spanish temperament in this diverse and colourful country. I am not at all surprised that the common people thought Don Quixote mad. Even today, they think that of anyone who comes wandering into their remote villages from the outside world. It is more than probable that if Don Quixote was not already mad when he set out on his travels, the local people would have driven him crazy. They almost did the same thing to me.

It is worthwhile persevering with *Don Quixote* for it has some fine tales as the knight roars about Spain on his bony nag, tilting at windmills, falling in love with barmaids, retelling parts of Cervantes' own life in his encounters with former galley slaves, and returning to sanity on his deathbed.

*   *   *

Thinking of Cervantes and Don Quixote gave me something to do as I circled south towards Corchuela, a dusty hamlet set in the middle of this bleached and inhospitable plain. Here I refilled the water bottles and wished that the sun, now scorching down full in my face, would slip behind some convenient cloud. Meanwhile, as the day and I marched on together, the castle of Oropesa drew slowly – oh so slowly – closer. You can see the hill of Oropesa from a long way across the *meseta*, which is one of the worst factors on any walk across Spain. You can often see your destination for hours, but somehow you can't get there. Try as I might I could go no faster, and it was nearly four in the afternoon before I crawled across the main Madrid–Cáceres road and then the railway line and finally up to the foot of the hill which supports the town and castle of the counts of Oropesa. Below the castle is a petrol station, and behind the petrol station a bar. There I found a friendly face, a glass of water and a helping hand off with the sweat-drenched rucksack, and sat down outside to think about the Peninsular War.

*   *   *

In the early years of the Napoleonic Wars, Spain was allied with France. Then Nelson shattered the Combined Fleets of France and Spain off Cape Trafalgar in 1805, and the future of the Alliance began to look less attractive, although Napoleon remained as strong as ever in the Continent of Europe.

Napoleon realised that to defeat the British he must somehow establish naval superiority, and in particular control the Mediterranean. The way to seal the Mediterranean was to capture Gibraltar, and that meant overrunning Spain. Napoleon's chance to seize the Peninsula came in 1807, after the British had seized the Danish fleet at Copenhagen to prevent it falling into French hands. Napoleon then ordered that all British ambassadors must be banished from Continental Europe, and all Englishmen arrested. This edict was intended even for neutral nations and brought him into conflict with Portugal, which refused to comply.

A French army was assembled at Bayonne and permitted to march across Spain to Lisbon, where it arrived on 30 November, just in time to prevent the Regent of Portugal fleeing to Brazil. Once in the Peninsula, Napoleon intended to remain there, and his subsequent moves were unsubtle. Spain was then ruled, in fact if not in name, by Manuel de Godoy, Chief Minister to King Carlos IV and lover of the queen. Both the king and queen adored Manuel de Godoy but their heir, Prince Fernando, hated him with equal passion. Forged letters accusing the prince of treason caused Carlos IV to order Fernando's arrest. The prince was popular and this action provoked riots, after which the king abdicated, and with the queen and Godoy, fled to France. Presently the turbulent times in Spain persuaded Prince Fernando to join his parents in Bayonne, and he was then persuaded by Napoleon to abdicate in his turn, leaving the throne vacant. The throne was offered to Napoleon's brother, Joseph, who entered Spain at the head of another army in October 1807. French troops then poured into Spain, occupying all the major towns, looting and abusing the citizens, living off the country. The Spanish ex-king and his court may have been overawed by all this; the Spanish people were outraged.

On 2 May 1808, the *Dos de Mayo*, a famous date in Spanish history, the people of Madrid rose against the invaders and cut the throats of every French soldier they could lay their hands on. French artillery soon blasted the mob to pieces, but the revolt, once started, broke out everywhere. These are the scenes shown in the paintings by Goya at the Prado in Madrid. Committees of Popular Resistance, Juntas, were formed in every major town and province, troops were enlisted and proclamations issued declaring support for Prince Fernando and death to the French.

Spain is a country where, as one general remarked, 'Small armies are defeated and large armies starve'. The French had no difficulty in destroying any Spanish force which had the temerity to meet the conquerors of Continental Europe in the field, but when the Spanish took to the hills, it was another matter. The Spanish word for war is *guerra*, and these wild bands of Spanish irregulars, fighting in small groups by ambush and surprise attack, gave 'guerrilla' warfare to the world. Meanwhile, the Spanish Juntas sought an alliance with the British, begging them to send arms and powder and, if possible, an army. The first British force, 13,000 men under General Arthur Wellesley, landed north of Lisbon in August 1808.

Wellesley, better known to history as the Duke of Wellington, scored some swift victories over the French at Obidos, Roliça and Vimeiro, but then not one, but *two* senior officers arrived to command the army and chaos soon reigned. The French army surrendered Lisbon, but were allowed to sail away with all their arms and equipment, an act which so enraged the British people that all three generals were summoned home to face an enquiry and possible court-martial. It was *not* our finest hour. Into the breach, as Commander-in-Chief in Spain, stepped the charismatic figure of Sir John Moore, father of the Light Brigade and one of the finest generals in Europe.

I found myself thinking about the Peninsular War from my little seat outside the castle at Oropesa, for both Moore and Wellington sent armies this way, and Talavera is still listed in the colours of many British regiments. This is the nearest I would come to scenes of the Peninsular War because most of the major actions took place to the north or west, at Badajoz, Ciudad Rodrigo, Salamanca or Vitoria, and I am saving these for another day and another book.

Moore joined the army near Lisbon and there, familiar words, he met a snag. The Juntas in Spain were in marvellous disarray, and a combination of bad roads, appalling weather and useless maps meant he could not move his army. He therefore decided to send the heavy artillery on the main road to Madrid via Talavera, while the light troops, cavalry and infantry, headed across Extremadura on rough mountain roads. The entire force would meet at Salamanca, and advance to attack the French forces at Valladolid.

I don't propose to follow the course of Moore's campaign, or the famous Retreat to La Coruña, and the battle there at which Moore was killed. However, this campaign did mark the beginning of a friendship between the Spanish and British which has somehow endured. After Moore was killed by a cannon ball and buried under the ramparts of La Coruña, Sir Arthur Wellesley returned to the Peninsula with a fresh army and

began the series of campaigns which finally drove the French out of
Spain. One of his greatest battles took place at Talavera de la Reina,
a few miles east of Oropesa, in July 1808 and a plaque commemorating
Wellington's victory decorates the walls of the castle *parador*.

Wellesley was attempting to co-ordinate his army with that of General
Cuesta, Captain-General of Extremadura, and after a great deal of
marching and counter-marching the two armies finally met at Talavera.
Here they were attacked by the combined corps of Marshal Victor, King
Joseph Bonaparte, and Marshal Sebastiani, a force numbering some
50,000 men. The Spanish never became engaged because, when the
battle started, General Cuesta was asleep in his coach and had left
orders that he was not to be disturbed.

The brunt of the French attack, therefore, fell on Wellesley's 20,000
British and German infantry. The battle lasted from dawn to mid-
afternoon, when the French launched 25,000 men in columns against
the British (and German) line. Rolling volleys blew the French columns
away, and although the Guards of Wellesley's First Division charged the
enemy and left a gap in the line, somehow Wellesley held the position
until the French withdrew, leaving 7,000 men on the field. On the
morning after the battle, General Robert Crauford arrived with three
battalions of the Light Brigade, which had marched forty-two miles in
twenty-six hours under the July sun, and still arrived too late for the
battle. Only someone who has walked across Spain in summer can
understand what a feat of arms that must have been.

Little good came of the battle of Talavera. An even larger French
army came up and Wellesley was forced to retreat along the Tajo. He
left his wounded with Cuesta, who promptly abandoned them. Led again
by the Light Brigade, the army withdrew to Portugal through Badajoz,
and Wellington never again attempted to combine his efforts with those
of his supposed allies.

*   *   *

Oropesa is one of the great castles of New Castile. Like Old Castile
on the northern side of the Central Cordillera, New Castile is full
of castles. During the latter half of the Reconquista this line of the
Tajo was a frontier between the warring Christian and Muslim kings.
The land between the Cordillera and the next big mountain range, the
Sierra Morena, was eventually given to the Spanish Military Orders, in
particular the Order of Calatrava, on the understanding that if they could
capture it from the Moors and hold it, then they could enjoy the benefits
of any wealth created.

Apart from thinking of Cervantes and Wellington, this is the time to take another look at the background to this journey, the Reconquista, which took another step forward when Alfonso VI captured Toledo in 1085. This put the Christians firmly on the line of the Tajo and delivered both Old and New Castile into their hands. This success did not, however, last long. The loss of Toledo forced the Muslim emirs of Al-Andalus to ask for help from Africa, and a warlike emir, Yusef Ibn Tashufn, led a new band of invaders, the Almoravids, into Spain.

Emir Yusef soon proved as big a menace to the Spanish Muslims of the small *taifa* kingdoms as he did to the Christians. He beat Alfonso at Sagrajas, as we have seen from the story of El Cid, but he could not take Toledo, which King Alfonso was determined to defend. Alfonso asked the French for aid and a huge army of so-called Crusaders crossed the Pyrenees in 1087, but they contented themselves with ravaging the Ebro Valley and returned home when they had gathered enough booty.

The Almoravids attacked Toledo again and again for the next fifty years, and were constantly crossing the Sierra Morena to burn crops and villages south of the Tajo. In 1109 a new emir, Ali Ibn Yusef, brought another army across the Straits to ravage the Tajo valley, but although he sacked Talavera a number of Christian castles, including Oropesa, held out until this army, too, withdrew across the Sierra Morena.

* * *

Much of the credit for this steady advance of the Christian kings to the line of the Tajo must be given to the Military Orders, of which there were now several. Among the most famous and efficient were the Orders of Santiago, Calatrava and Alcántara, which though exclusively Spanish were modelled on the Templars and the Hospitalers. There were also smaller Orders like the knights of Ávila and the Order of Montesa. The kings of Spain used the Military Orders as shock-troops, and developed a system of land grants where they would cede Moorish land to one of the Orders on the proviso that they must take it first. The knights of Santiago had the special duty of guarding pilgrims on the Road to Compostela, and a number of hostels on the Way, like the *Hotel San Marcos* in León, still bear the blood-red, sword-like cross of Santiago. Examine a map of Spain closely though, and you can still see relics of the Knights in the placenames. Look east of Ciudad Real and you will find a whole clutch of places dedicated to the Knights of Calatrava: Carrión de Calatrava, Torralba de Calatrava, Calzada de Calatrava, and many more. Then follow the Tajo west, towards Portugal and between Cáceres and the frontier the knights of Alcántara once ruled and built castles at Valencia de Alcántara, Herrera de Alcántara and many more.

From these seized lands, the Orders grew very rich. In 1243 there arose a memorable quarrel between the Templars and the Alcántaras over the ownership and grazing of 40,000 sheep in the Tajo valley. The Order of Santiago lasted the longest; founded by Fernando II of León in 1170, it was not disbanded until the end of the 15th century, when Fernando of Aragón invited the knights to elect him their Grand Master and so absorbed the Order and its wealth into the royal household. The red cross of Santiago became the emblem of royal service and courtiers can be seen wearing it in paintings by Velásquez. The Order of Calatrava was created and founded by the Cistercian monks, who needed knights to protect their sheep flocks in the Tajo valley, on which their wealth depended, for the Cistercians were great sheep farmers. These Orders, for glory, profit or the Christian faith, were the spearhead of the Reconquista.

*   *   *

The country of Calatrava lies to the east, beyond Toledo, though the fortress of Oropesa also lies in the province of Toledo. The present castle, which was built for the counts of Oropesa in 1366, has been rather well restored and is now a *parador*. A huge plaque in the stairwell of the inner courtyard records the fact that one count of Oropesa, Francisco de Toledo, became the Viceroy of Peru late in the 16th century. The original castle, much fought over by the Moors and Christians, was rebuilt in the 15th century and much of that work remains in place. From the small square outside the main gate I could see right across the plain I had crossed that day, all the way to the mountain tops of the Gredos, even to the Puerto de Candeleda, the plain between dotted with the regular squares of olive groves, the mountains behind a solid, jagged wall against the sky. It is easy to see why the castle of Oropesa was so important, because it dominates the landscape for miles around and bars the roads from Andalucía to Old Castile.

Tired as I was when I got there, it was worth pushing on to Oropesa, for many historic figures have been there over the centuries. Charles V stopped at Oropesa on his way to Yuste, as did Santa Teresa on one of her missions from Ávila. The castle was one of the first *paradores*, opening for business in 1930, and is a very fine example of the best. The inside, so dark and cool after the dazzling sun on the plain, is paved with dark red tiles marked with the blue star of the counts of Oropesa. There are rich hangings, and much oak furniture, thick walls and a private vineyard. A rare place indeed, is the *parador* of Oropesa.

Seen from below, or far away, the castle at Oropesa is a fine sight, the golden stone glowing against the blue sky. As I walked through the streets towards it I began to realise that Oropesa town is not a place to miss either. Many of the houses are faced with green and yellow tiles from Talavera. There are two huge churches to complete the skyline and, apart from one or two old ladies in traditional Castilian costume – black skirts and shawls and lacy coifs – there were little groups of women on chairs gathered in every shady corner, working away in groups at their embroidery. A donkey trotted past, then a small herd of cows came clattering through the streets, and all this less than a hundred miles from the centre of Madrid.

I made my way wearily up the hill towards the castle, hunting about to find the way in, which is through a short cobbled tunnel. This debouches into a sunny courtyard. A wood-built terrace draped with flowers and hanging baskets occupies one wall of the inner courtyard, and I climbed a flight of creaking stairs into the hall. Here, in the cool dark interior, the floor covered with glazed tiles, I slipped off my rucksack and collapsed onto a bench.

All this was enchanting, but matters picked up even more when I arrived at the reception desk where I was greeted with '*¡Dios mío!*' and a smile, and 'Ah, you must be *Robin del Bosque*,' from the receptionist. Smiles had been rarer than summer snowfalls over the last few days, but a joke to go with it was remarkable. *Robin del Bosque* is Robin Hood. Since Robin is not a Spanish name and my surname is virtually unpronounceable in Spanish, I usually clear the air and avoid error on the telephone by suggesting that they reserve the room for *señor Robin del Bosque*. They don't forget that. This does not work in Latin America, where they have never heard of Robin Hood. There I am, '*el amigo de Batman*'.

The walls of Oropesa were built in the 12th century and parts still remain, with the castle as the citadel. There was a castle here from about 1150, but this was rebuilt in the mid-13th century when the lords of Oropesa seized this land from the Moors. Parts of the present work are Mudejar, other parts Renaissance, but the total effect is very fine, and the people are charming.

I was definitely out of the province of Ávila. It was easy to see that. One porter carried my rucksack to my room, another hung about until I had stripped off my filthy clothes, whereupon he carried them off to be washed. A third turned up with a chilled bottle of Torres, on the house. No praise is too high for the good people of the *Parador Virrey Toledo* in Oropesa. I went out that evening in my freshly cleaned and pressed clothes, while the nightshift battled with the other set, and met smiles everywhere, from people in bars and those little knots of busily-tatting ladies. The art of embroidery at Oropesa goes back to the time of Cervantes and the town makes a fair living from it. The women fit the embroidery around their other domestic duties, and while the men retire to the bars in the evening, the women take a chair to the nearest corner and gather in a group, some working on their own piece, some sharing the work on a large item like a tablecloth.

The walls of the houses in Oropesa are all whitewashed and though the streets are wider than those of Andalucía, I took this as a sign that I was making progress and getting a little further south, where whitewashed houses and narrow shady streets deflect the sun. I quite enjoyed my evening limp and returned to the *parador* for an excellent evening meal with a local speciality, *ternera lagarterana*, a kind of veal stew, a pudding called *suspiros de la monja*, which, taken literally, means the nun's sighs, and some Manchega cheese. This hard cheese is La Mancha's contribution to Spanish cuisine. All this went well with a bottle of wine from the castle's own vineyards. I then collected my clean, ironed clothes from the reception desk, requested an early call and floated upstairs to bed.

*   *   *

I could have used a lot more time in Oropesa, but there is no point in making a schedule for a long walk like this unless you stick to it. The distance you don't do today is added to the distance you must do tomorrow. Besides, I was fit enough. My cuts and scratches did not look very pretty, but they were already healing at a rapid rate, which is a good sign of health. I needed an early start to make a good beginning on the eighty kilometres, or fifty miles which lay between the castle of Oropesa and my next significant stop at the Royal Monastery at Guadalupe, deep in the sierras of Extremadura.

*   *   *

Guadalupe actually lay off my direct track to Tarifa, but I had never been to Guadalupe. When Geoff was planning my route, I told him that apart from including as many castles as he could cram into the itinerary, my road *must* lie past Guadalupe. Next to Santiago de Compostela, Guadalupe is the greatest Catholic pilgrimage centre in all Spain and, not having seen it, I intended to go there on this journey. The only snag was the fifty miles of barren plain and mountain and, inevitably, an *embalse*, which lay between here and there. Well, that was the only snag at the moment.

The hill town of Guadalupe and the shrine of the Virgin, Santa María de Guadalupe, lie south-west of Oropesa, across a rugged range of rivers and sierras. From Oropesa a metalled road runs south for ten miles to El Puente del Arzobispo, the only crossing over the Río Tajo, the major river in these parts. This meant a long road-walk to start the day. The Tajo flows out of the Guadarrama across Spain and Portugal, to empty at last into the steep Atlantic stream near Lisbon. The great river has now been dammed at intervals all along its length, and this stemming of the river is a source of great contention between the Spanish and the Portuguese. One of the largest dams, the Embalse de Valdecañas, lay a little to the west of my path, backing up the river for a hundred miles and blocking any idea of a cross-country compass march directly to Guadalupe, by forcing me across the bridge at El Puente del Arzobispo.

So, first, nine miles due south to Arzobispo. Then, on a minor road, to Villar del Pedroso, and so on, always south and west, camping somewhere on the Sierra de Altamira overnight, and then on to Guadalupe. It was going to be a challenge, at least two days and maybe three, so I had better get on with it.

CHAPTER TWELVE

THE ROAD TO GUADALUPE

'Africa begins at the Pyrenees.'

Alexandre Dumas

I was out of Oropesa by seven-thirty, walking under the great Mudejar brick archway which supports the town clock over the south gate of the town, and after a kilometre or two, into the open country. This is still, just, *meseta*, but much more interesting than that flat plain which lies to the north of the Gredos. The land is much wilder, and more jumbled; great green lichen-covered rocks burst from the soil here and there forming a mass of rocky walls to carve up the landscape, and there are plenty of hills and valleys. This may be harder walking but your mind stays occupied, and there are views to enjoy. For fit, well-equipped walkers this road to Guadalupe is a good walk.

I made good time for the first few hours and, since tall fences barred the road on either side keeping me from the shade of the olive trees, the faster I went, the better. You need to claw back as much distance as possible before the sun gets up. I shot past the village of Valdepalacios, which seemed to consist of just one house, then paused for a brief look at my first *ermita*, the Ermita de Bienvenida, leaving my rucksack by the road to walk up to the hermitage, which seemed deserted. By ten-thirty I was having my first beer of the day in the *Bar Romay* in the wide, central, cow-dung-splattered main street of El Puente del Arzobispo. The archbishop's bridge is a medieval structure, much wider than the present brook, but in winter the Tajo must become a wide, swift torrent. Even now, at the end of a parched summer, it was a significant stream; it had played a significant part in the history of the Reconquista, a landmark on the march south, and on my march too. By crossing the Tajo I left Castile behind and entered Extremadura.

Once across the bridge, I picked up a track to the south-west and set off hard, taking bearings off the hump-back Sierra de Ancha to my left. At a distance, this hump-back hill had looked like a formidable obstacle, but closer to it looked rather less steep and difficult. This was some comfort as the long line of the Sierra de Altamira was beginning to appear as a dark line on the southern horizon. This was the mountain range which barred my road to Guadalupe, and one I had to cross directly, avoiding the long and winding road.

The idea of someone coming to Extremadura is a new one, but people have been leaving this province for centuries: soldiers, *conquistadores*, land-hungry peasants, people worn out from struggling to extract a living from this hostile soil. The word Extremadura was originally given to the land between the Duero and the Portuguese border, a buffer zone, stark and empty, between the Christians and the Moors. Even today, perhaps especially today, Extremadura is quite remarkably bleak. The upland plateaux are given over to grain, not fields of it but whole plateaux, an arching void of golden wheat or, at this season of the year, stubble and dusty plough. Half a mile into Extremadura I thought myself back in Africa, surrounded as I was by the plain desert, the sierras, the *jebel*. Only where there is water, here as in the desert, is there any green. Even the villages are burnt dusty gold, each church tower topped off with an untidy stork's nest, the streets empty. People are still leaving Extremadura and this golden land is probably more empty today than it was fifty years ago. No one wants to live on the land here any more.

It was now about noon, and very hot, but after my rest in Oropesa I felt fine. Any worries over water also proved unfounded, because little horse-troughs or small farms came up now and again and I could easily recharge my somewhat battered water bottles. This, incidentally, is essential; always keep your water bottles full. I drank like a camel at Villar del Pedroso, fifteen miles or so south of Oropesa, and then put my foot down for a final charge to my projected night-stop somewhere beyond, or even on top of the Sierra de Altamira, which was still eleven miles away. By now the full-length of the Altamira was in plain sight and although it rises in parts to the 1,000 metre mark – over 3,000 feet – I took comfort from the fact that my road, or rather my compass bearing, which bore directly for Guadalupe, pointed to a lower part, a saddle, on the range. The main road, at least on the map, took a great hairpin bend to get across, so if I cut this corner, my over-the-ground distance might be much less than the ninety kilometres indicated to Guadalupe on the signpost at Oropesa. I passed Carrascalejo on my left, another dusty hamlet where not a thing seemed to be moving in the full heat of midday. About a mile south of there I struck off across country on another compass bearing, aiming to hit the main road again on the far side of the sierra and so reach my night-stop at Navatrasierra. I was getting pretty tired, but if I could get there I would have broken the back of the road to Guadalupe.

*   *   *

By the time the main road swings sharply right or north-west, it is already over the 800 metre mark. The scramble to the top of the sierra, with the road glinting to my left, was no more than a panting plod across hot rock and thorn and, with the usual series of false crests to add a little frustration to the exercise, I was crossing the top of the Altamira within the hour and stumbling down through the scrub towards the distant ribbon of the road. I ran across a water course beside the road, complete with a welcome trickle of water, and entered Navatrasierra in the growing dark by just after six. By half-past I was camped in a small group of cork trees, half a mile outside the village, boots off, sucking hard on my blessed bottle of water. I had walked about twenty-five miles that day and every yard of the way had been fought for. Apart from the fact that I had only a couple of sugar cakes and some fruit left to eat, I felt fine.

So far, so good. By getting to Navatrasierra in one long day I had certainly cracked the back of the distance between Oropesa and Guadalupe and, by cutting corners across the winding mountain road, had done so at some saving in distance. The snag now was the country ahead. This was, if anything, even more jumbled and desolate than the country I had crossed already. I saw that early the following morning, when the eastern light and the cooler air made the next obstacle stand out quite clearly. This was the Sierra de la Palomera, which rose to 1,443 metres at one point and lay squarely across my road to Guadalupe. I lay back in my sleeping bag, eating a peach and wishing, not for the first time, that I had brought my binoculars. Lacking them I stared at the sierra as hard as I could. After a while it seemed to lie back a little and I thought I could get over the top without undue difficulty. If I could go directly across I would save miles off the road route, which wandered all over the place and offered, at the least, a wearisome twenty-five mile plod. Besides, I hate roads. They are very hard on the feet and no one ever offers you a lift, so what's the point? I got out the map and compass, worked out another course to Guadalupe, and had a good think.

The high point of the Sierra de la Palomera is the Pico de Cervales, a distinctive shark's fin of a mountain. However, the range in general seemed more open and less steep than the Altamira crest and got lower still at one point, a saddle, some distance south-west of the Pico de Cervales. If I could get across that I would certainly reduce the climb, and I could hardly get lost because on the far side lay the small but still

The jagged mountains and deep gorges of the Picos de Europa.

Left *One of the few tracks through the Picos.*

Below *The imposing Picos – the only part of Spain to resist the Moorish invasion – where a picnic turned into a battle for John Lloyd.*

The ***campo*** of Castile and, below, one of the many flocks of sheep to be found there.

Cervantes' house in Valladolid, the heart of Old Castile.

The castle of La Mota in Medina del Campo.

Madrigal de las Altas Torres, birthplace of Isabel la Católica.

The walls of Ávila, one of the great fortress cities of Europe.

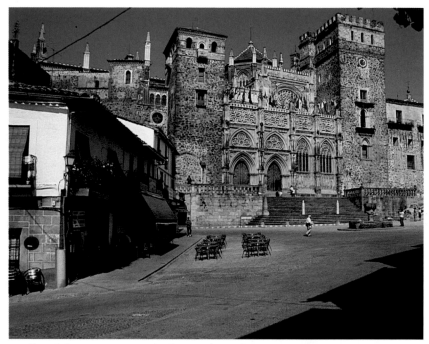

Guadalupe, a centre of pilgrimage and a popular tourist attraction.

The plains of Extremadura, a real desert set in the centre of Spain.

Right *The crenellated tower of the Moorish fortress at Belalcázar.*

Below *The view of Córdoba across the Río Guadalquivir and, inset, the Calahorra tower.*

Benadalid, one of Andalucía's typically picturesque White Towns.

Last lap: the Rock of Gibraltar and the shores of the Mediterranean.

significant Embalse de Alia. If I kept on south-west from there, I must eventually hit the roads around Guadalupe. Even if there were a lot of 'ifs' in all this, it still seemed a decent plan.

There were, as ever, snags. It is no good calculating bearings from a map if the map is inaccurate. On the other hand, the one advantage of old maps is that, if anything, there are more houses and signs of civilisation on the ground today than they indicate – at least close to the main centres, where urban sprawl has started. Only the heart of Spain is less populated than it was, and generally I found more farms than I had been led to expect from the maps. Although a number were deserted, at least the wells were still there. I crammed everything back into the rucksack which seemed to weigh a ton even as I slung it on: a sure sign that I was tired. My boots felt full of feet, but at least I had a plan and a compass bearing to buoy me up as I set off across the sierra towards Guadalupe, a distance, as the crow flies, of about twelve miles.

I crossed the Sierra de la Palomera with considerable effort, but without great difficulty. However, once on the top I saw no sign of Guadalupe – just another line of hills ahead and then another beyond that, all shimmering in the heat haze. But what can you do? I went on, through olive groves and thick patches of oak forest, across ploughed red earth and along dry water courses, up and down, over ridge after ridge. It was again shatteringly hot and very dusty. I saw a glint of blue that was surely the Embalse de Alia and even thought of turning towards it to put myself back on track, but then I struck a footpath. This was marked, praise be, with boots and hoofprints, and led more or less in the right direction. I followed it due west, into the descending eye of the sun.

After far too long, when a river of sweat had invaded my wrist-watch and stopped it, I finally hit a wide rough road which bore no resemblance to any highway and was not shown on my map. This ran off, empty of traffic, towards the north and south with no sign to Guadalupe. I sat down wearily on a pile of stones and was contemplating suicide when a truck swept past heading south, covering me with dust, followed by a car and then another. Whatever this wide road was, it clearly led somewhere. I got up and began to plod south, following the cars into their whirling clouds of dust, as the sun began its final dive across the mountains.

After about half an hour, I saw a strange domed brick structure off to my left and started towards it. When I got there, I found a plaque on the side which said that it was the Ermita del Humilladero, and this, thank God, was marked on the map a few miles north of Guadalupe. As I reached the chapel I saw, a mile or so below me, the lights and towers and flags of the Real (Royal) Monasterio of Guadalupe, a happy sight indeed at the end of a very long day.

*   *   *

One of the rules I was beginning to learn was to use local tracks whenever possible, not least because they were often shorter than more modern roads. I could now work out where I was and this road, which led nowhere on my map, was the one heading towards Navalmoral. At present an unmade track, it concealed the old road from Guadalupe and was currently being widened and improved. By the time you read this, it may even be a three-lane, metalled highway. About a mile down the road towards Guadalupe a small track struck off right, heading directly into the town. I followed it on stumbling feet, past a tethered donkey, past a large recumbent pig snoring against a wall, then gradually through more and more houses where the owners were sitting out in the gloaming, enjoying the cool air. These people fell silent to stare, except for a brief 'Hola' or a 'Buenas noches' as I tottered past. From the Humilladero it is nearly four miles to Guadalupe by the main road, but less than half that by this mule trail. Even better, the track brought me around the monastery and directly to the steps of the *Parador Zurbarán*.

I was again a terrible sight, covered in dust, and I had not reserved a room, but this fortunate arrival seemed a good omen so I entered and presented myself at reception. Did they have a room? Indeed they did. Could I have it for two nights? Certainly. None of that Castilian arrogance here, but even offers of help. Could they help me with the rucksack? Would I like a glass of water? Also, since I had come so far on foot, could they offer me one of their best rooms? Glass of water in one hand and one strap of the rucksack in the other, I accompanied the porter towards Room 207. From there, come the following dawn, I had a splendid view of the Real Monasterio of Guadalupe, floating over the rooftops just across the courtyard of the *parador*. It was too good to miss in the morning light, but it was also time for a rest. I closed the shutters carefully and went back to bed.

*   *   *

What a dream is Guadalupe! Coming out again onto my balcony at about ten in the morning, there it was. The red-tiled roofs of the town just below, all set out above whitewashed walls, while the russet stone walls of the monastery just across the road from the *parador* seemed near enough to touch. It was the clamour of the monastery bells that drove me out onto the terrace, for this is no gentle carillon but a steady *dong!* soon partnered by a sound not unlike that of someone beating a metal plate with a hammer. There is no music in it, but it certainly gets you out of bed.

After visiting Santiago de Compostela, Guadalupe is a surprise. Both places are beautiful and very striking but Santiago is a big town, a city, all grey and green like the province of Galicia itself, while Guadalupe is just a village, and glows in the southern sun. Guadalupe is a small place of slanting streets and white walls, set about the great Gothic-Mudejar monastery, which draws people to these parts from every corner of Spain and the New World.

This little dream of Guadalupe is a place of pilgrimage and, like Santiago de Compostela, owes its fame and fortune to a relic. The monastery started out in the Dark Ages as a hermitage consecrated to an image of Our Lady of Guadalupe which, legend says, had been carved by St Luke. When Al-Mansur came rampaging through here in 981 the image was hurriedly buried. About 1280, a local shepherd girl rediscovered the image still intact, and it was placed in a small hermitage close to the present town of Guadalupe. A string of miracles followed and the image of Santa María de Guadalupe soon became the one invoked by penitents and prisoners. The cult of the Virgin was very strong in the 13th and early 14th centuries – many chapels and churches dedicated to Our Lady were founded at this time – and the Virgin of Guadalupe soon came to rank with the Shrine of St James at Compostela as a place of pilgrimage for all Spaniards, but most especially for the people of Extremadura. The monastery which now guards this dark, faded little image, and dresses her in glorious garments, dates back to the 15th century, as does the Hospital of San Juan Bautista, St John the Baptist, nearby. This was originally built as a pilgrim hostel and now serves, most appropriately, as the *Parador Zurbarán*. Zurbarán was a famous Spanish artist in the early 17th century, and there is a fine collection of his work in the monastery.

Successful shrines soon attract a faithful following. Over the centuries the Royal Monastery at Guadalupe attracted the favours of many Spanish monarchs, especially Fernando and Isabel, who came here to give thanks for their final victory over the Moors at Granada in 1490. They were followed by Christopher Columbus, and it was here that they finally gave him money and ships for the projected voyage to Cathay, during which he discovered the New World. The island of Guadalupe in the Caribbean, found on this first voyage, is named after the shrine in Extremadura. One of Columbus' ships, the *Santa María*, a model of which hangs in the cathedral, was named for the Virgin of Guadalupe, and she is the most popular saint in the former Spanish-American colonies. Columbus returned to Guadalupe after every voyage to take part in the religious processions, and he was not alone in this. That unlucky lord, the Duke of Medina Sidonia, came here to pray in 1589 on his way home to Sanlúcar after the defeat of the Spanish Armada, and Miguel de Cervantes came here to give thanks after the Virgin's intercession had secured his release from Moorish captivity in Algiers.

The shrine of Guadalupe has also become a centre for that *Hispanidad* I have talked about, defined here as a community of thought, language and literature between the Old World and the countries of Spanish America. I had just missed *El Día de la Hispanidad* which is celebrated in Guadalupe each year on 12 October, the day of Columbus' landfall in the Americas. The flags of all the Spanish-American countries flutter from a line of flagpoles outside the monastery, and few dignitaries visit Spain from the New World without visiting the shrine.

The discovery of the New World must have been a godsend to the so-called Catholic Kings, Fernando and Isabel. The Moorish wars were over, the country full of unemployed soldiers. If Columbus was right, his discoveries offered an outlet for the turbulent soldiers of Spain, the possibility of treasure, and perhaps a trade route to the East. Columbus, for one, firmly believed until the end of his days that he had found a new route to Cathay.

Christopher Columbus – or Cristóbal Colón to give him his Spanish name – was not a Spaniard. He is said to have come from Genoa, that republic of seafarers, though years ago I met a man in the Balearics who swore that Columbus came from Ibiza. Columbus had been touting his ideas round the courts of Europe for years, trying to find a backer for his voyage to the west, and been pestering the kings of Spain since before the fall of Granada. Now, here at Guadalupe, in the flush of victorious celebration, they gave him what he wanted.

Columbus sailed from the port of Palos on 3 August 1492 leading an expedition of three small ships, the *Santa María*, the *Pinta* and the *Niña*, making a landfall at the Canary Islands, which were then the limit of the known world, and then sailed due west. After two or three weeks, his sailors began to get anxious. Many of them believed that the world was flat and that sooner or later they would sail off the edge. Columbus kept them hard at work and well fed on 'wine, salt meat, oil, vinegar, cheese, chickpeas, lentils, beans, salt fish, honey, rice, almonds and raisins'. Even so, mutiny was in the air on 8 October, when Columbus noted: 'Thanks be to God, the air is as mild as April in Sevilla, and fragrant'. Land birds were seen and gulls flew off the sea and headed west. Early on the morning of 12 October the lookout on the *Niña* saw the flash of breakers on a low green island and let out the cry, '¡*Tierra!*'. This was the coral island which is now San Salvador in the Bahamas.

Columbus returned to Spain on 15 March 1493, to a fame that has never died, although he gained little else from his exploits. On this first voyage, where the explorers reached Cuba and Hispaniola, all the voyagers returned, but when he sailed again for the Indies in 1493, he led a fleet of seventeen ships bearing 1,500 colonists to explore and exploit the New World. Columbus made two more voyages, visiting Venezuela and the coast of Central America from Honduras to Panama in 1524. But Columbus was to die in poverty, almost forgotten. The wealth of the Indies came later, extracted from Mexico and Peru by other explorers, men from the deserts of Extremadura: the great *conquistadores* of the New World.

Today, Guadalupe is still a centre of pilgrimage and a popular tourist attraction, though you would never know it. The town does not even have a tourist office. Although there is the beautiful Zurbarán *parador* and several hotels (including one in the monastery), if you wander even a few yards from the Plaza Mayor, here called the Plaza de Santa María de Guadalupe and formerly called the Plaza General Franco, you are back in a Spain of narrow cobbled streets. Old whitewashed houses lean out to block the sky, their upper balconies propped up on pillars and cloaked with a tumble of vine-leaves and geraniums. Back there, in the steep side streets and alleyways, old men doze on benches or sit in the bead-curtain covered doorways of the houses, only their feet and ankles in view: a curious sight. Donkeys clop about, some ridden, others carrying heavy loads up and down the hills. The chief sounds you will hear in Guadalupe during daylight hours are the braying of donkeys and the crowing of cocks. At all too frequent intervals, day and night, comes the clamour of the monastery bells.

*   *   *

After a night's rest at the *parador* I felt pretty good, all things considered; certainly well enough to contemplate a closer look at the town. The *parador* is itself worth inspection because, although it has been much enlarged and modern rooms added, the old pilgrim hospital of John the Baptist still remains, set around a central courtyard which is full of lemon and orange trees and provided with a fountain. There are more olive trees in the outer courtyard and, from my room at least, a splendid view of the monastery; a huge, fortress-like building with two crenellated towers and a number of steeples, each roofed with beautiful blue and yellow glazed tiles from Talavera. The monastery of Guadalupe is the centrepiece of the town, so when I went out for my stroll round, I decided to start there.

The way into the monastery church is through two huge 15th century bronze doors, each bearing scenes from the New Testament from the arrival of the Three Kings at Bethlehem to the Resurrection at Jerusalem, all beautifully done. The facade is in Mudejar brick. Inside, the church is rather small, though tall and quite wide, with the tiny dark image of the Virgin of Guadalupe set high above the altar behind a great iron grille. From here you are taken on the inevitable tour of the monastery and, although I am no great lover of guided tours, I trailed along behind an array of broad-beamed Spanish ladies into the Manuscript Room. Then we went through the Treasury, which contained a vast halidom of saints' relics (mostly arm bones), and up to the highlight of the visit, an audience with the Virgin of Guadalupe. This tour lasted about half an hour and left me exhausted.

There are some evocative sights though. When Ford came here in 1855 the convent at Guadalupe was a barracks, and he remarked that the *posadas* of Guadalupe were iniquitous and the town but a 'network of dirty, narrow wynds'. The walls of the shrine were hung with the chains and manacles of returned captives and freed slaves and, although the French Marshal Victor had plundered the shrine and removed a great deal of treasure – nine cart-loads of silver alone – he had left the Virgin behind, but taken the lantern of the Turkish flagship captured at Lepanto. The *hospedería* next door, which still receives pilgrim guests, was built from the assets confiscated by the Inquisition from burned heretics.

The Virgin of Guadalupe is an adaptable lady. Her image is set on a swivel and for much of the day she resides above the High Altar of the church, gazing down benignly on the praying folk below. When the pilgrim throng comes surging up the stairs behind her, a Franciscan monk of the resident community is on hand to turn her round and so presents a relic for the faithful to kiss. I am a Scots Presbyterian, but I owed a candle to the Virgin of Guadalupe for getting me safely off the Gredos so we settled for that.

*   *   *

Once the visitor has paid due respect to the cause of all this splendour and survived the sightseeing, Guadalupe remains an agreeable place to spend the day. I decided that if my legs were not to seize up solid, I must take some exercise and go back up the road for a closer look at the Ermita del Humilladero I had passed on the way in the night before. I took a leisurely stroll up there in the fag-end of the afternoon, and found at the end of it a little Mudejar chapel: just four grilled walls under a cupola, with a cross within. According to the plaque on the outer walls, it was built at the start of the 15th century to mark the spot from which pilgrims and penitents would catch their first sight of Guadalupe. Here the devout pilgrim could kneel and give thanks for the completion of any vow; Cervantes prayed here after his return from captivity in 1580. Many have followed him, even down to the present day, when pilgrimages are undergoing a revival.

Strolling out before dinner that night, down into the Plaza Mayor, I had another pleasant surprise. Guadalupe is full of good restaurants and during the daytime hours they are full of tourists, who fill every chair and crowd around every table. After dark though, when most of the tourist coaches have gone, Guadalupe reverts to itself. The people spill out into the streets to talk and drink or just doze in the dark doorways, resting after the heat of the day. Since you dine late anywhere in Spain, and even later as you move south, I decided to take a last look in the church and entered to find the organ going full blast. About fifty people were sitting in the pews listening, some of them facing the altar, some staring up at the organ loft. There were even a few teenage girls, twined about the pulpit rails. More surprising still was that when the music stopped, the audience burst into applause. I was brought up to believe that you *never* clapped in church, but it appeared that there was a concert in progress, not just of sacred music but of more popular stuff. I stepped back to where I could see the organist, high above the stalls, playing away in his full rig of white tie and tails. I stayed there for an hour, listening to the music, thinking that Spain will always surprise me.

*   *   *

I enjoyed Guadalupe, and I got myself back together there. One day I may even return, but now Time's winged chariot was again pushing me on. This sort of walking – the Commando-style yomp – can become something of a drug. It's rough and tough, but it gets you. After a day off the trail, you want to get back at it. On the morning after the concert, I was up with the sun, ate my breakfast on the balcony where I could look out again, feasting my eyes on the monastery. By eight I was off down the road, heading south towards my next destination of Córdoba, which lay a week's walk away across the Sierra Morena and the plains of Extremadura. I had recuperated in beautiful Guadalupe, and was very glad that my road had taken me there. Now I had to pay for my rest in sweat and effort, before I reached my next reward in the city of Córdoba.

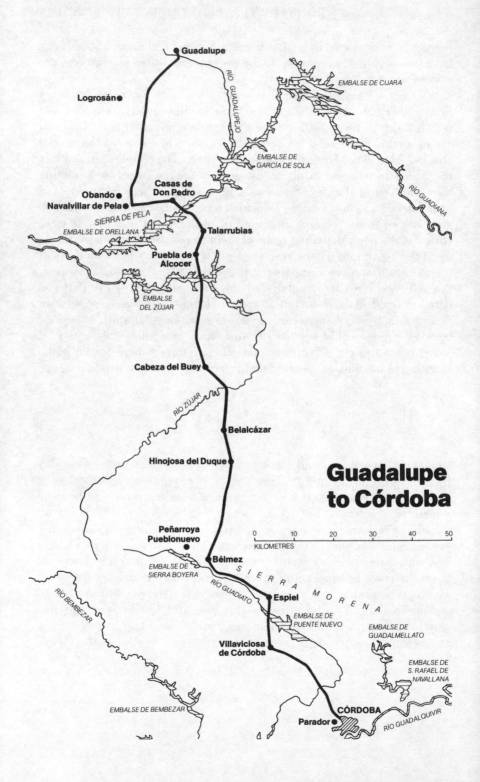

Guadalupe

Logrosán●

RÍO GUADALUPEJO

EMBALSE DE CIJARA

EMBALSE DE
GARCÍA DE SOLA

RÍO GUADIANA

Obando●
Navalvillar de Pela●

Casas de
Don Pedro

SIERRA DE PELA

EMBALSE DE ORELLANA

Talarrubias

Puebla de
Alcocer●

EMBALSE
DEL ZÚJAR

Cabeza del Buey●

RÍO ZÚJAR

Belalcázar●

Hinojosa del Duque●

Guadalupe
to Córdoba

0   10   20   30   40   50
KILOMETRES

Peñarroya
Pueblonuevo●

Bélmez●

EMBALSE DE
SIERRA BOYERA

RÍO GUADIATO

S I E R R A   M O R E N A

Espiel●

EMBALSE DE
PUENTE NUEVO

EMBALSE DE
GUADALMELLATO

RÍO BEMBEZAR

Villaviciosa
de Córdoba●

EMBALSE DE
S. RAFAEL DE
NAVALLANA

EMBALSE DE BEMBEZAR

CÓRDOBA

Parador●

RÍO GUADALQUIVIR

CHAPTER THIRTEEN

ACROSS
EXTREMADURA

*It is mostly very flat, and consists of boundless, trackless
plains, with villages, like happy days, few and far between,
with a want of roads, wretched accommodation and a lack
of subjects of interest in the towns. However, the very
features of this country, its loneliness and silence, may
tempt some travellers of a peculiar class and disposition.*

H. O'Shea on Extremadura (1865)

Hardly anyone was stirring as I slipped away from Guadalupe, taking
the road out, past the hospice of the monastery, heading for Logrosán,
though by no means certain if I would arrive there. I might decide to
turn south across country though, at least from the map, this country
looked suspiciously empty of people and places. It might be a long dry
day before I reached the next *embalse* and a certain supply of water.

My first surprise on leaving Guadalupe was to find a great rail viaduct
spanning the road ahead, seemingly intact and operational, except that
just as I went underneath a car whirled past overhead raising a cloud
of dust. This explained the inclusion of the railway line across my map
marked with the word *abandonado*. Some old railway line had been
closed and the track taken up for conversion, in part, to a roadway.
This smooth and level track ran away to the east and west, and was
therefore of no use to me. My road, as ever, lay south.

I had seen my way out the day before, from the heights by the
Humilladero. Just a notch in the hills to the south, but a way through
which I could see evidence of an open plain, ideal for a compass march. I
headed for this, staying off the road in short grass where I could follow the
track of what seemed to be yet another railway track. At least there was
a flat track and periodic embankments, so it resembled a railway and it

helped reduce the overall distance, for the road, as usual, wound in and out of the side valleys. I was definitely moving south now. Although the weather had never been really chilly, give or take a few morning frosts, it was becoming uncomfortably warm, even in the early morning. By eleven sweat was pouring off me and I was already moving carefully, sticking where possible to the shade of the abundant olive and eucalyptus trees that occupied the plain.

Fortunately, the scenery was stunning and therefore a real distraction from the problems of the day. Once out of the dry valley of the little Río Guadalupejo, I emerged onto a rolling plain, barren certainly, but full of beauty, with far blue hills, great misty sierras and sweeping views on every side. The flatter parts were thick with olive trees, but to the east the land fell away into open, parched grassland, dotted here and there with great flocks of sheep. Here were the barren plains of Extremadura, the country of the Spanish *conquistadores*, the birthplace of the conquerors of the New World.

It is not hard to see why this bleak country of Extremadura produced so many soldiers of fortune. The conquerors of Mexico, Peru and Chile were soldiers who knew no other trade but war. With the fall of Granada in January 1492, the Moorish wars were over and their employment gone. They knew that their pay would stop, their efforts go unrewarded. Lacking some other employment, they must starve or turn to brigandage.

This is probably why Fernando and Isabel leant a more than usually attentive ear to Christopher Columbus when he came yet again to the court of Guadalupe and requested men and ships for his projected voyage to Cathay. Los Reyes Católicos now had time on their hands, the treasure of Granada was theirs to play with, and a whole army of unemployed soldiers stood in need of occupation. If Columbus could indeed find a way to busy these wild spirits at the cost of three small ships, it would be a wise investment.

By the 1530s, the exploration of the Caribbean islands was complete, and Spanish explorers were already cruising the jungle-clad shores of Central America. The time was ripe for the coming of the *conquistadores*, and the best of them came from Extremadura.

The greatest of the *conquistadores* was probably Hernán Cortés, conqueror of the Aztec empire of Mexico. He was born in 1485 in Medellín, a city in Extremadura, the son of a small landowner. Cortés was nineteen when he took ship for the Indies, and in his thirties before he had mustered enough men – all wild spirits like himself – and obtained a commission from the Governor of Cuba to explore the coastline of Mexico. Cortés intended to do much more than explore. He had to sell his lands in Cuba to equip the expedition, and many of his followers did likewise. If the expedition failed to find new lands, they would lose everything but, as the world now knows, Cortés' expedition to Mexico was a success beyond anyone's wildest dreams. The exploits were chronicled by a native of Medina del Campo, Bernal Díaz del Castillo, and he records how, when Cortés' men faltered at the sight of the huge Aztec armies and at the thought of marching inland away from the relative safety of the coast, he ordered that they should burn their boats, and march on to conquer or die. On the way to Mexico they fought countless battles, winning victories over the Aztec hordes thanks to their metal armour, their horses, their artillery and most of all, to the Mexican belief that Cortés was a god. Cortés was more of a devil, but he had, and needed, the Devil's own luck. He overran the empire of Mexico with about six hundred men, eighteen horses and ten small cannon.

The Aztec empire of Mexico was ripe for conquest. The Aztecs had conquered all the neighbouring territories, and yet they continued to make war on their subject people because the worship of their gods required human sacrifice by the thousands. Prisoners captured by the Aztecs were taken to the tops of vast pyramids, or *teocalli*, some of which still remain outside Mexico City and in Yucatán. There they had their beating hearts cut from their living bodies. Bernal Díaz recorded that this fate befell those Spanish prisoners who fell into Aztec hands, and how the Spanish army, mustered far below and unable to help, could even see their captured comrades being carried to the tops of the *teocalli* and slaughtered like cattle on the Aztec altars.

With the loss of much blood, Cortés finally captured and destroyed Tenochtitlán, the old capital of Mexico (now Mexico City), overthrew the Aztec emperor, Montezuma II, who died of grief in captivity, and sent a vast hoard of treasure back to Spain. Cortés himself gained very little but an enduring fame. The Holy Roman Emperor, Charles V, heaped honours and titles on Cortés' head, giving him the title Marqués del Valle de Oaxaca, but he kept most of the treasure for himself. Cortés was soon forced to go voyaging again, and he cruised the coastline of Southern California before his luck and his money ran out. He returned to Spain in 1547 and died near Sevilla at the age of sixty-two. His star had faded so quickly because a new conqueror had found and destroyed yet another American empire in Peru.

The next great *conquistador*, Francisco Pizarro, another Extremaduran, came from the town of Trujillo. Trujillo was the birthplace of other *conquistadores* and explorers, like Francisco de Orellana, who explored the Amazon delta. Francisco Pizarro was illegitimate, but he lived in the house of his father, Gonzalo Pizarro, a poor but honest *caballero*, and had a legitimate brother, Hernando, and two more from the wrong side of the blanket, Gonzalo and Juan. The barren family lands could not support such a tribe, and the brothers soon departed for the New World. Francisco and Hernando were both in their fifties, and tough as old boots, before they set out to conquer Peru.

Cuzco fell to the Spaniards in 1533, who numbered less than a hundred men, and the great wealth and working silver mines of the Andes soon outmatched anything that Cortés had taken from Mexico. There is a statue to Francisco Pizarro in the main square of Trujillo, and one exactly like it in the Plaza in Lima, Peru, where Francisco's bones can still be seen mouldering in a glass coffin in the cathedral. As usual, though, the Pizarros hardly benefited from the conquest. Juan died in the fighting, Francisco was murdered by rivals at his house in Lima, Gonzalo was beheaded for rebelling against the king's Viceroy of Peru, and Hernando was kept in a Spanish prison for over twenty years, though he was eventually released and lived to be a hundred. They breed tough men here in Extremadura. As if to prove that this really is the country of the *conquistadores*, Extremadura also bred Hernán de Soto and Vasco Núñez de Balboa. It was Balboa and not 'stout Cortez' who actually crossed the Isthmus of Darien and gazed with 'a wild surmise' at the Pacific Ocean.

During much of the Reconquista, Extremadura was a march, a bufferzone, and crossing it on foot one can see that an army of any size would be hard pressed to survive here. This may have been the reason why the main thrust of the Christian armies was to the east, out of La Mancha and Calatrava, south towards Bailén, rather than across these barren wastes.

The Almoravids eventually succumbed to the languor of the Peninsula and the Christian kings marched south again. But in the middle of the 12th century a new wave of Muslim fanatics, the Almohads, arrived from Africa. The resistance to this fresh attack came mostly from the Portuguese, and the Order of Calatrava, but with great efforts, even from the petty Christian kingdoms, the line of the Tajo was held. A new hero, Geraldo the Fearless, came out of Portugal into Extremadura and proceeded to recapture a number of cities. Trujillo fell to him in May 1165, Evora in September, Cáceres in November. Geraldo entered these cities alone and at night, scaling some dark sector of the wall with a long ladder, then letting his followers in to kill the Muslims and pillage the town. The Order of Santiago was founded in Cáceres in 1170, but then another Arab chieftain, Yusef I, arrived in 1171 and drove the Christian army from these southern strongholds, raiding as far north as León. In 1195, the Christians were soundly defeated at Alarcos, after which even the great castle of Calatrava fell into their hands. This defeat so depressed the Christians that Alfonso IX of León swore that he would not 'shave or cut his hair, sleep in a bed or with a woman or mount a horse or mule' until the defeat had been avenged. The revenge for Alarcos, the worst Christian defeat since Sagrajas, was

to come in 1212, at Las Navas de Tolosa, the most decisive battle of the
entire Reconquista.

The Christians had been raiding Muslim lands from the castle at
Salvatierra, which fell to the Muslims in September 1211. This defeat
was the last straw for the Christians – perhaps the name had something
to do with it – and the Pope, Innocent III, allowed his bishops to preach a
crusade. By the spring of 1212, thousands of French knights had crossed
the Pyrenees to join the Castilians, the Navarrese, and the knights of
Aragón, and the advance began. Alarcos was quickly recaptured, along
with several other towns and strongpoints, and on 16 July the two rival
armies met on the plain of Las Navas de Tolosa, near the Despeñaperros
Pass, north of Bailén.

The battle began soon after dawn, and fortunes ebbed to and fro
for some hours until Castilian reinforcements arrived, the Basques of
Navarra overwhelmed the caliph's bodyguard, and all Muslim resistance
collapsed. The Christians pursued the Muslims for twelve miles, killing
thousands, and taking hundreds into slavery. The victory of Las Navas
in July 1212, which few people outside Spain have ever heard of, was
celebrated at the time throughout Christendom. The Cathedral Chapter
at Winchester gave a special Mass, and all the Cistercian abbeys of
England sent thanks to the victors of Spain. This defeat so shattered
Muslim power that as a Spanish monk recorded, 'Alfonso VIII won at
Las Navas and so greatly that King Fernando his successor won all
he wanted'. Within fifty years the Almohad empire lay in ruins and
by 1252, the Christians ruled throughout much of the Peninsula. The
Reconquista, however, was not over, for although they now paid tribute
to the Christian kings, many Muslim kingdoms remained.

*   *   *

As a counterpoint to all this history, I met a party of young Spanish
walkers – my first such group since leaving the Gredos. They stopped
for a chat and we compared notes and maps. They were staying on a
rancho (they have ranches down here, not *fincas*, or farms), but since
none of them could ride a horse, they had been sent out for a walk.
My rucksack was duly tried on by everyone, with much grunting and
slaps on the back. Then we retired to the shade of some olive trees to
discuss my route and share their water. I was quite determined not to
part with a drop of mine.

The simplest thing, they suggested, was either to follow the road south
and a little west for a while, across this soaring country to the road
junction at Navalvillar de Pela, or, if I was so inclined, I could strike

off across country, directly for the Sierra de Pela and the town of Obando. The sierra could just be seen rising out of the heat haze far ahead across the plain. That was quite far enough for one day – about forty kilometres – but I was sure to find a bed in Obando and, since the ground was flat and the trees offered some shade, this might be a good route.

On the other hand, if I struck off due south across the flat country, I would hit the main road from Mérida that much sooner, somewhere east of Obando, and so perhaps cut down the distance. This would also knock a few miles off the next day's march and I might then stay somewhere on the road, perhaps at Casas de Don Pedro. This was just a dot on the map, but the map was old. It might be bigger now. Accompanied by my new-found friends, I trailed down the road until we reached the junction where another road ran north to Logrosán. There, directly opposite the junction and running due south, was a genuine track! I know a sign when I see one, and a track on the map which I could also find on the ground was almost a miracle. My water bottle was still full so, shaking hands with the walkers, I set off at a good clip across the waterless southern plain. If I tend to go on about water remember that I wrote this when I was actually on the trail and the lack of water was all too fresh in my mind. When you think of Extremadura, think of the North African desert and you will have a clearer picture of the country in your mind.

*   *   *

Perhaps I should try to describe the countryside. They tell me that in the spring, after the winter rains have drenched the land, Extremadura blossoms into a carpet of grass and flowers: great rolling plains of colour, stretching as far as the eye can see. When I came to cross it in October, there had been no rain for four months and the sun was unseasonably hot. I met old, semi-literate peasants who became almost lyrical when they talked about this area in the spring, when it must indeed be marvellous. In October there was not a flower or a blade of grass, nor a drop of water in the streams or rivers. The dams were empty, great olive trees, heavy with fruit, drooped in dull green exhaustion, their roots sucking some moisture from who knows how deep in the soil. Here and there a tractor crossed some vast field, trailing a great cloud of brown dust, but otherwise nothing moved under the hammer of the sun. The whitewashed houses and farms were empty of cattle and people and, in the few villages, people stayed indoors or in the cooler depths of bars. Even so, and in its own stark fashion, Extremadura is beautiful, but if I ever go there again, I will go there in the springtime.

So, it was hot. In fact, it was very hot. I tried to stay in the spattered shade of the olive trees, but it was still hot. At this time of the year, the temperature hereabouts in Extremadura should vary between 18°C and, say, 25°C. I had checked this carefully before departure. On this day, the temperature was at least 30°C, the upper 80s°F and probably higher out in the open. I stayed in the shade where I could, drank sparingly from my water bottle, and moved exceedingly slowly. Even so, it was desperately hard work. On a walk like this, it is time rather than distance that you go by. It was just three in the afternoon, and I had been walking for about eight hours when I came over a low crest among the trees and saw before me the main *carretera*. I do not remember much of this walk. There were trees and rough plough, and the occasional dry stream bed, perhaps a fence or two. I don't really remember; it was just too hot. I was pretty well exhausted and I was also mildly lost. There was no sign at all of my new target for the evening: the *pueblo* of Casas de Don Pedro. I could see the Sierra de Pela off to my right, so I knew the town could not be terribly far away, but I was, in a word, done-up. I had about an inch of water left in my water bottle and so I sat down on the edge of the road to suck on this and have a think. While I was thus engaged I heard the popping sound of an approaching motorcycle.

Until then I had not accepted a lift. There was no nobility in this, just that no one had offered me one. On those occasions where I could stand the slog no longer and stuck out my thumb beside the road, I had simply been ignored for, as a rule, the Spanish do not pick up walkers. This may be because hitch-hiking is illegal, though I hardly think that would bother them. I think it is because the Spanish driver is, in all but fact, a fighter pilot. He gets in his car and goes on a mission. Foot flat on the floor, he flies along until he hits his objective: a wall, a tree, another car, maybe even his destination, whatever comes first. One thing he does *not* do is stop for large, loaded, sweating idiots walking on the wide *carretera*.

Having accepted this as a fact, it took me a little time to realise that the rider on the two-stroke moped had stopped. His engine in neutral but still popping away, he was inviting me to hop on the carrier for a lift, by jerking his head invitingly. I have to say that my would-be benefactor was not the most engaging sight. He was clearly a mechanic, for he was clad in once-clean pink overalls. These were now liberally drenched with oil. More oil adorned his hands, hair and unshaven face, but he was cheerful, smiling, and most insistent, shouting at me above the noise of the engine.

'Hop on . . . it's too hot to wait here,' he bellowed. 'Come on . . . *venga, hombre.*'

'Well. . . .' I struggled to my feet and indicated my rucksack. 'This is very heavy . . . it will affect the . . .' I waved my hand from side to

side, '. . . the balance.' I don't know the Spanish word for balance but
he got the idea and dismissed it.

'Hop on,' he said again. 'I'll go slowly.'

Well, mock me not. If you had been crossing Extremadura on a hot
afternoon and had already walked for eight hours that day, you would
not have turned a lift down either. Besides, I'm always one for a dare.
I squeezed onto the bare metal carrier behind him and, engine popping
madly, we set off. It was not too comfortable. There were no pedals to
put the feet on and nothing to hang on to but my host. Also, as I had
predicted, we wobbled – wildly.

There are times in life when you realise rather quickly that the action
you have just taken is unwise. So it was here. Within about two minutes
of mounting the bike I realised that my benefactor was as drunk as a
skunk. With a little experience you can soon spot things like that. When
the driver sticks to the wrong side of the road, talks incessantly, sings a
lot and gives the finger to other drivers as they swerve wildly out of his
way, you can be pretty sure all is not as it should be. If, added to this,
you get a blast of brandy fumes and a stream of sparks blown back into
your face from his cigarette, you will soon experience a combination of
fear and discomfort that can really make your day.

'*¡Cuidado!*' I shrieked as a coach roared past, blasting us up onto the
verge. This was when I realised we were on the wrong, or English, side
of the road.

'*No tenga miedo*,' he yelled back, swerving the bike into the middle
of the road, taking a hand off the controls to wave his fist at the
white-faced passengers peering back at us out of the rear window.
Having fear was the least of my worries. Sudden death seemed much
more possible. On the way uphill, when our pace slowed somewhat, I
even contemplated rolling off onto the road, balancing the possibility
of a cracked skull against the certainty of catching a foot in the rear
wheel. You are not too agile with a rucksack on your back. On the
downhill sections our combined weights plus the rucksack gave the
moped much unwelcome velocity. I think we even passed a car at one
point, but I can't be sure. What with one thing and another, I kept my
eyes shut.

Suddenly – thank God – some houses came into sight, a garage, a
café: rescue. With another wild swerve we were off the road, bounding
up the bank and skidding to a stop outside a café.

'*Las Casas*,' he said. 'Now I must go and see my girlfriend.' At this
point he slid out of the saddle and off the bike, to lie on his side giggling.
I caught the bike and helped him up, being rewarded with another blast
of brandy fumes. Then I held the moped while he got back on, cranked
the throttle and shot off.

'Be careful,' I pleaded. 'Don't you think. . . .' Too late.

'*Adiós*,' he cried, swerving away again into the traffic. I watched the cars scatter and swerve as he vanished out of sight over the hill.

'*Adiós, y gracias!*' Well, I had a few miles to be thankful for and it always pays to be polite. When I turned towards the café a small knot of people had gathered by the door and were standing there staring at me. One of them helped me off with the rucksack and they all followed me inside as I headed towards the bar.

'You shouldn't ride with him,' said the barman. 'That's Alonzo . . . and he drinks a lot.'

'I found that out for myself,' I told him. 'Make that a large one.'

*   *   *

The Don Pedro of Casas de Don Pedro turned out to be yet another *conquistador*, Pedro de Valdivia, the discoverer and conqueror of Chile. I know more than I might about Pedro de Valdivia, as my wife is from Chile and is full of information about him. Pedro de Valdivia was one of Pizarro's captains. After the conquest of Peru he was sent by Francisco Pizarro to extend their dominion to the south. This meant crossing the great void of the Atacama Desert in the north of what is now Chile. The Atacama is a dreadful place, a region where it never rains, is still full of rough soldiers from the Chilean army, is freezing cold at night and well frequented by vampire bats. I have been up there, fleeing from a constant round of cocktail parties in Santiago de Chile, but unless you are very anti-social, I can't really recommend it, though it may be like home if you were born in Extremadura. Valdivia eventually crossed the Atacama and made his way south to the green country around what is now Santiago de Chile, where he spent some years trying to subdue the fierce Mapuche Indians. Unfortunately for Don Pedro, he eventually fell into their hands and since he had come for gold, they gave him some. They melted gold in a cauldron and poured the molten metal down his throat.

The excitements of the last half-hour had given me quite enough adrenaline for one day. After a few drinks in the bar, I wandered through the streets of Casas, past the fine fortified church, and spent the night, quite cheerfully, at the *Bar Estrella* on the far side of the town. Apart from the church and the two bars, there is nothing else of note in Casas, but on the whole I preferred it like that. What with one thing and another, it had been quite a day.

CHAPTER FOURTEEN

THE ROAD TO AL-ANDALUS

When men travelled through Spain they
were nearly always in a bad temper.
And they had cause to be.

W. Somerset Maugham *Don Fernando* (1935)

South of Casas the road falls away steadily across the barren plain to yet another of those great reservoirs that barred my direct route to the Mediterranean. On the following morning, the first of these, the Embalse de Orellana, lay within an hour's march. This *embalse* is normally as big as an inland sea, but was now very low and hardly noticeable, just a thin, slimy trickle of water in a shallow valley. A small *ermita*, the Ermita de las Vegas, stands on the north side of the bridge across. There was no one about that I could see, so I walked on over the bridge, racing the sun to get as far south as I could before midday. I had my tent and my water bottle and a little food in my rucksack. Perhaps today I would give up walking in the heat of the day and take to the Spanish siesta. When in Spain it usually pays to do as the Spanish do.

I might talk a little about this Spanish day. In the cities of Madrid and Barcelona, international trade has changed or curtailed the Spanish day, but not much has changed in the countryside. The great object is to avoid the heat, so people get up early, avoid the afternoons, and eat late. I was often up and out by six, well before dawn, but even in the smallest village there was always a café open and plenty of people inside. The great sight in an early-morning café is the huge raft of coffee cups and saucers laid out along the counter, ready for the morning rush of people on their way to work. My normal eye-opener was a cup or two of milky coffee, *café con leche*, and a couple of *magdalenas*, small, sweet cakes. Most of the other men in the bar drank beer or hard liquor.

My friend Peter Chambers has described the French as 'drip-feed alcoholics', from their habit of tippling throughout the day. The Spaniard does not waste time tippling; he gets stuck in to double measures of brandy, or a half-tumbler of whisky, maybe two, and all this at the crack of dawn. That done, to the accompaniment of the usual bellowed conversations and the blare of a television set, everyone departs for work. The Spaniards are not lazy. That image of Latins sitting under a cactus, sound asleep in their *serapes*, is Mexican imagery, and is not true either. The Mexicans know how to work. By the time the average visitor stumbles from his or her hotel, the Spaniards have been at work for hours.

Whatever hour of the day you go into a Spanish bar, it will be full of men; you rarely see a woman in a bar, and never see one alone. The men come in for a coffee or a beer or an afternoon snack, a few *tapas*, because people eat late, and later as you go south, where it gets even hotter. You can get *comida*, lunch, any time from two until five, during which time some people also fit in a siesta, and though the siesta seems to be dying out, the long lunch break, of two or three hours, seems to be lingering on. People then go back to work at about four or five, until seven or later, with some shops staying open until nine. After that, you can dine at eleven or later. This all makes for a very long day, but since you can't get to sleep in the heat you might as well stay up. This also applies to the children, who can be seen or heard running about at all hours. No wonder the average Spanish child looks small, pale and wan. They don't rest. As for their parents, they avoid the sun and work like dogs.

I was still nursing my resolve to do as the Spanish do, when I drew near Talarrubias. This little town seemed worth a look before I swept on to my chosen siesta spot at Puebla de Alcocer, three miles further south. Alcocer looked rather more interesting than Talarrubias, mainly because the sierra behind it is crowned by a fine Mudejar castle. However, I thought Talarrubias looked a nice town, even though Ford said that it had 'iniquitous accommodations'. For some reason, Ford makes no mention of the castle at Alcocer, although this is a splendid place seen across the plain. When I found a small *fonda*-restaurant in the centre of Talarrubias, I decided to stop for an early lunch. Practically the entire male population of the town was there, watching football on the television, and when the word spread that I was English, I was invited to comment on the game.

'In Spain, we really only have two teams that matter,' said the barman. 'Real Madrid and Barcelona. There are others, but every year it is Real Madrid at the top, Barcelona second, or vice-versa. Now, in England you have Manchestershire United and Liverpool. . . .'

'*Y* Everton,' another man brought me a beer. I rather liked Manchestershire United. I could support them, and said so.

'*Sí*, and Arsenal,' said the barman. 'You have many, many good teams.' He looked wistful.

Half the bar supported an English team and demanded an account of their prospects for the coming season. The snag is – why is there always a snag? – I know nothing about football. I don't like football; I actually loathe football. As for football supporters, never mind English football supporters, you could drown the lot and leave me smiling, but this was not the place to say so.

Truth to tell, I was more than a little fed up with football. The Spaniards are mad about it, but the conversation inevitably comes round to '*los hooligans*', one of our few gifts to the language of Spain. Other loan words include the one hanging over a strike-bound oil tanker in Santander harbour, which called for a '*boicott a Shell*', and there is, before I forget, *baicon*, which you have with *huevos*. Defending *los hooligans* is impossible, and accounting for their actions difficult. I settled for the Spanish shrug and said that the British are not all like that. The hooligans are the ones who make the papers, though. Still, in a situation like this, with everyone hanging on your words, what do you do? What can I tell them about football? You tell lies, that's what you do. When I ran out of lies and they ran out of beer, I got up and reeled down the road to Alcocer. At least I didn't have to stay and watch the match.

*   *   *

Outside the towns and *pueblos*, there is nothing in Extremadura. Like the Sierra de Gredos, the plain of Extremadura is the real thing. The Gredos are real mountains and Extremadura is a real desert set in the centre of Spain. Alcocer is overtopped by a magnificent castle, one of the finest I had seen in all my travels, built on the sierra above the town to protect the road and overawe any Moorish raiding party coming up across the Sierra Morena from Andalucía. Like the castle of La Mota at Medina, it took me all the next day to shake it off. As I plugged on across the plain, the castle of Alcocer was always there, mocking my efforts to leave it behind.

*   *   *

Leaving Puebla de Alcocer next morning, my road south, for about twenty miles or more, crossed an area of Extremadura known as La Serena, a region encircled to the north and south by the great sweep of the Río Zújar, and more like North Africa than anywhere else in Europe. I left Puebla de Alcocer easily enough, my head tilted up to that magnificent castle which crowns the hills behind the town, filled up my water bottles and myself at a washing place by a garage just out of town, and after sucking in the water like a camel, I set out across the void for Cabeza del Buey. I had actually intended to take a bus across this bleak, inhospitable terrain, but there are no buses. That lamentable fact discovered, I intended to stop every two hours to rest in the shade, but there is no shade. The Serena of Extremadura is the nearest thing to a desert I was to encounter, and crossing it, heavily laden and in a single day, was to prove a real challenge. The reason for crossing it in a day and not two days was simple: water.

$$* \quad * \quad *$$

It began pleasantly enough. A few miles down the road I had an encounter on the far side of the Sierra del Castillo with an old man from Galizuela, a small village nearby, who came trotting along on his donkey. He stopped, we chatted. He had never met an Englishman before, and this will give you some idea of the remoteness of Central Spain. Millions of Britons have been descending on Spain every summer for the last thirty years, and this old gentleman had never met one. You don't actually get many English afoot in the middle of Extremadura and though I'm actually a Scot, life is too short to explain all that. We walked on together to his village, discussing the weather, the lateness of the autumn rains and the difficulty of scratching a living from this inhospitable terrain. Even so, bleak as it is, with weather that can change from heat to chill in the space of hours, my new best friend was very proud of his province. Nowhere, he assured me, was as green and beautiful as the sierra of Extremadura in the spring. Seen now, when there was nothing but brown undulating downland for twenty miles in any direction, I found that easy to accept but hard to believe. I trudged on, thinking to refill my water bottles and find green grass near the Embalse del Zújar. When I got there the *embalse* was empty and I had a problem.

Various bridges, raised high on great metal pillars, span the Embalse del Zújar. All were now quite unnecessary, for the lake bed was as dry as any bone. I made my way down to the bed of the reservoir and saved a mile or so by walking directly across the lake bed to the distant shimmer of the road running around the edge, reflecting that in any normal year I would have had thirty feet of water above my head. That would have been nice. I tried not to think of water, for the day was already hot and I had exactly a quart of water left to get me across this desert to the safety of Cabeza del Buey.

There are various schools of thought on how to ration water. One opinion has it that you sip a little bit often, and try never to become too dry. The other school, fearing that sips may all too easily become gulps, advises that you drink only at specific times, say once an hour or every five kilometres . . . whatever. I opted for the latter school, stopping once every hour to drink exactly two finger-widths of water from my scanty supply. Sometimes, when I was crouched in the shade of a roadsign to do this, a car would sweep by – God knows what the people inside thought – but they made no attempt to stop and offer help. Later that afternoon, when I attempted to stop a car by standing in the middle of the road, arms wide, the car braked, hesitated, then swung off the road, bumping across the prairie to one side in a cloud of dust, then came back onto the road ahead and raced away, hostile faces staring back at me out of the windows. By then down to less than a pint of water, I hoped they crashed.

To ration your water by a road in a Western European country at the end of the 20th century sounds ridiculous, a throwback to the great days of exploration. In Africa or some desert terrain, a shortage of water might seem acceptable, but now, here, in Spain? I would not have died crossing the sierra, but I could have, and did, become somewhat distressed. I ran out of water with half the distance still to do, and owe a fairly trouble-free crossing to a farmer I met by the road. He was resting by his tractor when I stopped for a chat and he offered me a drink from his supply. A long, cool draught from an earthenware pot, with a plug over the filling hole and a teat-like spout from which a jet of water can be directed into your mouth; it was nectar. I was reluctant to accept the water – well, I pretended to be reluctant – but he insisted, so I took it as he said he had plenty and I could drink the lot if I wanted to. I took several good swigs but within half an hour I was thirsty again. Half the snag in something like this is not the lack of water but the loss of body salt. My shirt was now encrusted with sweat marks, and no amount of water could replace the salt I was losing. Well, that's life. I hitched up the rucksack and plodded on, head bowed, across the plain, the dried earth crumbling under my boots, putting up little puffs of dust, the sun smiting me for all it was worth.

As usual, I tried to cut the distance by cutting the corners, using the road only as a guide and a possible source of water. Where there are roads there are people, and where there are people, there is water. Right? Wrong! Not in Extremadura. I tried a few farms and whitewashed barns, but they were either empty or abandoned, and a well with water in it far below, did not have a bucket or a windlass. My next real find, late in the afternoon, was a well-equipped well. I saw it to the left of the road, a small patch of green around a stone wall. Green was so rare, I limped over to see if it could possibly be what I hoped for. There I found a spring-fed well. Behind that lay a couple of stone troughs for watering the animals, and with all this went a leather bucket and a rope with which I drew up a quantity of rather sludgy water from the depths and drank long and deep. Anyone who has ever gone thirsty will know how little you get to care about small living bodies in the water. If it's wet, you drink it; the living bodies must look out for themselves. I drank and drank until the water ran out of my pores, and refilled the water bottle. Then I pressed on across the plain.

With evening coming on fast, I reached another five kilometre point and treated myself to the last two fingers in my water bottle. Then I heaved on my heavy, sweat-drenched rucksack for the umpteenth time that day, and plodded on for Cabeza del Buey. This town had stayed stubbornly out of sight all day but finally came into view late in the afternoon, a glimpse of white houses from the top of a low hill. Seeing it was one thing, getting there another, for it took hours to close the distance. I wandered hither and thither across the parched earth, until finally and wearily, about six in the evening, I crossed the Badajoz–Madrid railway line and made my way into the town. First, I found a *fonda* but there was no response to my knocking. Then I found a bar where I had a *Fanta naranja*, an orange juice, then a beer and a glass of water, and then another beer in rapid succession, before asking the owner if there was a hotel in town. What I needed now was some tender loving care.

'There is one,' he told me, 'but it may be full.' Leading me outside, he pointed out the way to the *Hotel Polideportivo*, which was rather far away on the other side of town, but had, he assured me, plenty of rooms and plenty of baths. This *Polideportivo* sounded like Paradise. I heaved on the rucksack yet again, and made my way, oh-so-slowly, up to the main street of the town and then right towards the *Polideportivo*, which seemed from a distance to be surrounded by cars and was therefore probably booked solid. This gloomy thought had just crossed my mind when I was accosted by a brace of youths. I had become wary of such people since Ávila, but this pair had a question. Had they not seen me only this morning in Alcocer? They had. Had I *walked* all this way, across the plain? I had. Without a lift? Without a lift. They were stunned. '¡*Maravilloso!* ¡*Hombre!*' I thanked them for their congratulations but said that all I wanted now was a bed at the hotel up ahead, and only hoped that I could get one. If not, I intended to burst into tears. The two lads offered to carry my rucksack, and insisted on buying me a drink; this could be useful, so we went on together.

I had already experienced a certain amount of difficulty getting into respectable accommodation on this walk, but that was nothing new.

Hotel receptionists are not overburdened with charm, even at birth, and since guests simply add to their workload without any increase in pay, if they can turn you away they feel happy. There are exceptions to every rule, of course, but by and large, hotel receptionists are an obstacle that has to be surmounted rather than a step towards bed-and-board.

In my particular case, since I usually arrive at the reception desk looking like a survivor from the wreck of the *Hesperus*, turning me away takes on the aspect of a public duty. Fortunately, I have been around the world a bit and various techniques can be employed to prevent getting what the Americans aptly describe as the 'bum's rush'.

The first trick is to leave your cycle or rucksack outside. Quite apart from attracting hostility, lugging them in takes time. If the hotel has a doorman as the first line of defence, treat him like dirt. Whatever you do, do not offer him money. If you can snap your fingers to attract his attention, so much the better, but otherwise when it dawns on this lackey that a hobo has the temerity to attempt to enter the august portals of his five-star Carlton-Splendide-Ritz-Plaza, and he promptly claws for the scruff of your neck, take him up short:

'Ah you . . . what's your name, eh? Never mind. Look after this,' (handing him the rucksack or the handlebars). 'If there is so much as a scratch on it when I return, I shall have you sacked.'

If you can do this in the local language, so much the better. 'I will have you sacked,' is one of those phrases, like 'My friend in the corner will pay', that any serious traveller should learn in as many languages as possible.

So, leaving the porter with his mouth open, guarding your valuables, you enter the hotel. Once inside, never hesitate. You must sweep up to the reception desk at speed. The tip here is *never speak the local language*. Anywhere abroad, speak English. Even in America they will hardly understand you, while in Britain, where you must speak English because everyone in the tourist trade is too lazy to speak anything else, do so with a foreign accent. No one is quite sure about foreigners; for all the hotel receptionist knows, foreigners may be covered with dust and sweat all the time – and time is what you must gain at this point.

Then, before the receptionist has collected his or her wits, produce your wallet, scattering as much money and credit cards on the counter as possible. This establishes your credentials as an eccentric millionaire. Eccentric millionaires are known to be big tippers. Then, my final piece of advice, ask for a suite. If you say, 'Have you a room for the night?' and they say, 'No,' you have no option but to withdraw. Hotels usually let their suites early, so there is no real danger that you will actually have to take a suite, but you have established the fact that you are horribly rich, and given everyone a fall-back position. They do not have a suite . . . pity. All right, and very reluctantly, you will accept a room. Eventually you will get the single room with bath or shower that you really wanted in the first place.

I am exaggerating, but not much. Hotels do not like oddly attired guests, however well-behaved, and if the alternative to acting like Napoleon is sleeping in the streets, I say, no contest. One final, final tip. If the hotel receptionist simply ignores you or vanishes, or attends to everyone else, the answer is to say, politely but very loudly, 'If you persist in being insolent (Sir or Madam), I shall send for the Manager *now*'. It is the word 'now' that freezes their blood, because even if the manager throws you out, he will remember that the receptionist caused an embarrassing scene in the foyer and this is something which receptionists are hired to prevent. I am not alone in having developed techniques for handling hoteliers. My friend Ken Ward, who runs a walking holiday company, told me that some hotels were very reluctant to accept his bookings when his company was known as Backpack Man. He then changed it to Lord Winston's Walking Tours, and hoteliers have been grovelling round his boots ever since.

*   *   *

The two lads, my new best friends, burly, sporty types, aged about eighteen, even offered to come with me and get me in, but in this case I need not have worried. While I was shrugging off the rucksack on the outside terrace, preparing to carry all before me, my companions went inside to prepare the ground and set up the drinks. I entered the bar to a turned sea of faces and a certain amount of popular acclaim. This bar at the *Polideportivo* is a circular, sunken affair in marble, rather like a swimming pool, and seems to be the social centre of Cabeza del Buey, and home to the local sporting club. Everyone was in there, staring at me.

'*Éste señor*,' said one of my companions, addressing the throng from the top of the steps, '*es inglés. . . .*' (Mild applause, cries of '*¡Bienvenido! ¡Viva Everton!*', etc.) 'He has walked from Santander . . . *y por España, a pie . . . ¡con destino a Tarifa!*' (Whistles, thumping of counter, head-shaking, etc) and, wait for it, 'He has walked today . . . *sin coche . . . ¡desde Alcocer!*'

The roof came off.

I had a pretty memorable evening in the bar of the *Polideportivo* at Cabeza del Buey. The barman kept lining up glasses of *Cuba Libre*, made with gin rather than rum; there was a lot of noise, two or three fist-fights and a great deal of talk. I think there was singing and there was certainly guitar-playing. I had a good meal, a hot shower or two, several gallons of water and far too much of the hard stuff. They can kill you with kindness at Cabeza del Buey.

Next morning, feeling rather better than I deserved, I paid my dues to the hotel. Studying the bill I discovered that I had only been charged for dinner, bed and breakfast, and not for any of the drinks I had had or ordered during the previous evening. After that night and the rigours of the previous day, I did not feel like doing too much, so I began with a stroll round the town. My first task now was to find out why Cabeza del Buey had such a curious name. The Bullock's Head is not a name you expect to find, even in Extremadura. I asked some old men in the park, but they had no idea and I have still to find the origins of that strange title. Fortunately, Cabeza has various other attractions, because here the arid plains end and the hills begin again. There were small farms and orchards, green grass and the occasional flower, even streams with water in them. After the hard times further north, I now stood on the doorstep of Andalucía and I was very glad to be there. I had been on the road for a month and getting towards the last third of my journey.

Doctor Footpath had also done wonders in improving my health. I felt pretty good; that worrying tingling sensation had gone from my arm, I had lost weight and I had a tan. Even the kit was holding up well, though I was becoming very fed up of swapping round my wardrobe of two shirts and two pairs of Rohan trousers on a twice daily basis: on in the morning, off in the evening, wash, then on again in the morning. My social life was about zero, but I could have worn some party clothes just for a change. Ah well, perhaps in Córdoba or the Costa del Sol. I wondered idly what would happen if I walked up to the Marbella Club, rucksack and all. Perhaps I should go and find out.

With a mercifully chill breeze pushing me down, once again, to the Río Zújar, a river which seemed to pop up everywhere hereabouts, I set off again for the south. The countryside was softer and more pleasant. I even saw a patch of real green grass, my first in days, and it is some measure of the country that I stopped to stare at it. The farms were well-kept, and surrounded by cherry trees . . . it looked delightful. Even better, after about an hour, when I had just crossed the dry bed of the Río Zújar, I was greeted by two notices. The first announced that the Río Zújar was the frontier of the *Provincia de Córdoba*. The second bid me welcome to the country of Al-Andalus: Andalucía! I seemed to be getting somewhere at last.

CHAPTER FIFTEEN

INTO ANDALUCÍA

In spite of everything, Spain does amuse
me. Every day a sky so blue you can scoop it
out with a spoon; a sun so glorious that the
shadows are palpably black; a dry, crisp air
which tightens one's muscles and makes life
easy; and people who are always good
natured if you do not insult them.

Henry Adams (1879)

Having come so far across Spain, following the halting steps of the Reconquista, the banks of the Zújar seemed a good place to stop and look a little closer into the Moorish history of Spain and the eight-hundred-year-old struggle between Christian and Moor. This struggle can only have been maintained by greed, land-hunger, religion or sheer human cussedness. It was certainly not a Civil War between Spaniards — that was reserved for a later time — but after an occupation lasting over seven hundred years, who can deny that the Moors of Granada were Spanish? Indeed, much of what we now recognise as the best in Spain comes from these Spanish Moors, who had a taste and style in architecture rarely found among the Christians.

I was heading now for the Río Guadalquivir, and the great Moorish capital of Córdoba. Córdoba is a good place from which to review the history of Andalucía because, although the kingdom of Granada endured until 1492, when it fell to Fernando and Isabel, many Moors continued to live in Spain for a long time after that. The Moors were not, in fact, finally expelled from Spain until 1614, but the capture of Córdoba by Fernando el Santo ('the Saint') in 1236 meant the end of Andalucía as a separate, happy kingdom. To see how that tragedy came about we must go back a bit, for although I have covered the path of the Reconquista regularly on this walk, the story of the Moors in Spain deserves separate and more detailed consideration.

The Moors who invaded the Spanish peninsula in AD 711 were Umayyad Muslims from Syria. The Umayyads had been conquering their way along the North African seaboard since the death of the Prophet in 632. They reached Morocco in 709, and in 716 the Muslim governor of Morocco sent a force of 7,000 Berbers across the Straits under the leadership of Tariq im Ziyad, the governor of Tangier. They landed beside the great rock that came to be called the Jebel-al-Tariq – or Gibraltar. Córdoba, then a Visigothic town, fell to the Moors in October 716, and Toledo in November. More Muslims then poured across the Straits to overrun all but Pelayo's little Asturian enclave by AD 717. By 750, except for that tiny kingdom in the Asturias, the Muslims held most of what is now Spain, south of the Pyrenees, with the distant Umayyad caliphs of Damascus as their overlords. The Umayyads of Damascus were overthrown in AD 750, but one who got away from the massacre, Abd al-Rahman I, reached Spain in 755. After defeating the governor of Córdoba with the support of the Berbers, he proclaimed himself Emir of Córdoba, and soon exerted his lordship over the entire Peninsula, which he called Al-Andalus, the Country of Light. The ruler of Al-Andalus, or Andalucía, remained an emir until 929 and Córdoba then became a caliphate.

Al-Andalus was not an entirely Muslim country. Many Jews lived there and a great body of Christians were allowed to remain and practise their religion, though under a number of restrictions. They were not allowed to ride horses or carry weapons, and had to pay a monthly residence tax and other charges, but while the taxes were certainly gathered, most of the other petty restrictions were tacitly ignored. The Muslims recognised Christ as a prophet and regarded his followers, like the Jews, as 'People of the Book'. The one thing they detested was church bells, and the Christians were forbidden to ring them.

Pelayo's victories in the Asturias at the start of the Reconquista began about AD 718 and the Christian advance never really stopped thereafter. So the history of the Reconquista is the history of a slow surge south by the Christian powers. Sometimes waxing, sometimes waning, the Christians never quite returned to their original positions once they had progressed south. By the end of the 8th century the Christians had advanced to the Río Duero and created a wide march as a barrier against the marauding Moorish armies. It is about now, in the early years of the 9th century, that the relics of St James, or Santiago, were discovered in Galicia. These were placed in a shrine at Santiago de Compostela, and this shrine brought knights and warriors from the north to add their arms to the Christian kingdoms. In the next century the kingdoms of Castile,

Navarra, Aragón, León and Galicia, with the county of Barcelona, came into being, and although these kingdoms were still small and regularly went to war with each other, the Christian advance continued. By the 850s their forces left the mountains and pushed on across the Duero towards the open *meseta* I had crossed so painfully weeks before. By the early years of the 10th century the Christian kings, especially those of León and the Asturias, had reconquered about a fifth of the Peninsula. They held their conquests by studding the land beyond the Duero with castles or *castillos*, and so created another great kingdom called Castilla: Castile. You know all this.

At this moment, when all was going so well for the Christians, a great warlord came to power in Córdoba. The caliph, Al-Hakim, had lost his territories in Morocco, and thereby a fruitful source of soldiers, but he still resisted the Christians stoutly, and was continuing to do so when he died in 976. His son, Hisham II, retired with several hundred concubines to his palace at Medina Azahara, outside Córdoba, and left his affairs in the hands of his chief minister, Muhammed Ibn Abi Amir, who swept north, retaking towns and castles, defeating any force the Christians sent against him. He returned to Córdoba taking the title of Al-Mansur bi' Allah, 'Victorious through the grace of Allah'. To celebrate his triumphs he put in hand the building of the great mosque of Córdoba, laying the bricks with his own hands. The rule of Al-Mansur saw the caliphate of Córdoba reach out to strike in all directions and enter a brief Golden Age.

The Christians soon gave up any attempt to defeat Al-Mansur in battle and many became his vassals – Sancho II of Navarra even gave Al-Mansur his daughter as a wife – and the other kings hurriedly offered tribute. Where they resisted they were defeated. By 997 Al-Mansur had swept north-east into Galicia, where he destroyed the church but not the shrine at Santiago de Compostela. The story goes that Al-Mansur rode his horse into the church and found an elderly monk kneeling before the shrine. 'Who are you and what are you doing here?' asked the conqueror. 'I am the familiar of St James and I am about my prayers,' replied the monk. Al-Mansur gave orders that the monk and his charge should be left in peace, but the other Christians were not so lucky. Taken into slavery, they were whipped back across Spain, carrying on their shoulders the doors and bells of Santiago. Once back in Córdoba, the bells, inverted and filled with oil, were used as lamps in the Great Mosque, while the doors provided timber for the roof vaults. After a long string of victories, Al-Mansur died in 1002, and all Spanish Christendom heaved a sigh of relief. True relief had to be delayed a little, for the rule continued under his son Al-Malik, who continued his conquests until his death in 1008. Only then did the power of Córdoba begin to wane. Civil war broke out between the heirs of the caliph and to gain the support of the Christian powers, both sides granted them lands in Central Spain and so let Christian power revive. Before long, Andalucía itself began to break up as petty chieftains took over the control of entire provinces and then set themselves up as kings. The caliphate of Córdoba changed hands fifteen times in twenty years before it finally collapsed in 1027, leaving Andalucía split into what became known as *taifa* kingdoms – Badajoz, Toledo, Zaragoza, Granada and many smaller ones. All wary of each other, all were prey to the Christians of the north, who had found a great warlord in Fernando I of Navarra. Fernando established the 'empire' of León and soon had his sons ruling over the subject kingdoms of Galicia, León and Castile. Fernando preferred to leave the *taifa* kingdoms intact, while extracting riches from them in tribute, but he eventually began to annex their territories, beginning with Badajoz.

Fernando had overrun much of the territory conquered by Al-Mansur by the time he died in 1065. His territories were divided between his three sons, Alfonso VI of León and Asturias, who also held lands in Moorish Toledo; Sancho of Castile; and García, who held Galicia and much of Portugal. These three brothers soon fell out. García was quickly overthrown and robbed of his inheritance, and, as we have seen, Alfonso, with the assistance of his sister Urraca, had Sancho murdered, which left Alfonso sole heir to his father's vast domains. He also had an able general in Rodrigo Díaz de Vivar, El Cid, and they quickly overran much of Central Spain and took Toledo and the great city of Valencia. Their task was made easier by the fact that the Church had declared a Holy War against the Muslims.

Alfonso funded his campaign against one Moorish kingdom by extracting tribute from the others, but his aim of total conquest was obvious when his army sat down to besiege Toledo, south of the Guadarrama, which he captured in May 1085. This success threw all of Andalucía into turmoil as in one blow it shifted the Christian frontier from the Central Cordillera to the Río Tajo and the Sierra Morena. Beyond that lay Córdoba itself. The greatest of the Moorish kings, Ali Mu-Tamid of Sevilla was soon forced to accept a Christian Spanish adviser in his court and surrender many of his castles, but in doing this, Alfonso went too far. Ali Mu-Tamid sent across the Straits for help and in 1086 the fierce Almoravids came swarming into Spain.

The Almoravids were a fundamentalist Muslim sect, with no great love for the soft Moors of the Peninsula, but they had a great general in Yusef Ibn Tashufn, who raised an army in Africa to conquer Christian Spain. He landed at Gibraltar in June 1086 and four months later shattered the Christian armies of Alfonso at Sagrajas. Yusef's failure to overrun Spain is usually credited to Rodrigo Díaz de Vivar, who took and held Valencia, so denying it to the Almoravids, who needed a second port from which to sweep west towards Castile. Rodrigo captured Valencia

in 1094. He showed that the Almoravids could be defeated in battle
and invited the *taifa* kings to send Muslim forces to his muster, pointing
out that should the Almoravids beat the Christians, they would take over
Muslim kingdoms as well.

*   *   *

The Almoravids continued to rampage in Spain until 1150, but then a
new power arose in Morocco, the Almohads. With the Almohads sapping
Almoravid strength across the Straits, the Christians slowly began to
recover. A king of Aragón, Alfonso I, called 'The Battler', was to prove
a hammer to the Almoravids. In 1125 he marched into Andalucía,
besieging Granada and Malaga, then returned north to capture other
Muslim cities and slaughter their Almoravid garrisons. The Christian
monarchs regained confidence and by 1150 the Almoravid terror had
been defeated. As a result, the *taifa* kingdoms flourished again, but
they were sickly now and offered little resistance to the Christian kings,
notably Alfonso VII of León. Alfonso, who reigned from 1126 to 1157,
now made war on the Almohads who were attempting to take the place
of the Almoravids in southern and south-eastern Spain. He was still on
campaign when he died in 1157, and until 1200 the Almohads' rule
included all the country of Andalucía south of the Central Cordillera.
Once secure there, they in turn set out to overrun the entire Peninsula
and might well have done so, but for their defeat at Las Navas de Tolosa,
south of Toledo, in July 1212. The defeat of Las Navas de Toloso proved
as devastating to the Muslims of Andalucía as the Christian defeat at
Hattin proved to the Franks of Outremer.

The Muslims still held the passes into Andalucía over the Sierra
Morena, but the victor of Las Navas, Alfonso VIII of Castile, soon
began to march south, outflanking the Sierra Morena by heading east
across Extremadura and cutting the road between Córdoba and Sevilla.
In these campaigns the three great Military Orders of Spain, Santiago,
Calatrava and Alcántara, played a leading part and received great gifts
of newly conquered lands as their reward. The Christians were now doing
well but nothing happened quickly in medieval times, or indeed at any
other time in Spain, and Alfonso's armies were still on campaign when
he died in 1214.

During the 1220s the Christian kings made advances in Portugal and
Extremadura, but the next monarch to make a real mark in the long
march of the Reconquista was Fernando III (El Santo) of Castile. The
Almohads had already begun to quarrel among themselves and in these
divisions Fernando saw his chance. He took a great army across the

Despeñaperros Pass in the summer of 1225, formed an alliance with an Almohad chieftain at Bailén, captured many towns and castles and received the tribute of the Muslims of Jaén. Ten years later, leaving the knights of Santiago and Calatrava to watch the Moors in the Algarve, Fernando returned to the valley of the Guadalquivir. In January 1236 his army appeared before Córdoba. He pitched his tent near where I was to spend the night, just south of the Calahorra tower, just across the river from the Great Mosque, near the road to Écija, but Córdoba was not to fall easily. The citizens held out until June 1236, until starvation had thinned their ranks and weakened their resolve. Then the governor, Abu Hassan, came across the Roman bridge and offered Fernando the keys of the city. On 30 June, Fernando III entered the city and, remembering Al-Mansur's action three centuries before, he took the great bells of Santiago de Compostela from the Great Mosque and had his Muslim prisoners drag them back all the way across Spain to Santiago de Compostela, where they still remain. In the next two years many other cities of Andalucía fell to the Christian armies, but after the fall of Córdoba the end was in sight for Muslim rule in Spain.

Spanish history is always complicated, partly because of the countless characters involved and the several kingdoms you must consider, but mostly because the Spanish monarchs all used the same few names. It takes time to discover whether the Alfonso VII you are reading about ruled in Aragón or Castile or León, and if Sancho was his son, his nephew or even his father. I found my brain growing tired trying to work this out, so I got up and transferred the effort to my feet.

*   *   *

Plodding up the short, steep hill from the Río Zújar, these thoughts of the past, of Andalucía, a land flowing with milk and honey, helped to keep my mind off the growing heat of the day. Even a mile or two into golden Andalucía, I could see great differences between this still rolling yet somehow prosperous countryside, and the bleak vastness of Extremadura which I had so recently left behind. The latter was clearly an inhospitable march; this country of Andalucía has been settled and farmed for a thousand years and it shows. Neat rows of trees, not olive trees as I at first thought but dwarf oaks, grown for their acorns which feed the pigs, seamed the countryside in neat rows which soon expanded into vast plantations. Here and there, whitewashed farms were set among cherry trees. Sheep bells tinkled from distant flocks and, given a light breeze or a little rain to cool down the day, walking in this part of Spain could be a most agreeable experience.

A few miles into Andalucía, strolling now along a track beside the road, I saw a yellow lorry parked on the verge ahead and a knot of men wielding picks, busy repairing the edges. Here again, what a difference from the province of Ávila. As I drew near, plodding uphill towards them, work was stopped, cries of '*¡Hola!*' came floating down to greet me and on arrival at the truck the earthenware pot of cool, delicious water was quickly produced. This was a little work-team led by Raphaelito, with his friends, Manolo and Eduardo. Eduardo, they had to tell me, spoke some English. In fact, Eduardo spoke English quite well and very passable French. Like many men from Andalucía, he spent the summer working in the tourist hotels of the Costa Brava and the Balearics – in his case at C'an Picafort in Mallorca – returning home to Hinojosa del Duque to take up any available work during the winter. I would have thought that anyone with two good languages might find less strenuous or more profitable employment than working on the roads swinging a pick in the heat, but Eduardo didn't think so. His day started at eight and finished at four, he had good friends and plenty of time to spend at home with his family, and an adequate income. Who needed more? Who needs more indeed? How nice to meet someone in this day and age who knows the value of a simple life.

I spent half an hour with those cheery Spaniards, sitting on the grassy bank beside the road, chatting about this and that. I then pressed on, in increasing heat, to the elusive shelter of my midway stop at Belalcázar. From the name, 'alcazar', this must be a Moorish rather than a Castilian fortress. Quite apart from leaving their mark on Spanish art and architecture, the Muslims have bequeathed many traces from their language to the Castilians. The word for a mayor, *alcalde*, comes from the Arabic *Al-quadi*, which means the same. The Arabic for a valley, *wadi*, became *guad* in Spanish, and so we have Wadi-al-Kabir, the 'great river valley', or Guadalquivir. Medina is Arabic for town, as in Medina Sidonia, while to come down to more utilitarian words, a mason – in Spanish *albañil* – comes from *al-banni*, a bricklayer in Arabic, and the word for shop, *almacén*, comes from the Arabic *al-maxan*. I could go on like this.

It took time to get to Belalcázar, but I cut the distance as usual by leaving the road and moving across the ploughed land under the oak trees, moving towards that distant crenellated tower which, as the last crest revealed to me, was just part of a much larger fortress.

Belalcázar shimmered in the midday heat, and by now my feet hurt. Having to walk along a road I had decided to wear trainers that day and give my feet a rest from the Daisy Root boots, but this was not a success. I removed the trainers in a cool, dark bar and discovered I had blisters; large ones. Before leaving for this walk, I had promised my family and friends that whatever tales I returned with, I would not moan on and on about my feet. Feet are not romantic; forget feet. Even so, it would be unfair to delude any follower or walker crazy enough to attempt crossing Spain in six weeks or less, to imagine that it can be done without punishing the feet. Fortunately, I now had only five miles to go to my destination for that day, Hinojosa del Duque, so I contented myself with swapping the trainers for the boots, and resting up a little in the dark bar, eating a ham *bocadillo* with a beer or two, before moving. Then, a hundred yards down the road a yellow truck screeched to a halt alongside me and amid a chorus of '¡*Holas!*' there were Eduardo, Manolo and Raphael once again. Lifts were no longer needed and rarely offered, but a ride in the municipal dust-cart is not one any traveller should turn down. The rucksack went into the back, with the tar and the shovels and the gravel, and I climbed into the front cab with the lads. We then drove directly to the first bar in Hinojosa del Duque, hid the municipal truck round the back and stayed in there until the sun went down, devoting the afternoon hours to some serious drinking.

*   *   *

Hinojosa del Duque is a straggling town, laid out along the main road, with a very busy Plaza Mayor and a fine church. It took me some little time that night to find the local *fonda* and once there I went to sleep and missed dinner. Another small advantage of this walk was that the weight was still falling off me. I found a set of scales in the *fonda* and if they and my mathematics were accurate, I had already lost about eight kilos, say a stone and a quarter. This was hardly surprising because it was quite hard to eat, even when I could find somewhere to do so. I got a meal of sorts every couple of days, but otherwise lived on beer, water, coffee and *tortillas*. I didn't even feel hungry but I was now almost gaunt . . . marvellous. No wonder I felt so healthy.

Next morning I made the usual early start and after a long look at the map decided that I could compass-march directly to the south, to Bélmez in the Guadiato valley some twenty miles away, using the road for a while and then, with luck, finding a few suitable tracks. For once this worked. I found a track to the left of the main road, just where I expected it to be from the map, and drifted south along it, past little farms and through shady dwarf oak and olive tree plantations, chatting to tractor drivers and shepherds, hurling stones at inquisitive dogs and hitting the road at the right point for the second bound to Bélmez. Here I found a crumbling monument to some skirmish of the Civil War, the first I had noticed on this walk across Spain.

The Spanish Civil War has left few memorials in Spain apart from the Valle de los Caídos outside Madrid, a vast mausoleum which Republican prisoners laboured for years to construct, and where General Franco himself now lies buried. The scars of that war, which killed around 700,000 people lie elsewhere, not least in people's minds. Every decade has its war; in the 1940s the issue was Nazi Germany, in the 1960s, Vietnam, but in the 1930s the battleground for rival ideologies was Spain. The Civil War of 1936–39 was simply a proving ground for a larger, later conflict.

The Spanish trace the origins of the war back to 1805, when Nelson destroyed the Combined Fleets off Trafalgar. This broke the link between Spain and her Latin American colonies, and by 1820 all the old viceroyalties had thrown off the Spanish yoke and become free if chaotic republics, as many remain to this day. The Spanish are not good colonisers.

In 1814, the Crown Prince Fernando became Fernando VII, who accepted both the throne and a constitution he was promptly to ignore. Those liberals who had framed it were shot or exiled or retired to the hills. Fernando even attempted to restore the Inquisition. An army revolt in 1820 forced Fernando to restore the constitution, but this last move worried authoritarian rulers north of the Pyrenees. A French army invaded Spain and among many other victims shot General Riego, the army general heading the liberal revolt. After Fernando died, his widow, Marie Christina, liberalised some of Spain's institutions, but her brother-in-law, Don Carlos, denied the right of Fernando's daughter to ascend the throne and the Carlist Wars which followed devastated Spain, only ending in 1839 when Princess Isabel's claim was fully recognised.

From 1840–75 the most significant feature of Spanish political life was discontent among the working classes. This was quite justified for they were little better than slaves. In 1982, riding to Compostela, I met a Spaniard who had returned from Australia after forty years away. 'It has changed but it had to,' he told me. 'When I was a boy there was terrible hardship, even starvation. If you protested, you could be thrown off your land or beaten or shot by the Guardia Civil.' And that was in the early 1940s.

The famous, or notorious, Guardia Civil, a paramilitary force, was created in the 1840s mainly to fight 'banditry' here in Andalucía. Most of the so-called bandits were farmers driven to the hills by poverty and bad treatment. Periodic outbreaks of civil unrest continued in the countryside and eventually spread to the cities. Then, in 1868, the anarchist Mikhail Bakunin arrived from Russia. Anarchy has a great appeal to the Spanish mind and before long the new Anarchists' Party, or International, had over 50,000 active members.

Queen Isabel had become mentally ill, and was replaced on the throne by Amadeo, a prince of Savoy and brother of the King of Italy. He abdicated in 1873, and his reign was followed by the First Republic. Anarchy followed, the Army took over and placed Isabel's son on the throne as Alfonso XII. He ruled in a feeble fashion with their support, but still discontent grew. In 1910, moving on a little, the first national trades union was formed, the Confederacíon Nacional de Trabajo, the now famous CNT. Growing working class exasperation and discontent in the regions, especially from the Basques and Catalans, kept the pot bubbling, and the Moroccan Wars of 1909–27 did nothing to unite the nation. Rather it gave the Army useful experience in quelling revolts with artillery and brutality.

Spain took no part in the Great War of 1914–18, but the workers were greatly influenced by the Russian Revolution of 1917. The large and growing Socialist Party made common cause with the CNT, and in the same year called a General Strike, which was crushed by the Army.

Civil War was now simmering, as governments came and went, seemingly incapable if not actually unwilling to ease the lot of the people. The anarchists of Cataluña took up arms in 1920 and there was street fighting almost daily in Barcelona for the next ten years. Then the Spanish army suffered defeat in Morocco and in the outcry which followed, General Primo de Rivera came to power. He became virtual dictator of Spain in 1923, but ruled with some success until 1930. De Rivera followed an economic path pursued with more success by Hitler; he put people back to work, held down inflation, built roads and railways. A hard-drinking, womanising Andalucian, he was popular with all sections of society, and only fell when the crash of 1929 ruined the European economy. The king decided to abdicate and the Second Republic was formed, first by the military, later by the Socialists, Republicans and Liberals, who had the reins of power by 1931.

This popular government tried to introduce a wide range of necessary reforms but ran at once into opposition from the industrialists and the landowners. The Republicans also managed to upset the Church, by attempting to take over church schools. Agrarian reform, autonomy for the Basques and Catalans, removal of the Army from the political arena – every sensible move brought the government into conflict with a vested interest on the Right or Left. Before long the country was split; the Left had tasted power, the Right saw the end of all their privileges, and the first period of Republican government, between 1931 and 1933 was a shambles. Then in 1933 the coal-miners of the Asturias rose in revolt and set up a Revolutionary Guard of their own. This was crushed by the Spanish Foreign Legion, who were led by a new general, Francisco Franco. In 1936 fresh elections gave a clear mandate to a Popular Front government, an alliance of Socialists, Communists and Liberals, but by now outside influences were also at work. Germany and Italy were supporting the Right and the Fascists, notably the newly-formed Falange Party led by José Antonio Primo de Rivera, son of the old dictator. Meanwhile Russia and the Left everywhere were supporting the Republicans of the elected government, although this government proved itself quite incapable of ruling. There were strikes and shootings every day, scores of churches were set alight, and the landowners raised forces to keep the peasants from occupying their land. The long-simmering Civil War broke out in July 1936, after a Right-wing coup led by several army generals.

The Army declared that they had been forced to seize power from a government that could not maintain law and order. The generals began by occupying towns and declaring martial law, but the townspeople promptly rose against them, and the bloodletting on both sides was enormous. The Right shot teachers and students and intellectuals, the Left shot officers, priests, nuns; both sides shot their prisoners. Within weeks the Spanish had fallen upon each other and were tearing their country apart. The two sides became divided into the Republicans – the Reds – and the Nationalists – the Fascists. Aid came to the Fascists from Italy and Germany who sent men, arms and money, while the Reds were supported by the famous International Brigades, raised in the USA, Britain, France and elsewhere. The Spanish Civil War was the catalyst of the 1930s, when every Left-wing idealist worth his salt went to fight in Spain. Many died there, but their deaths, however tragic, were but a drop in the ocean compared with the suffering of the Spanish. Over 300,000 died in battle; over a quarter of a million, mainly women and children, died from hunger or disease, and at least 100,000 were shot or murdered, and over 300,000 Republicans were driven into exile when their forces collapsed in the face of Franco's advance in 1939.

The reasons for General Franco's victory are not hard to work out. He received adequate support from Germany and Italy, who sent him up-to-date war material, including tanks and aircraft. The Russians gave fitful support at best, and sowed enmity between the various Left-wing militias at the same time. The democratic nations, particularly France and Britain, were locked into appeasement, and did nothing to help the Republic or the suffering Spanish people for fear of upsetting the Fascist dictators and igniting a European war. It is not a pretty story and, as usual, appeasement did not work. The Spanish Civil War ended in March 1939, and the Second World War broke out six months later.

Travel writers should be careful of commenting on politics. It may be everyone's business but it is not their field. Even today, fifty years after the end of the war, the subject of Spain is still a sensitive issue, which tends to centre on the matter of General Franco. Clear-cut views about Franco are clouded by the facts that he refused to join with Germany during the war, that he carried out major and necessary reforms, that he worked wonders for the Spanish economy and, as promised, he eventually returned Spain to democracy and passed the succession as Head of State to King Juan Carlos, who is generally and rightly regarded as a fine man and a good king. On General Franco, the jury is still out.

*   *   *

Bélmez is not hard to find for like many other places hereabouts it is guarded by a huge ruined castle, another relic of the Moorish wars, which crowns a huge rocky hill just south of the town centre. I came out on the crest of the ridge to the north, high above the town, and there it was far below and quite unmistakeable. Bélmez seemed just a small place, but as I trudged down towards it, so it grew, and grew, a great mass of narrow, empty streets lined with whitewashed houses, all now tightly shuttered against the late afternoon sun. It took a little time to find someone to talk to and ask for help, but when I did, this friendly Andalucian insisted on leading me to the best *fonda* in town and hammering on the door until the owner came to let me in. My clothing went into the sink and I went into the shower, the normal end to yet another long, hot walking day. That done, I set out in search of a decent meal, failed to find one and dined at the *fonda*, on shoe leather steak, some cheese, an apple and a bottle of very rough red wine. I have eaten worse.

The next morning brought back another preoccupation. My bowels had been inert for several days. I don't normally keep track of such matters, preferring to let nature take its course, but if it had been several days since the last time, I would not have been at all surprised. Perhaps the problem arose because I was scarcely eating anything. Dinner the previous night, my first proper meal in two days, had hardly been an adequate repast, bearing in mind the mileage I was putting in each day. Before that, some time the day before (or was it the day before that?), I had a ham *bocadillo*. As a result I lost a lot of excess weight and was now positively sylph-like.

While pondering my reluctant bowels, I could at least admire myself in the mirror. It is, in fact, quite difficult for a walker to keep up the carbohydrates in Spain because the eating hours work against you. Breakfast is around seven or half past, far too early for anything substantial, even without the sight of the locals knocking back tumblerfuls of whisky and brandy to set them up for the day. I hit the road while the air is still fresh. Lunchtime comes between two-thirty and four-thirty, when I am either slumped, totally exhausted, in some fly-blown bar or still crossing the *campo*. There is a great shortage of wayside restaurants in the remoter parts of Spain. Dinner is at nine-thirty or even later, and by that time I am usually either in bed or have gone off the whole idea. I can't eat after about eight at night. On the other hand, I am drinking like a fish. Only beer and wine and water mind you, and am usually so dehydrated by the end of the day that alcohol has no visible effect – but the bowels are different. I was brought up at a time when regular bowel movements were considered essential to health, even by the medical profession, often, or so it seemed to my youthful ears, to the virtual exclusion of all else.

'Hmmm,' the family doctor would intone, arriving like a spectre at my bedside. 'Broken every bone in his body, has he, eh? Well . . . let's not worry about all that. Tell me, Mrs Neillands, have his bowels moved?' You could be bleeding from a hundred holes, but the doctors were still only interested in your bowels. I don't want to labour this distasteful point, but I did promise a full account of the events of the day and my preoccupations on this journey. No doubt, sooner or later, the bowels will move. I just don't want to be there when they do.

CHAPTER SIXTEEN

CÓRDOBA

The narrow streets, or rather alleys, so well
adapted to give shade in summer, are a relic of
the Moorish dominion, under which Córdoba was
the rival of Bagdad and Damascus.

Augustus Hare *Wanderings in Spain* (1873)

There seem to be no rules in this walking business. In the past week I had put up some fairly substantial daily mileages, always in great heat and over arid terrain. This had passed, if not easily, then at least with no lasting effects, and whatever happened I was always able to go on again next day without too much trouble. Then, coming out of Bélmez on a bright morning when I should have been pleased that I had crossed the Sierra Morena and was now deep in Andalucía, I actually felt totally drained. My first problem was to avoid the main road down to Córdoba, already obvious on the previous day as a traffic-jammed chaos, very narrow and full of large trucks. There was no footpath and the narrow verge and steep banks forced me to walk among the traffic. This struck me as very dangerous and, besides, I hate roads.

I therefore walked south from the town, through some tumbledown suburbs and across the line of the single track railway in search of the Río Guadiato. There is usually a path of sorts along any riverbank and so it was here, although the river was now little more than a few slimy green ponds set among a tumbled mass of boulders. I thought at first of walking along the railway track, but apart from the fact that railway sleepers are never quite the right distance apart for a proper stride, the line was still in occasional use for the passage of trains from the coalmines at Peñarroya. To begin with though, and in spite of my weariness, it wasn't a bad day. The sun was not too hot, and for a while I had the company of a farmer on a horse, who came cantering up from behind and rode beside me for a mile or so, complaining about the heat and the lack of rain. When the rain does finally come, he said, the ground will be so hard and dry it will run off without sinking in or, where they had ploughed the fields, simply turn the dusty earth to mud and then wash it into the river. Spanish farmers, like farmers everywhere, are permanently discontented.

When he had cantered off again, whistling up his dog, I had a chance to take a look at the country. I was now walking south-east, down the Guadiato in the direction of Córdoba. A high, wooded sierra ran off south-east to my right, while the hills of the Sierra Morena I had crossed yesterday stopped fairly abruptly just to the north, forming a steep escarpment above the N432 road. Here in the valley the air was hot and still. I even saw a patch of green grass, and then another, and it is some indication of how dry the country had been that I stopped to stare at them. Green grass has been rare in the last couple of weeks. There were a great many magpies flitting about and even the occasional hoopoe which went whirling away across the plough like a firecracker. Great buzzards or eagles rode the thermals rising off the sierra to my left, and all of this might have kept me entertained had I not been feeling so exhausted. It should have taken me no more than five hours' walking to get to my night-stop at Espiel, even across country by the riverside footpath, but it took nearly eight. I was quite done-in by the time I reached the village and fell into a *fonda* in the village square.

*   *   *

Much of this exhaustion was probably due to a lack of food. Since I was still in time for lunch, I sat slumped in the *comedor* and let Miguel the chef ply me with soup, a good stew, several beers and many questions. Most of the questions were, inevitably, about football, of which my ignorance is profound. After a while, and half a bottle of chilled *rosado*, I began to feel better. Even so, I had no intention of going another yard that day. This *fonda* at Espiel was one of the better ones with marble halls and well-appointed bedrooms behind the usual rustic bar facade. I was given a room with a bath, into which I dived, and I followed that with a long, deep siesta. It was ten o'clock at night before I came down to dinner, much refreshed but still hungry. The bar was crowded, the *comedor* quiet, and I was just beginning to think I had finally found the one dining room in Spain without a television set, when Miguel rushed in from the kitchen, full of apologies, and switched it on. After dinner I went out for the evening limp, and found Espiel to be a pretty little town, full of friendly people, as mining communities usually are. There were a number of rustic bars, lots of steep streets lined with whitewashed houses, and a great moon rose above the sierra to bathe the streets with light.

*   *   *

My task now was to drift gently through the countryside, south and east over the next two days into Córdoba, the great city of the Moors, and do so, if possible, on tracks or minor roads. I was up early next day since Miguel came to hammer on my door at six-thirty, and I was fed and away by just after seven, back down to the railway line and so off to the south again. I followed the railway for a mile or so, and then out across it to the western end of the half-empty Embalse de Puente Nuevo. Like the other, larger reservoirs further north, this one too was now almost dry, which was a good thing as I was able to walk along the flat, dry lake bed, rather than round the rocky, tree-lined shore. I retreated into the trees as soon as the sun got up. Any shade is very welcome after weeks of walking in the heat, and I was already in the habit of looking out of the window every dawn and groaning, 'Oh no . . . not another bloody beautiful day'. Good weather is all very well, but not when you are walking.

The southern or south-western shore of the *embalse* took me to a track which led up the hill and through the woods to a little town, Villaviciosa de Córdoba. Here I might have called a halt, except that the previous day's fatigue seemed to have disappeared, and I still had plenty of daylight left. Having just had a night in a *fonda*, I was not averse to a night out in the open, before meeting the noise and crowds at Córdoba. I filled the water bottles and bought some ham and a packet of *magdalenas* in Villaviciosa, and pushed on uphill to the Puerto del Aire. Here I stopped for the night, quite content, camping in the shelter of a clump of oak trees, looking out across the valley of the Guadiato, back to the dark green bulk of the Sierra Morena.

*   *   *

It took most of the next morning to wander down the south face of the hill into Córdoba and the valley of the Guadalquivir. Córdoba is a large city, rather overendowed with suburbs, and when I got there I met a problem. Every hotel was full. When arriving in a strange town my normal routine is to head directly either for the old town centre, which is usually near the cathedral if there is one, or for the railway station. Both areas are usually full of hotels. Once in Córdoba I therefore headed for the Mezquita district round the Great Mosque. This part of the city is jammed with hotels, hostels and *fondas*, but all of them were full or claimed to be on spotting the rucksack. This was a city and you cannot leave your possessions on the pavement in a city. I trailed up and down a dozen narrow streets and enquired at many hotels, but all to no avail. There was no room for a man, or at least not for a single man or, most probably, a single man with a rucksack anywhere in Córdoba. It was the feast of the Virgin del Pilar, and once again there was no room at the inn.

However, as you will know by now, we have our little ways. I crossed over the Río Guadalquivir by the bridge at the Calahorra tower and stopped to ask directions from a man near the old gate on the far side, and he indicated a hotel. Once there, I hid the rucksack outside, brushed my hair flat with a grimy hand, and entered. Yes, the receptionist confirmed, they had a room. Having signed the usual forms, handed over my passport and got the key, I then went back outside for my rucksack. When he saw it, the receptionist's face was a picture. People with rucksacks were clearly not welcome. It was interesting to watch him, racking his brains for some way to get the key back and throw me out. I knew it, he knew it, and he knew I knew it, so there was a certain amount of humming and hawing. Did I understand the room was only for one night? I did. Well, he still wasn't sure that they actually had a room at all. 'You haven't now,' I pointed out. 'You've let the last one to me.' While he babbled on, I pointedly began to study the section of a notice on the wall which offered irate guests the *hoja de reclamaciones*, the complaints book. When he failed to take the hint, I asked sharply if he preferred that I paid up front – was my honour in question? At this he finally melted and we began to chat about my walk, the heat and dust and so on. It was insincere but it broke the ice. Then I went off to change and returned looking a much more respectable figure, to his ill-concealed relief. After a further exchange of pleasantries he went off for a siesta and I went off to explore Córdoba and began my rest day with lunch.

My lunch here in a restaurant in the Plaza José Antonio was enlivened by reading the English translations on their menu. For the life of me I cannot understand why Spanish restaurateurs do not let one of their English customers check out the menus. This would deprive everyone of some harmless fun, but I don't know what anyone could make of some of the following offerings. Thistles with mussels; the homme pate (shades of Sweeney Todd the Demon Barber, perhaps?); garlic soup homeley style; brochette of gizzards; stag-legs; fried tick beans; fungi with scramboil eggs. Translation from the Spanish is no help either. I can't see any Englishman enjoying *caldo de perro*, or dog soup, or another Cádiz speciality, *caldo de gato*, cat soup, though neither contain a morsel of domestic pet. The former is a fish soup, the latter reeks of garlic. The great dish of Andalucía is, of course, *gazpacho*, but here in the south *tapas*, tidbits of food, are the great delight and are more varied than in any other part of Spain. Shrimps, slices of *tortilla*, *jamón serrano*, kebabs, octopus – some bars offer a selection of fifty or more, and with a glass of beer or Jerez, they make a good meal.

*   *   *

Córdoba was the largest city I came across on my travels, and the only one full of tourists, at least in the old quarter around the Mezquita, where tourists of all nations abound. Even in Ávila that coach-borne breed had been largely absent, but here in Córdoba they were out in force, debouching from lines of gasping, wheezing monster coaches to flood across the Calahorra bridge and along the narrow streets around the Mezquita. The chief attraction that draws visitors to Córdoba is this Mezquita, the Great Mosque of Córdoba, which now enfolds within its confines a great Gothic church. I thought I would spend the afternoon in there, out of the heat.

The Great Mosque of Córdoba was begun during the reign of that indolent monarch, Hisham II, who directed the work from his palace out on the sierra at Medina Azahara, a few miles to the west. Al-Mansur himself worked on the foundations and the walls of the Mosque in the intervals between his campaigns, and brought back gold and silver and the bells of Santiago to decorate the structure. When it was finished the Mezquita was one of the greatest mosques in the Arab world, rivalled only by the great Umayyad mosque in Damascus. When Fernando III entered the city with his Christian army in 1236, he stripped the Mosque of many treasures but left the structure intact. There it remained, surrounded by the city and the Patio de los Naranjos, crumbling gently away until the building was consecrated as a Christian church dedicated to Santa María in 1238. Various chapels were then built into the fabric over the next two centuries, but the great drama came in 1523 when the Bishop of Córdoba began to build what is, in effect, a Christian cathedral within the old Mosque. This act of vandalism shocked the Emperor Charles V when he came to Córdoba in 1526. 'You have built something which you or I or anyone could have built anywhere, but in doing so you have destroyed something unique in the world,' he told the Bishop. The cathedral was not completed until 1593, but the damage had been done.

You see the truth of the Emperor's remark after you have crossed the great dusty Courtyard of the Orange Trees outside the Mezquita and stepped through the doors into the dark interior. The best way to imagine the interior of the Mezquita is to think yourself lost, at the end of evening, in a great forest. Slim pillars, hundreds of them, like the trunks of innumerable pine trees, run off into the darkness inside this echoing monster of a building. You could easily get lost in here, and the Christian church in the centre, built in space torn from the heart of this splendid building, is indeed a desecration.

The best way to approach the old part of Córdoba is from the west bank, across the great Roman bridge over the Guadalquivir, which is guarded by the fortified Calahorra gate which was built by Enrique of Trastamara in 1369 to defend the city against his half-brother, Pedro the Cruel, who ruled hereabouts from his castle at Carmona. Crossing the river, three unusual sights met my eye, or unusual anyway in a large provincial city. To my left, a herd of cows were grazing along the grassy shore beneath the bridge; to my right a man was herding goats beneath the old walls. Further downstream, on a small island in the river between the two bridges, a flock of white egrets were settling down for the night amid the trees. Even here on this bridge, in the heart of the city, the Spanish countryside intrudes, and so does the Catholic religion. There is a small shrine to St Raphael resting in a smoke-blackened, candle-wax-splattered niche, halfway across the bridge, and a great winged statue of the Archangel stands on a column outside the Mezquita. All this and the narrow streets lined with old white houses are but a prelude to the Mezquita itself, the glory of Córdoba and Muslim Spain.

Córdoba existed long before the coming of the Arabs, but the modern city, which lies on ground high above the river and spreads further out, is much like any other modern metropolis: a place of noise and traffic and large shops and cinemas, interspersed with small squares and parks. It is nice enough, but you could be anywhere. The old part of Córdoba, however, the old quarter which lies around the Mezquita, is quite delightful, a maze of white houses in narrow streets and squares, the squares all endowed with fountains and olive trees, the streets lined with orange trees still heavy with dusty, shrivelled fruit. As elsewhere in Spain, all is not as it seems. These terraced houses are much larger than they appear to be when seen from the street. The doorway is usually blocked by a massive wooden door in dark walnut wood, well-studded with brass nails or rivets, but behind the door lies an iron grille, and once through that, the main house will lie set around a small Moorish courtyard, all in marble, an arbour usually full of flowers and ferns, but always with water tinkling somewhere and often with a sparkling fountain. However hot the street outside, these interior courtyards are always cool and a great relief from the heat of the day which seems to be intensified by the glare from the white walls, though these, in practice, help to keep the houses cool. All the buildings are painted white, all have shutters in green or blue or red, and every balcony is a mass of flowers, but all are slightly different and the total effect is quite beautiful.

I got a closer look at all this when I was attempting to photograph one of the streets and, stepping back, nearly trod on an old man on his way out to buy the evening paper. I apologised and we started to chat. 'This is not the best street to photograph,' he told me. 'Wait here, and I will show you.' He rushed into a shop but in a minute he was back, wearing a flat, black Cordoban hat, and led me up a number of alleyways into an even narrower but much more beautiful side street near the Mezquita. 'This is where I live,' he said. 'The Calle de las Flores is the most beautiful street in Córdoba.' He was quite right. From the square with fountain at the far end of the Calle de las Flores, you can get the perfect picture-postcard shot back down the street to the bell-tower of the Mezquita. My new friend was a silversmith, working beautiful filigree in fine Cordoban silver, and after a tour of his house, where he explained the advantages of the fountain and the courtyard, we went into his workshop, which was tiny and crammed with hundreds of items in filigree silver. There we inspected his work-bench and a couple of favourite items. 'These are two special pieces,' he said. 'This one here is a model of the cupola inside the Mezquita. People can turn it over, so, and then it holds sweets or biscuits – for the children. And this, in filigree silver, is a model of the ship of Christopher Colombus, the *Santa María*.' The ship was the size of a coffee cup, the cupola no bigger than a saucer, both of them most intricately worked, but he assured me neither took him longer than two days to make. 'But I have been working in silver since I was twelve,' he said, 'and my father taught me. There have been silversmiths working in Córdoba since the time of the Moors, the Romans even, maybe even before that.' Córdoba is famous for silver and leather and has a great flea market in the Plaza de la Corredera.

*   *   *

Prehistoric Córdoba was the capital of an Iberian tribe, the Tartessos. They were overwhelmed by Hamilcar Barca the Carthaginian, and the country became a province of their empire under his son, Hannibal. This eventually brought in the Roman legions, in about 206 BC. The Romans stayed until the Visigoths arrived in AD 572, and the Visigoths ruled until the Arabs crossed the Straits in 711.

History apart, Córdoba is a city of famous men and the citizens have commemorated most of them with statues. Just by the walls of the castle, the Alcázar, stands a statue of the Roman senator, Seneca, who was born in Córdoba in 4 BC and died in Rome in AD 65, his lifetime spanning the start of the Christian era and the reign of some formidable emperors. Considering his own waspish nature, and his later occupation as tutor to Nero, it is a wonder Seneca survived to die in his bed. A number of famous Romans came from Andalucía, including the Emperors Hadrian and Trajan, and the author Lucan.

Córdoba is also a great city for walkers, not least because it is hell to park. The Mezquita will certainly take up a couple of hours, even for the less dedicated traveller, but this is not the end of the sights. The Roman bridge across the river has sixteen arches, several ruined watermills dating from Moorish times, and was once part of the great Via Augusta, an Imperial road. The gardens of the Alcázar de los Reyes Cristianos form part of a fortress built by Alfonso XI in 1328. The poor King of Granada, Boabdil, was imprisoned here for a while after the fall of Granada in 1492. Fernando and Isabel lived in this Alcázar during the siege of Granada, watching from the ramparts as three thousand mules loaded with arms and food set out to supply the besieging army, and Christian slaves released from Granada came here to thank *Los Reyes Católicos* for their deliverance. The castle was then handed over to the Holy Office – the Inquisition – who remained in possession of the citadel until as late as 1821, when it then became a prison. It is now owned by the municipality, who are restoring it to its medieval splendour and it may become a museum.

Then there is the *Judería*, the old Jewish quarter, perhaps the liveliest part of the city, which has a synagogue dating from 1315, one of the oldest European synagogues, and a rare survivor of centuries of terror. There is also a great quantity of museums, palaces and churches, too many to absorb on one short visit, even without a visit to the caliph's palace at Medina Azahara, some miles outside the city. This was once a paradise, a place of fountains and flowers, music and poetry, built by Abd al-Rahman III in 936, as his summer palace, but now it lies in ruins, a little tragedy to go with all the rest, for it was destroyed by the Berbers in 1010.

Wandering away from the Calle de las Flores, heading through the old town towards the Mezquita, I passed the bronze statue of a Moor, complete with turban and shiny bronze slippers. This is Maimonides, who was, in fact, Jewish. He was born in Córdoba in 1135 and became a noted scholar, but his great fame was as a doctor. At the end of his life he was called to Cairo as personal physician to the mighty Saladin. I think it useful to have such statues as fingerposts to the past, but they do have a lot more meaning if you know a little about the lives of the people they represent. My next statue of note lay in the newer part of the town, an equestrian statue of Gonzalo de Córdoba, El Gran Capitán, conqueror of the kingdom of Naples, general to the Catholic Kings and jailer of Cesare Borgia.

Córdoba is full of statues but my next one was no more than a bust, although it recorded yet another mighty man, that prince of matadors, Manolete. I am no great lover of *los toros*, or the bullfight, and have not been to see one for years, but you can hardly cross Spain and spend a lot of time in their television-infested bars without realising that the attraction of the bullfight is as strong as ever to the Spanish male, whatever claims are now made for football. There is, however, a great shortage of good *toreros* – the last one with any popular following was Manuel Benitez, who soared to fame in the 1960s and 1970s as El Cordobés: the man from Córdoba. Manolete, Manuel Rodriguez, also came from Córdoba, which has been producing great bullfighters since the middle of the last century. Manolete was born in 1917, and was killed by a Miura bull in the ring at Linares in 1947. You will find faded yellow or sepia photographs of Manolete in little bullfight bars all over Spain, stuck in between the posters advertising past *corridas*, underneath the horns or heads of long-dead fighting bulls. There is even a bullfight museum in Córdoba, but it was closed and I was not too sorry to miss it. Besides, there is another one inside the bullring at Ronda, where I am due to meet Geoff in seven days' time. I can take a closer look at the life of the *toreros* there, but it will be brief. American writers are the ones most fascinated by the bullfight, but the sport rather baffles me, for it is at best a bloody business.

I spent most of that evening and most of my time in Córdoba in and around the Mezquita, having a drink in some dark bar or at a pavement café in one of the squares, dining in one restaurant after fleeing from another where, in lieu of the usual television set, one whole wall suddenly leapt to life, revealing a full-size screen packed with flamenco dancers, all stamping away. No one else in the room paid any attention. Later that evening, I found a bar under the walls by the Alcázar, at no great distance from the Tourist Office, where real flamenco was being danced, not by a bored professional group entertaining tourists, but by a group of young people in their teens and twenties, who were whirling and stamping and clicking their fingers in a corner of the bar, while the rest of the customers beat on the counter in the usual way, tossing in the occasional *¡olé!* to keep the youngsters happy. It was all great fun.

I had never before seen flamenco danced by anyone other than professional dancers, though when I talked to the lads afterwards, their girlfriends having rushed off into the night, they told me that they were dancing *sevillanas*, a variation of flamenco which comes from the city of Sevilla, further west. They had learned to dance at school and enjoyed it. True flamenco, I learned later, is much more than a dance, for it combines guitar playing, singing, that explosive hand-clapping that is very hard for non-Latins to do and, of course, the dance itself. Some say flamenco came to Spain with the Moors, others that the gipsies are responsible. It hardly matters. The important thing is that flamenco, or this *sevillana* has survived and is danced not only by professionals to entertain the tourists, but also by teenage boys and girls in a local café on a Saturday night, just because they enjoy it. That sort of folk art will survive.

Later that night I wandered back across the river, downed a few cold beers in a *cervecería*, and returned to my hotel where the night porter told me that there *had* been a mistake. They needed my room back in the morning. You can't win.

* * *

The *parador La Arruzafa* in Córdoba lies some distance back towards the north sierra and outside the city centre, quite near the excellent municipal camp site I could have used the night before. I decided to stay at the *parador*, which had a room available. This *parador* stands on the site of a manor built by the Emir Abderamman I, who was the man who introduced palm trees into Europe and planted them here; the word *arruzafa* means a palm tree. Next day, as I walked across town towards the *parador*, the weather began to change, and change quickly. Within an hour grey clouds had swept in across the usual blue, and a chill wind was blowing, bringing with it a deal of mist and low cloud to screen the southern hills from my view. That afternoon I went out onto my balcony and strained my eyes south to spot a track beyond the city. All I could see were lowering grey clouds and sweeping drifts of rain. Ah well, I had wanted a change in the weather and now I had it. Whether I liked it any better than the heat and dust of Extremadura remained to be seen. Meanwhile, I could enjoy a little rest and relaxation at this modern *parador*, which serves the most excellent food. Their lunch buffet is a marvel and the dinner superb. The menu included *gazpacho de almendras*, vegetable soup with almonds; *huevos espárragos*, eggs with asparagus, and another local dish, *estofado de rabo de toro*, an oxtail stew, all this with a fruity local wine from Montilla, the vineyards further to the south. I now had a week to go before I met Geoff in Ronda ('four o'clock outside the bullring'), and I was looking forward to his company.

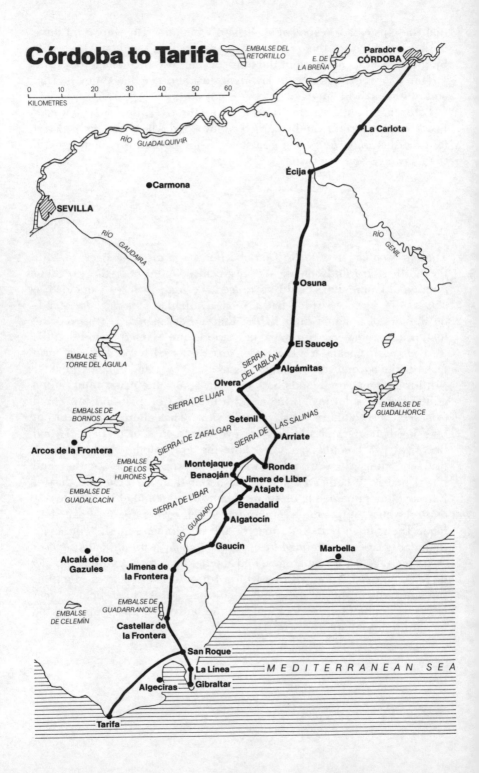

Córdoba to Tarifa

EMBALSE DEL RETORTILLO

E. DE LA BREÑA

Parador ● CÓRDOBA

| 0 | 10 | 20 | 30 | 40 | 50 | 60 |
KILOMETRES

● La Carlota

RÍO GUADALQUIVIR

●Carmona

Écija ●

RÍO GENIL

SEVILLA

RÍO GUADAIRA

Osuna ●

EMBALSE TORRE DEL ÁGUILA

El Saucejo ●

SIERRA DEL TABLÓN

Algámitas ●

Olvera ●

EMBALSE DE BORNOS

SIERRA DE LIJAR

EMBALSE DE GUADALHORCE

Setenil ●

SIERRA DE LAS SALINAS

Arcos de la Frontera ●

SIERRA DE ZAFALGAR

Arriate ●

EMBALSE DE LOS HURONES

Montejaque ●
Benaoján ●

Ronda ●

Jimera de Libar ●
Atajate ●

EMBALSE DE GUADALCACÍN

SIERRA DE LIBAR

Benadalid ●

RÍO GUADIARO

Algatocín ●

Gaucín ●

Marbella ●

Alcalá de los Gazules ●

Jimena de la Frontera ●

EMBALSE DE CELEMÍN

EMBALSE DE GUADARRANQUE

Castellar de la Frontera ●

San Roque ●

La Línea ●

MEDITERRANEAN SEA

Algeciras ●
Gibraltar ●

Tarifa ●

CHAPTER SEVENTEEN

THE ROAD TO RONDA

*The country is wild and stony, eminently
lonely but picturesque.*

Richard Ford *A Handbook for Travellers in Spain* (1882)

The weather broke in Córdoba, to the great delight of everyone in
Andalucía who was not a tourist. I sat eating breakfast on my balcony at
the *parador La Arruzafa*, watching the rain slanting down across the city.
In the fields between the suburbs and the *parador*, a man was dancing
with delight under the downpour, paddling in the fresh mud about his
feet. Within half an hour the ditches were full, great puddles occupied
every hollow in the fields, the water-starved Guadalquivir had advanced
from a noisome trickle to a wide, muddy flood. Even the parched grass
regained life, and the pines around the *parador* were giving off a great
air of freshness. Even I, who have no great liking for walking in the rain,
felt glad for the people of the *campo*, and not entirely sorry for myself.
Anything was better than another week frying on the grid-iron of Spain,
but I was again dithering over my route.

Between Córdoba and Sevilla lies the town of Carmona, which has
one of the great castle *paradores* of Spain, a place I have long wanted
to see. This castle, the Alcázar del Rey Don Pedro (Pedro the Cruel of
Castile), was the king's favourite castle and, or so the story goes, he
would steal out from here by night to creep about the streets of the
town and stab to death any hapless subject who came across his path.
That juicy tale apart, the castle of Carmona looked a splendid place, if
only judging from the postcards. The snag was that it lay off my route,
so reluctantly I turned my eyes south, saving Carmona for another time.
This is the problem with walking; you cannot see places which are just
off your route, as you cannot spare the time to get there.

From my balcony I could now actually see my way south, the road a grey slash in the brown hills beyond the city. When the rain had slackened back to a steady drizzle I made my way towards it, leaving the *parador* by way of the garden, crossing over the fields beyond, my boots collecting great clods of mud, negotiating a concrete bridge across a brimming drainage ditch, then the streets of the city, and finally across the Guadalquivir. By the time I reached the southern outskirts of Córdoba, I was already fed up with the rain and the rain was again torrential. I do not mind being wet. Provided I can keep moving during the day and dry out in the evening, being wet is supportable, but the muddy ploughed fields were almost impassable. Great clods of earth stuck to my boots and if I was to knock up my daily stint of twenty miles, it would clearly not be across country. On the other hand, the road from Córdoba to Écija soon becomes a motorway, where great trucks thundered past, sending up sweeping sheets of spray. Walking on the *autovía* was illegal as well as dangerous, so what was I to do?

Lurking in a garage by the *autovía* which ran out to Écija and Sevilla, I decided to call on that supply of rat-like cunning with which all journalists are supposedly equipped. First, I hid the rucksack. Second, I stripped off the streaming oilies. Third, I donned an ingratiating smile. This done, I approached every motorist with a car-bonnet pointing south and asked for a lift, just to the end of the motorway. On my third try I struck lucky, and not even the subsequent appearance of the damp waterproofs and the muddy rucksack led to a rejection. Within minutes we were hurtling south at great speed, and when I was decanted at the end of the *autovía*, by the junction of a single track road some fifteen minutes later, even the rain had begun to relent. This lift was the only way down the *autovía* from the city, so I felt fairly lighthearted and blameless as I heaved on my rucksack and stepped out fast for the next stop. Given this headstart I decided that my target for today should be the city of Écija, now only twenty-three miles away. Much of the country between Córdoba and my next destination, Ronda, is largely occupied by the wide valley of the Guadalquivir, which drains the Sierra Morena to the north and irrigates the arable, cattle and wine-growing country to the south.

The Guadalquivir is indeed one of the great rivers in Spain. It rises in the distant Sierra de Cazorla in the province of Jaén, and flows through the Guadalquivir gorges out onto the Andalucian plain around Córdoba, Sevilla and into the sea, through the great marshland and National Park of the Coto Doñana. The river is always brimfull in winter but subsides rapidly in the summer and is only navigable as far as Sevilla, a city which was once the main port for all the treasure fleets arriving from the New World. I should have liked to walk west down the river to Sevilla, but the south kept tugging me on.

To the walker in the rain, the southern portion of the Guadalquivir country lacks drama, but the scenery here, as in La Mancha and many other parts of Spain, picks up remarkably when the sun comes out. When that happens, as it did on this day around noon, there is a transfiguration. The rolling brown hills turn into patterns of red, yellow, ochre and bright green, patched increasingly with the dotted squares of the olive groves and supplemented here and there with what appeared to be great patches of salt, or even snow. Only when I was closer, did I realise that set among these miles of unfenced plough were vast fields of cotton, now in full bud, the great white cotton bolls full to bursting. I have passed through cotton fields before, in the Southern States of the USA, in Egypt and Turkey, but the cotton here in Spain (until this moment I had no idea that they even grew cotton in Spain), is grown on low, knee-high bushes, all at a uniform height, looking from a distance exactly like a field of snow in that clear Andalucian air.

Andalucía was, and to some extent remains, a land of *latifundios*, huge estates on which poor labourers, *braceros*, once made a thin living and longed for land of their own. Here in the valley of the Guadalquivir, the peasants did rather better as the land is fertile and well watered, supporting figs and almonds and good cash crops like olives. The peasants may have been malnourished but they did not starve, although most of them have long since given up the land and gone to work in factories. The estates remain but a few men with tractors can cope with the work.

To pick up the history theme again, we might begin with Felipe II, son of the Holy Roman Emperor Charles V (Carlos I of Spain), and continue through his successors, including Carlos III, and finish with the arrival of the French, and so fill in the remaining historic gap in this journey. Felipe II squandered his inheritance and the wealth of the Indies in fighting the wars of the Counter-Reformation, on building the great palace at El Escorial, and by building the Spanish Armada, of which more later. By the 1590s, the Spanish economy was on the point of collapse, and the country's economic situation was not improved by the expulsion of the Jews and baptised Moors, who ran the professions, business, and many of the arts.

In spite of this, Spain enjoyed an outburst of artistic life in the 16th and 17th centuries, the time of El Greco, Murillo, Velásquez, Lope de Vega and Cervantes, but in the economic and military sphere her decline continued. Between 1635 and 1665, there was war with Portugal, which led to that country regaining her independence. In 1643, the French shattered the Spanish army at Rocroi. The successors of Felipe II were unable to stem this decline in Spain's fortunes.

Felipe was succeeded in 1598 by his son, Felipe III, of whom he said, 'God, who has given me so many kingdoms, has denied me a son capable of ruling them after my death'.

Felipe III was a genius compared with his 17th-century successors, Felipe IV and Carlos II; during their reigns the wars continued and wealth-producing territories, like the island of Jamaica, were seized by the French or English, who regarded Spain as an empire in terminal decay and set out to prey upon the remains. In 1700, Carlos II, the last of the Hapsburgs, went to his reward, and a war – the War of the Spanish Succession – broke out across Europe. Louis XIV of France backed the old king's nominated successor Louis' grandson Philip of Anjou, while England and Austria, alarmed at the thought of any extension of French hegemony in Europe, backed his rival, Charles of Austria, heir to the Holy Roman Empire. In the end, Philip of Anjou secured the throne of Spain, but the price was high. He lost his Austrian lands, and by the Treaty of Utrecht, which ended the War, had to cede Gibraltar in perpetuity to Great Britain.

The Spanish Bourbons were, if anything, more autocratic than the Hapsburgs, and they ruled an increasingly discontented population from 1701 until 1808. Carlos III, who is commemorated here in La Carlota, made some attempt to resolve the national economy and ease the lot of the land-hungry peasant. During his reign, from 1759 to 1788, the Jesuits were expelled, land reforms introduced, and trade revived, although the privileges of Church and nobility remained virtually intact, and most of the people remained in the grip of poverty. Then, in 1789, a fresh wind came blowing across the Pyrenees from Revolutionary France. The execution of Louis XVI and Marie Antoinette angered and alarmed their kinsman Carlos IV of Spain, but his anger soon subsided when the French threatened to invade, overawed his chief Minister, Manuel de Godoy, and marched across Spain to invade Portugal. The Spanish had never seen or imagined troops like the soldiers of Revolutionary France. In 1808 the king and his son Fernando were persuaded to abdicate. Then came the brief rule of Joseph Bonaparte, the *Dos de Mayo* and the outbreak of the War of Independence. Since then, until the end of the Second World War, Spain has been in turmoil, a long, self-inflicted agony, from which she is at last beginning to emerge. When you consider their history, it is surprising that a people can endure so much and remain so pleasant.

*   *   *

The main road runs fairly directly south and west from Córdoba to Écija. There is empty, rolling farmland on either side, but plenty to see and occupy the mind; a sudden whirl of hoopoes, a circling eagle, a small herd of horses cantering to water. In the occasional garden set beside the track which lay to one side or the other of the main road, were oranges and peaches, red pomegranates, jasmin shrubs, heavy with flowers and perfume after the rain. I passed through La Carlota, a straggling town where a group of statues recalled the fact that it was here in 1767 that King Carlos III dispensed land rights to emigrants from all parts of Spain and Europe and so turned 'this arid desert into a region of farms and prosperous towns'.

*   *   *

The day was now sunny but not too hot, just right for walking. By mid-afternoon I was sitting in the *Bar Gasolina* in the Plaza de España at Écija, eating a ham *tortilla* and getting ready for the evening limp around the sights. Écija lurks out of sight of the road in the deep valley of the Río Genil, a tributary of the Guadalquivir, and you come upon it suddenly. A sprawling 'White Town', the mass of tiled roofs overtopped by many tall church towers, each more or less decorated with glazed tiles. To be truthful, Écija has rather too many churches, ten in all, plus two convents, but most of them are now in ruins. The town itself is very clean and a pleasant place, and for the moment even cool, though in summertime Écija is known as the frying pan, the *sartén*, of Andalucía. Écija is older even than Córdoba, for the Greeks had a city here, *Astigi*, and according to Richard Ford, in the time of the Romans it ranked in importance with Córdoba. The Plaza Mayor is the real centre of the town, as all such plazas should be, and comes endowed with an Amazon fountain, spouting water. The Amazons are also well-endowed, and water spouts exuberantly from every breast.

Écija's churches are dotted about the streets around the square, and although I try to avoid ABC (Another Bloody Church) tours, some of them are worth inspecting. The Church of San Gel is built in a delicate Gothic-Mudejar style, the Church of San Juan has fine paintings and Baroque decor, and the Church of Santa Cruz contains the pilgrim shrine of Nuestra Señora del Valle – the Virgin of the Valley – which dates from the 13th century and is venerated in the town. Those who cannot face another church have a choice of two palaces, one of which, the Palacio Benameji, is a national monument.

I found a *fonda*, washed my socks, and then spent a quiet evening wandering about and wondering how I could get south to Osuna without too much road time. The country was drying out and soon, if no more rain came, the fields might be passable. There is no pleasing me. When I am in the sierras, I long for the flat, easy walking of the valleys, and now I am in this most pleasant of valleys, my eyes are straining south for the sierras. They are out there, somewhere, under the clouds ahead, and in a day or so I shall reach them.

*   *   *

East of Sevilla, in a rough triangle drawn between that city and Écija and Osuna, which lies twenty miles to the south, lies the country called *La Campiña*. This is horse country, like much of Andalucía, and so the local poets rave about it. 'Its freedom, its horizons, those vast expanses, green today and gold tomorrow. . . .' this is lyrical stuff indeed. Walking south next morning, down the wide, rutted track from Écija to Osuna, I found this fervour a little hard to understand, for under grey and dripping skies, *La Campiña* is somewhat lacking in drama. It rolls on, relentlessly, towards the southern sierras, and the road rolls across it, past a number of ranches, one of them with gateposts bearing the crossed lances and pennons of the Spanish cavalry. There was not a horse in sight all day, but *La Campiña* is home to some famous Spanish horse herds, the Abades, the Alcorín, the Turquillas, all bred from Arab stock. Perhaps the most celebrated of these is the Remonta de Écija, which supplied, and still supplies, horses for the Spanish Cavalry from its base at Isla Redonda on the Río Genil. Given all this, I had expected to see horses all the way, but none was visible and nor was it easy to see what they might feed on; the land only seemed to grow grain, olives and cotton. In fact, the reason for this lack of horses is rather more sinister. African horse fever is decimating the herds of Andalucía. This fatal disease is carried by a mosquito and every summer the ravages increase.

There are some 120,000 horses in Andalucía, but only about six thousand are the pure Spanish-Andaluz breed, famous the world over for their beauty and docility. A good Andaluz horse will fetch more than £10,000 at any horse-market in the world. Hundreds of horses have died, and the great horse fairs of Andalucía are being boycotted for fear that the fever will spread. This is both an economic and cultural disaster, for while horse-breeding is important, the horse ranks second only to the fighting bull in the country life of Andalucía. At Sevilla, at Jerez, at a dozen other fairs and festivals, one of the great attractions is the arrival of the horsemen, in their wide-brimmed Cordoban hats and tight riding suits, their ladies in flamenco costume riding behind on the horse's rump, or more gracefully perhaps as Amazonas, riding *a la vaquera*, left hand guiding the horse by the reins, right hand negligently on hip. If the current outbreak of horse fever does not end, and it has now lasted since the spring of 1987, the prospect for the great herds of Andalucía appears bleak. No cure has yet been found, no prophylactic injection yet exists, and the Andalucian horse trade is at a standstill.

As I walked on, I saw no sweeping grassy plains, at least not in this October. Here and there were small lakes, *lagunas*, but most of them were dry, and my only excitement in a rather long day came from putting up a number of very large hares, which bolted from under my feet and shot off across the fields at a great rate, their sudden appearance scaring me half to death. I tramped on, under the leaden sky, watching the steady wheeling of eagles far above, and counted any number of magpies, and so, at last, after a rather long day, I came to Osuna and Osuna was a delight.

*   *   *

As had happened all too often on this walk, I saw Osuna hours before I got there. The town occupies the slopes of a great hill, a foretaste of the approaching sierras, and this hill is crowned by a great church and a castle, the seat in former times of the dukes of Osuna. The present town is a fine place, a White Town, with a maze of narrow streets, all leading up to the *Colegiata* on the hilltop. I decided to do the sightseeing before I found a bed for the night, so leaving my rucksack in a bar, I made my way up to the heights and the terrace of the *Colegiata*. The *Colegiata* was firmly closed but the views were worth the climb. To the north lay the plains, to the south the rumpled indications of fresh sierras, and to the west the sun was sinking in red glory behind the purple clouds. Spain can be so bleak and so splendid, you remain confused.

Ford says that Osuna takes its name from the goddess Osuna, daughter of Hispan, who married Pyrrhus, the killer of bears. Who these gods and goddesses are I have no idea, but it's a good tale. Osuna held a large garrison in Roman times, the base for two legions, and then after centuries under the Moors, it fell to the Christians in 1240 and was granted to the Order of Calatrava. The great days came later, in the reign of Felipe II, he of the Armada, who gave the city and the dukedom that went with it to Pedro Giron, the first Duke of Osuna. The castle dates from the Moors, the *Colegiata* from 1534, and much of the town from the 15th and 16th centuries, but one can have too much monumental Spanish architecture. I was quite glad to trek back down to the town centre, collect my rucksack and find a bed at *El Caballo Blanco*. This lies in the town centre and is a very agreeable inn, but then Osuna is a very agreeable town. Full of bars and good restaurants, it contains as a novel touch a great cage full of songbirds in one of the main squares, all twittering away. It also has some very splendid houses down the side streets, each with a great wooden walnut door, highly polished and studded with shiny brass nails, all most imposing. To the east of Osuna lies the wine country of Montilla, and Montilla was the birthplace of El Gran Capitán, Gonzalo de Córdoba, a nice historic touch. So, having ordered a good meal and a bottle of wine, I lingered in a restaurant and did myself rather well at the end of a busy day, thinking about Spanish wine.

It will probably produce irate letters, but Spanish wine used to be dreadful. I can recall it in the early 1960s, when try as you might and pay what you would, you could not find a mellow bottle untainted by a resin-like taste. Lord knows, I tried. Therefore, it is pleasant to record that the wines I drank on this journey, from Rioja, Valdepeñas, Navarra, Montilla . . . wherever, were always palatable, definitely smooth, and at worst, drinkable.

The Spanish sold wine abroad even in Roman times, and it is said that Hadrian and Trajan were partial to the wines of Alella, which comes from the Catalan coast, north of Barcelona. I have never tried that, but the best-known of current Catalan vintages, Peñedes, is a very good wine indeed. Most of these are red, but Peñedes also produces Cava, a *méthode champenoise* that is very bubbly and very cheap. I can recall drinking it for 30p a bottle, but it might cost a little more now.

The best-known Spanish wines come from the Rioja, but the greatest quantity, more than half the total production, comes from the central plateau of New Castile, the whites from La Mancha, the reds from Valdepeñas – the valley of the Stones – where the wines mature, not in casks, but in earthenware pots not unlike *amphorae*. The Rioja has the great names, like Marqués de Riscal and Marqués de Murieta, which are great reds, very dark and quite tangy, but there are some good dry whites and red or white, the quality improves every year.

Wine is produced in most of the Spanish regions, even in Mallorca, but the most famous of all must be the wines from Jerez, Xeres, or sherry. In Elizabethan times, the English used to call this 'sack', since the casks came wrapped in sacking. Falstaff was a great lover of sack, and praises it endlessly in both parts of Shakespeare's *Henry IV*, and there is still a brand called Dry Sack to keep the link going. I like a glass of wine to go with my *tapas* during a pause in the evening limp, but if you ask for a *copa de vino*, a glass of wine, you invariably get served a glass of sherry. Getting what I really want, a glass of red Rioja or a cool, white Peñedes, is often quite a struggle.

*   *   *

My route out of Osuna led me gradually back into the sierras. From Osuna to Ronda is a two to three day walk across always empty but otherwise not too demanding country to my long anticipated meeting with Geoff. This was anticipated not least because Geoff is the most agreeable companion, and I was now in sore need of a little company. Apart from my meeting with Jochem up in the Sierra de Gredos, I had not spoken English for over a month, and however good this might be for my Spanish, it can also be remarkably wearing. No one here speaks the sibilant Castilian I had attempted to learn all those years ago in London, or Madrid, or has accents as familiar now as those of Chile or Mexico. Andalucian Spanish is very thick and fast. Fortunately, the range of subjects under discussion is often rather limited – food, wine, weather, football, manure – so I usually have no difficulty. I have.also stepped back into the second stage of language learning. They can understand my questions, but I can't understand their replies. That problem apart, I'm steadily going native. Last night I even caught myself watching the television set in a corner café at Osuna. I couldn't hear it, but I watched it. I am also starting to shout, when I am normally accused of mumbling. Even worse, I am getting tolerant of Spanish excesses. The Spanish have perfected the art of excess, down to the smallest detail. They cannot do anything in moderation, let alone by halves. In any room they might have three television sets and if they have three sets, they are all on. All will be showing the same channel, which usually is football. Background music has to be played with the maximum amount of decibels, and while I was brooding on all this in the bar last night, someone switched on the extractor fan and introduced a great gale. If I had not hung onto the bar I might have been blown away. No one else even noticed. I have also given up shaving every day, and I am beginning to like beer at breakfast. Looking at my thin, brown, stubbly face in the mirror, I hardly knew myself.

I therefore decided to ring Geoff for a chat and got the bad news. Geoff, one must remember, has a real job, and therefore cannot slope off and enjoy himself like an itinerant writer. The pressures of business were such that he could not now make our Friday rendezvous, 'four o'clock, outside the bullring in Ronda', which had been fixed upon months before. We therefore settled for same time, same place, Sunday. Reflecting on the fact that I could therefore slow down a little, I got up later next morning and took my time over breakfast at *El Caballo Blanco*, before heaving on my battered rucksack and addressing myself again to the road.

Crossing the railway track and motorway south of Osuna, looking back from time to time at this agreeable little town, I began to climb away from the plains for what I hope will be the last time. The eternal plains and *mesetas* of Spain could daunt the spirits of the stoutest traveller. So, as I plod out of Osuna and take the road to El Saucejo, fifteen miles or so to the south, I hope I have left the plains behind at last and can take the most direct route I can find over the hill to Ronda. It was a fine, if somewhat overcast morning, with a chill wind whistling past my ears, and a steady stream of cars flowing south, all full of olive-pickers. From every height and every bend in the road, I could see the olive groves. From this road alone the trees blanket the countryside for miles in every direction, a million within my view at least, maybe two or three million, all heaving with fruit. This poses a question I must get answered. If the entire population of Spain turned out to pick olives they could not gather in even a tiny percentage of those I can see from this road – so how is it done?

You have to become a nosey-parker to find some diversion from the daily plod, so when I saw a car parked in an olive grove and a ladder leading up into a tree, I wandered over, to stand on the plastic collecting mat spread on the ground, and looked up into the foliage. All I could see was a pair of legs projecting from the branches, but there was the regular rattle of a stick against the branches and a steady hail of olives onto the matting and my head. After a few bellows and '*¡Holas!*' a man came down to answer my questions, offer me a drink and stop for a chat.

Olives are a major crop, maybe the major crop, certainly the big tree crop of Andalucía. The crop is counted in quintals, a nice archaic word, at about ten quintals to the ton. From the olive comes a lake of highly profitable olive oil, and a crop of almost equally profitable olives for the kitchen and the cocktail market. Millions of olive trees can supply the wherewithal for a million litres of Martini, but little of the resulting money comes back to the farmer. This one told me that his entire crop, picked over several months with the aid of his entire family and friends, brought him in about 15p a litre. You have to pick an awful lot of olives to make a profit on a price like that, and the labour is considerable. They can tell when an olive is ripe by rattling a cane among the branches; only the ripe ones will fall off, and some of these go to the oil press and others go for bottling. Once I had got him talking, it was hard to get away. We then had the usual inquest into my walk, and the various reasons why I did not do the sensible thing and take the train. He had his car, and if I cared to wait a bit or even lend a hand, he would run me down to El Saucejo. I gracefully declined. Therefore, after an exchange of back-slaps, he disappeared up into his tree and I plodded on over the hills towards El Saucejo.

*   *   *

This was another pleasant day, spent brooding on olives or persuading some people to take my photograph – for the publisher will surely need some and I still don't have any – and sitting in the ditch beside the road eating a pear. I can recommend this walk from Osuna to El Saucejo, not least because the hills and views are both very agreeable and there is plenty of shade. Just before El Saucejo, the road, which has been climbing steadily all the way from Osuna, finally tops the sierra at the Puerto de los Barrancos Blancos, a fine breezy spot. There, with El Saucejo in sight across the valley, the road makes a violent swing to the left. I decided to save distance and cut directly across country, down through the fields and the olive groves below, and pick up a direct track into the town. After half an hour or so, this brought me out onto the track just ahead of an old man riding up into town on his donkey. We pressed on uphill together, with me just managing to match the donkey stride for stride, until the old man offered to take my rucksack onto one of the panniers. I thanked him but again refused. I was feeling fit now, and when I am not tired, the rucksack weighs little. Even so, this offer was a good introduction to El Saucejo, a most agreeable little town. This day's march, a fairly gentle fifteen miles, also gave me a good leap forward towards the last sierras. Like a lot of these little Spanish towns, El Saucejo is actually bigger than it looks, for the houses are tucked away on either side of the ridge which supports the main road and the church. I found a *fonda*, with dinner and *comida* available, for just 1,500 pesetas, about £8, and then went out before dinner to buy some fruit and cheese, and inspect the locals. They inspected me back. Not much happens in El Saucejo, and my arrival had been noted, but after a few glasses of remarkably nasty wine, everyone became very animated and wished me '*Buena suerte*' on my walk towards Tarifa. A nice town with nice people, El Saucejo. Pity about the wine.

CHAPTER EIGHTEEN

THE SOUTHERN SIERRAS

There is indeed but one Ronda in the world
. . . this favourite stronghold of the Moor.

Richard Ford *A Handbook for Travellers in Spain* (1855)

Another minor road, blessed with very little traffic, leads over the hills from El Saucejo to Algámitas, a road which, for all its twists and turns, heads relentlessly up to the distinctive green bulk of the Sierra del Tablón, which bars my path like a huge hand, telling me there is no way through here. Fortunately, as I had looked across the valley to the village on the previous evening, I caught a glimpse of the track I was after, leading south out of El Saucejo towards a distant col, just to the east of the sierra. After a little poking about in the back streets, I finally found it. On the way out I was set upon by a black and white puppy that must have been all of a month old yet hung onto my boot-laces with full-grown intensity, growling happily until I put the handle of my stick under his tummy and lifted him into the air. Back on the ground again, mouth open, he ran off, yelping with surprise.

A stick was essential on my walks across France and Spain. In either country there are far too many half-crazed dogs to ward off. You can do this easily and quite painlessly, simply by showing the dog your stick, at the sight of which even the most impetuous cur will pause, but I would not hesitate to clout a persistent dog around the ear. Down here, a bite means, if not rabies, then the possibility of rabies injections. These are given in the stomach and are said to make the eyes water. I do not know why French and Spanish dogs are so ferocious; I have two dogs, a flat-coat retriever and a Jack Russell, and even the Jack Russell is friendly. Dogs are not a problem for walkers in Britain, but abroad they are a menace.

However, wary as I am of them, many Spanish dogs are rather pleasant mongrels, who only want a little company. They lie in wait outside villages, paws crossed, dying to go for a walk. Whistle them up and they will come lolloping over and trot with you for miles, sniffing about in the rocks, as delighted as you are with the company. The only difficulty is to send them back home when you think they have travelled far enough. I met a number of walking dogs on this journey through Spain, and they spared me a lot of loneliness.

I found the track, just where it should have been according to the map – wonder of wonders – and followed it uphill for one of the best days walking of the whole trip. Everything was just right. My feet were fine, it was hot but not too hot, there was shade among the olive and cork oak trees, and a cool breeze came sweeping over the col to cool me down as I pressed on uphill. Best of all, the track was clear and easy to follow.

*   *   *

Olive trees apart, there were lots of cork oaks up here, recently stripped, with piles of bark about their roots. The world's wine trade relies on this part of Spain for a regular supply of corks. I passed through grove after grove of cork oaks after I left El Saucejo, and a curious sight they were: rather splendid if somewhat gnarled trees, banded for a large extent of the trunk with deep red wood, where the outer bark had been stripped off. Why the trees do not die beats me.

About eighty-five per cent of the world's bottle corks come from Spain and Portugal. The trees grow wild in the mountains of the south and seem to thrive on sandy soil and excessive heat. The trees are first stripped of their bark when they are about fifteen years old, and reasonably mature. Once the cork bark has been stripped, it takes up to nine years before it regenerates and can be stripped again, but the tree can be stripped for about two hundred years, maybe more, before it dies. Apparently the bark has to be stripped off or it will go on thickening and eventually suffocate the tree.

When Richard Ford was touring Spain in the 1880s, he might have met William Rankin, an English cork merchant who visited the Peninsula every year and travelled about by mule to buy cork bark. The bark is piled in great curved swatches, just as it has been peeled off the tree, and shipped to cork manufacturers in all the main wine producing countries. And the cork trade must be profitable; a cork for the standard 73cl wine bottle costs about 1p, a cork for a port or champagne bottle 10p or more. For all their utility, corks are not cheap. Corks have survived the intrusion of plastic stoppers and metal caps because if the bottle is kept tilted and the cork moist, nothing provides such a good, long-lasting seal against the dire effects of fresh air.

*   *   *

I could put the map and compass away on this leg of the walk and just enjoy the scenery which, certainly on the southern side of the Sierra del Tablón, is quite stunning. I got my first glimpse of it from the very top of the col, and saw far away to the south-west, a White Town glittering in the midday sunlight, with sharp, rocky hills dotting the land between, and great misty mountains against the cloud-capped sky beyond. It was a breathtaking sight, particularly as I had spent days out on that interminable *meseta*. I sat on a bank beneath the pine trees and compared the view with my map, working out that the town must be Olvera. The hills behind must be the Sierra de Lijar, with the higher Sierra de Zafalgar beyond that. I was still contemplating the view when there came a great hullabaloo from behind and a herd of goats came pelting down the track, urged on by a galloping horseman and a brace of dogs. Finding me sitting in the way caused considerable confusion, but after I had scrambled up the bank, the goats streamed past and the horseman, as usual, dismounted for a chat. We walked along together down the track, urged on by periodic shoves in the back from the horse's head, while the goats, who seemed to know where they were going, clattered on ahead with the dogs.

The horseman was a farmer who owned a *finca* down by the main road at the far end of this track. He and his family farmed most of the mountain, grazing sheep, cattle and pigs, growing olives and cork and various cereal crops, as well as asparagus. Asparagus, he had to tell me, was the great cash crop hereabouts. The hotels on the Costa del Sol paid well for it. That was news; had I now come so close to the end of my journey? The profits apart, it was a good life, he said, certainly better now than in Franco's time. As for my walk, if I had walked all the way from Santander, I should certainly walk up and visit Olvera. As I could see, it was *muy bonita*, and so close too. If I didn't want to walk there, he would run me up in his car – a lift at last. In the end, down at the *finca* I consulted the map and worked out that I could drift up to Olvera and stay there without much extra time or distance, and still rejoin my main route to Ronda on a footpath. Since Geoff would be late anyway, I had time enough. That decided, I shook hands with my friend of the *finca*, and crossed the main road to pick up the track of another long-abandoned railway line. Three hours later I was at my hotel in Olvera, a place which supplied the perfect end to the perfect day.

*   *   *

If you must walk across Spain – and having done it I cannot recommend it – then do not miss this section of the walk, from El Saucejo to Olvera. My ancient map shows a road from one to the other, north of the Sierra del Tablón, but I somehow missed that and still got there easily enough. Olvera is a gem. Olvera was my first real White Town of Andalucía, and when I say it glittered, that's the word. Olvera shines like a jewel, dazzlingly white on the steep green hillside, with a church and castle to crown the crest, etching their turrets and towers against the sky. Olvera is almost impossibly picturesque.

It lies on what is now a tourist route, *La Ruta de los Pueblos Blancos*, the Road of the White Towns. Part of the deal for all the White Towns is that the inhabitants must whitewash their houses every year, but on reading my guide I discovered that Olvera used to have a much darker side. A Spanish proverb says you should '*Mata al hombre y vete a Olvera*', kill a man and flee to Olvera, and the inhabitants, especially the women, were particularly fond of slaughtering any French couriers or detachments who fell into their hands during the Peninsular War. Burning alive and nailing them to trees were just two ways of disposing of these unlucky prisoners. Today, even if the streets slope steeply up to the great church and the castle, Olvera is much more friendly.

I dumped my rucksack in the *Hotel Sierra y Cal*, a good spot for such rucksack dumping, and went on to see the town square, the great cool church, and follow a rather vertiginous scramble up to the keep of the ruined castle. From there, there are marvellous views over the surrounding countryside. I saw a track along a valley to the south that must take me eventually to Ronda, and picked my way gingerly down again, glad I had come to Olvera and wishing to stay longer. A man in the *ayuntamiento*, the Town Hall, gave me a small guidebook and a stack of postcards, so I sat in the shade to read the one and write the other.

According to this guide, Olvera, a city of the province of Cádiz, is the market town for a region devoted to farming and cattle rearing, and the growing of olive trees. A glance from the tower of the church confirmed that Olvera seems to have entered history with the Muslims, who called it *Wubria*, and they built the first castle on the hilltop. Olvera stayed in Muslim hands until quite late, and was not conquered by the Christians until 1327, after which the church went up and the town spread down a long street along the ridge. A poet wrote: '*Que Olvera, es una calle, una iglesia y un castillo – ¡pero qué calle, qué iglesia, qué castillo!*' – which hardly requires translation. The town's most famous son was Nicolás de

Laredo, born here in 1494, and the first *alcalde* of Lima, Peru, and the church contains a holy relic, La Virgin de los Cien Sierros, and a hundred sierras do lie within sight of the castle on the hilltop. All this is a way of saying that Olvera is not a place to miss.

The good thing about the rolling hill country between Olvera and Ronda is that it has people in it. I know travel writers who can drone on for pages about the beauty of solitude, but those who have not walked day after day across an empty land can have little idea how pleasant it is to cross a country dotted with white-painted farms, small orchards, great clumps of cacti and refreshing glimpses of green. Best of all, the map and the ground seemed to be in agreement for once. Granted, the map was old, and new roads and buildings popped up where they were not indicated on the map, but better too many than too few. I made my way with no great difficulty, first to Setenil, and then chancing my way across the Sierra de las Salinas, my last obstacle before Ronda, I got completely lost. That serves me right for giving up on the map and compass once Ronda was in sight. I then entered thick dwarf oak and scrub. The track I was on simply petered out. The paths off the hill to the south failed to appear where indicated on the map, and when I decided to go bush-bashing down through the dwarf oaks to the plain below, I found myself on the edge of a sheer drop. This was now a small-scale replica of my descent of the Gredos. That thought concentrated my mind and I was forced to make a retreat to higher ground for a re-think. In the process I lost my second (and last) compass. That was no problem at the moment because from the top of the Sierra de las Salinas I could actually see Ronda, but I would now need to ring Geoff and tell him to bring another one for our compass march to Tarifa, across the Serranía. Meantime, I had to get off this damned hill. That took some time and it was late afternoon before I reached the green valley around Arriate.

I finally got down to the plain by following the Río Guadalcoracín out through a gorge. This is never a very good way to get off a mountain, since water tends to take a steep line, but after an hour or so crashing about on the hill, clinging to tree roots and crumbling rocks, I was off the hill and trudging steadily on towards Ronda. On the way I ingested ants which had taken wing by the million on this hot afternoon, until the air was full of them. With this setback on the sierra it was very late before I got into Ronda, but I soon found a *fonda* behind the Plaza de Toros for only 800 pesetas a night, and having dumped the rucksack and rescued my feet from the boots, I set off to find a phone. Then I met another setback. Geoff could not meet me outside the bullring at four on Sunday. Business called yet again, and the best he could do was arrive next Thursday, just a day or two before the walk ended unless I slowed my pace down a bit. I hung up gloomily and went off for a think.

*   *   *

This painful arrival in Ronda might provide a good place to return to the Reconquista for one last time, because from this point on, the Christians advanced south-east to eliminate Granada, while my route lies to the south-west, towards Tarifa.

After the victory at Las Navas de Tolosa, the Christians moved on to capture Córdoba, and then conquer the south-east of Andalucía, a task in which the knights of Santiago played a significant part. Valencia, the old stronghold of El Cid, was recaptured from the Moors in 1238, after which Jaime I of Aragón marched south along the coast, an action which, with the Castilian advance to the Guadalquivir, had the effect of boxing the Muslims ever tighter into the Sierra Nevada and Granada. Jaén fell to King Fernando III in March 1246 and, this achieved, he marched against the last but one of the great Muslim cities, Sevilla.

At the middle of the 13th century, Sevilla was the greatest city in Western Europe, well protected by a string of fortresses which included Carmona and Alcalá del Río. Fernando overran most of these by the end of 1246 and by July 1247 the city was completely surrounded, and remained under siege until November 1248, when it fell to Fernando's army. The Muslims were expelled, some taking ship for Africa, others joining the remains of Muslim power in Granada, but all knew that the fall of Sevilla was another major step towards the extermination of Moorish life on the Peninsula. One exile, Abu 'l Salah, summed it up when he wrote: 'Sevilla, through our fault you are in slavery, and we have become foreigners in Spain'.

Well, not quite. The Moors were to live and rule in Granada for another one hundred and fifty years.

*   *   *

Flushed with their conquest of Sevilla, the Christians might have moved at once against Granada, but two events saved the last Muslim kingdom. In 1252 King Fernando died, 'the greatest of all the Crusaders, who alone has done more for the honour and profit of Christ's Church than the Pope, the Templars or the Hospitallers'.

Fernando was succeeded by his warlike son, Alfonso X, but before Alfonso could take the field, a fresh wave of warriors – the Marinids – arrived from Morocco, and with their help the Muslims of Andalucía were able to prevent further Christian advances until 1340. This did not mean that the Christians failed to erode the smaller Muslim enclaves, and both Alfonso and Jaime of Aragón snapped up towns and castles until their deaths towards the end of the century. The Marinids proved stout warriors in the field, but had no skill at siege warfare, so that once a fortress or city was lost, they seemed unable to retake it, and they were finally defeated outside Tarifa in 1340 by Alfonso XI of Castile, and his ally, Alfonso IV of Portugal.

Once again, the way seemed clear for a final advance on Granada, but the heirs of Alfonso XI gave themselves over to family and dynastic quarrels or to wars against Aragón. The Black Death, which swept across Europe between 1348 and 1350, killed about a third of the Christian population, including King Alfonso XI. The Muslims, who were cut off from contact with the rest of Spain, were spared the worst effects of this plague. The war on the frontier was increasingly left to local lords, one of whom, Guzmán el Bueno, Guzmán the Good, had a famous descendant, the Duke of Medina Sidonia. But I run ahead of myself.

We can leave the Reconquista at this point. Like the Christian armies we have come a long way, from the bleak hills of the Asturias, where it all began, to within forty miles of the Mediterranean. Granada fell on 6 January 1492, and the long march of the Christian kings was over. My own still has a hundred miles to run, but a day off in Ronda is a fair reward after coming this far.

*   *   *

You have to take your time in Ronda today and face a few facts. Ronda is beautiful, Ronda is different, but Ronda is a tourist trap. The English tourists were there in force, coached daily from their high-rise hotel hell-holes on the Costa del Sol, making every café terrace unsightly with their ghastly clothes and plastic souvenir bags. I was now unused to my fellow countrymen *en masse*, and decided to ignore them. I cheered myself up that evening with a good meal at the *Restaurante Romero*, just opposite the bullring, which is a rendezvous for the *aficionados de toros*, and not touristic at all. The *Restaurante Romero* is full of bullfighting memorabilia, and named for the great *torero*, Francisco Romero, founder of modern bullfighting, and I found out more about this *torero* on my visit next day to the Bullfight Museum underneath the stands of the Plaza de Toros. Although I am no *aficionado de toros*, I found the bullring beautiful, the museum interesting, and Francisco Romero a character. Born in 1698, Francisco Romero is the man who put bullfighting on the map and organised it into a sport – if bullfighting merits such an appellation. Although the custom dates from the time of

Felipe II, to Romero goes the credit for the popular bullfighting costume, the glittering *traje de luces*, the suit of lights. His son Juan introduced the other participants of the modern *cuadrilla*.

Before Romero most bullfights took place on horseback, rather as they do now in Portugal and sometimes in Southern France, the bull being killed with the lance as well as the sword. When Romero elected to fight on foot, it caused a sensation. Romero organised a *torero* which technically means all the men in the ring – the *matador*, the *picador*, who wields a lance on horseback to weaken the bull's neck muscles, and the *banderilleros*, who help place those darts in the bull's shoulders, though this is often done by the star of the show, the *matador* or *torero*. The team is a *cuadrilla*, and the complete bullfight, when six bulls are killed, is a *corrida*, literally a running.

My objections to bullfighting are the usual ones. It is a bloody, cruel business, and the end is almost certain. It is risky business and I wouldn't want to try it, but the odds are good. Only about twenty people died in the ring in the 19th century and before El Campillo was gored at Las Ventas in 1985, no *torero* had died in the ring since 1971.

The museum also contains relics of the great Manolete, who was killed in the ring at Linares in August 1947 just before his thirtieth birthday, by a Miura bull called Islero. There are posters and photographs, some of which feature such well-publicised *aficionados* as Hemingway and Orson Welles. Welles was a great follower of the bulls, and after his death his ashes were scattered on the *finca* of the great Ronda *torero*, Antonio Ordoñez. The other attraction of the bullring at Ronda is that you can walk out into the arena – *arena* is also the Spanish word for sand. Out there, in that lonely space, you get some idea of what it might be like to be all alone with nothing but a cape between you and half a ton of enraged potential corned-beef. Francisco Romero's grandson, Pedro (1754–1839) was the founder of the classic bullfighting style here – the Ronda style – and killed hundreds of bulls every season.

The Ronda bullring, built in 1785, is one of the oldest in Spain and a very beautiful building, but the great glory and attraction of Ronda is natural: the gorge of El Tajo. This great cleft in the mountain is about 200 feet wide and 350 feet deep, a sheer drop, spanned by a bridge, the Puente Nuevo. The central span once contained the town jail, and the man who built the bridge was killed when he fell from it into the gorge. The torrent of the Guadalevin pours through this gorge, a spectacular sight from the terrace of the *Restaurante Don Miguel*, high above the Mercadillo, or town side of the gorge. On the town side lie the bullring, the gardens of the Alameda, an attractive park, and most of the shops and restaurants. My favourite part of Ronda lies across the bridge in the Ciudad, once the Moorish fortress, protected on one side by the Tajo gorge, and on the other by a massive curtain wall. Much of this wall still stands astride the road to San Pedro de Alcántara. Over there in the Ciudad, are quiet squares, orange trees, cobbled streets and hardly any tourists. The Carrera de Espinal is the most picturesque street with wrought-iron balconies and walnut doors, most with a brass knocker shaped like a hand, the hand of Fatima, to ward off evil from the house. Other browsing attractions include antique shops, several small restaurants and the Casa del Rey Moro – the House of the Moorish King. The Moorish king in question was Al-Motahed, who built this palace in 1042, and used to toast his guests in goblets formed from the skulls of men he himself had beheaded. A real charmer, Al-Motahed. Christian prisoners cut out the staircase down to the Guadalevin in 1342, and the town only fell to the Christian kings in 1485, the same year the last Plantagenet king died on Bosworth Field. The Mercadillo is busy and bustling and modern Spain, but the Ciudad offers a real touch of the past. The Moors held Ronda until as late as 1485.

I spent most of the day strolling about Ronda, stopping for a drink at the pavement cafés behind the Plaza de Toros, writing my notes on a bench in the Alameda gardens, which hang 2,000 feet above the valley floor, lunching in the *Don Miguel*, watching the local lads fly paper aeroplanes into the Tajo gorge from the middle of the bridge.

So, I had arrived in Ronda, the sea lay only a week away and my walk across Spain was coming to an end. Another five days should do it and, cussed to the last, I was rather sorry. Now I had got used to it, I was enjoying myself a little more each day.

CHAPTER NINETEEN

THE WHITE TOWNS

And, as the cock crew, those who stood before
The tavern shouted, 'Open wide the door,'
You know how little while we have to stay
And, once departed, will return no more.

Omar Khayyam *Rubaiyat*

Ronda is a straggling town, laid out on both sides of the Tajo gorge, and my problem next day was how to get out of it. The aim now was to head towards Jimera de Libar and beyond, down the line of the *Pueblos Blancos*, the White Towns, but preferably avoiding the higher parts of the Serranía de Ronda, which bars the road from Ronda to the south. Fortunately, I had at last obtained some decent maps, scale 1:50,000, from *Librería Hispánica* in the Calle Espinal, the pedestrian precinct which runs through the centre of Ronda. Antonio Márquez, who runs the *Librería*, ferreted about in the back of his shop and eventually came up with the maps covering the rest of my journey, and helped me plan a route. Half an hour brooding over the map and the morning *café con leche* suggested that the best way out was to cut due west and hit the railway line and the Río Guadiaro, both of which run to the west of the town. By following one of these, I could glide round the western end of the Serranía and out towards Jimera.

I worked this out from a seat on the bandstand behind the Plaza de Toros, looking out across the valley I intended to cross. This route decided, I heaved on the rucksack. Like me, my Karrimor rucksack was showing signs of wear, the straps creaking, the fabric faded and dusty, the back now streaked a gratifying white from weeks of sweat. I made my way down to the bottom of the escarpment and then followed various tracks across the farmland, greeted at every turn by fresh yelps from yet more dogs. There is a good track to the west, and at about eleven o'clock I arrived at the *Estación de la Indiana*, somewhere south of Montejaque. Exactly where I hit the railway line hardly mattered. There is only one single track line running in a great sweep, first to the north of Ronda and then round to the south-west, so if I followed it I must arrive at Jimera. No problem. The station at the *Estación de la Indiana* was quite deserted, with no one to protest as I left the platform and followed the footpath along the edge of the track. This footpath, with an even wider path to one side or the other of the railway, or just beyond the rushing Guadiaro, took me south at an easy clip. From time to time the footpath vanished, as Spanish trails tend to do, but I soon picked it up again by returning to walk along the railway line for a few hundred metres. The station at Benaoján was open and even had a *cantina*, and the only snags that day lay a little south of Estación, where the railway line runs through two long tunnels. I crept through one by the light of my torch, ready to hurl myself flat on the ground against the wall if a train should appear. The next tunnel was a little too long for comfort, and after a hundred metres or so I retreated and climbed round the cliffs above, noticing as I did so that a road now ran along the Sierra de Libar, high above the railway line to the west, where the 1:50,000 scale map (dated 1974) I was using showed only a rough track.

By early afternoon, I had arrived in the station at Jimera de Libar, where a 'new' road and railway bridge now spanned the line. With more hills ahead, I refilled my water bottles at a tap outside the church opposite the station and began the climb to Jimera *pueblo*, higher up the valley, which has a Moorish minaret serving as a church bell-tower. I was accompanied on the way there by a farmer bewailing the price of olives. I had heard this tale before, but he also gave me the recipe for making cocktail olives. You crush the olives slightly, then put them, still with the stones, into a jar full of water. There you leave them for about a week. Then you drain off some of the water and add oregano and garlic and whatever sharp herbs take your fancy, and store it all away to mature. The result, he assured me, would be an olive, 'firm as friendship, sharp as love'. This is the first lyrical Spaniard I have ever met. Perhaps other travel writers *are* just luckier than I am.

*   *   *

Finding that new road, which had been joined by the none-too-new-looking bridge across the river at Jimera station did raise fresh doubts in my mind about cross-country marching with an out-of-date map, but the footpath I was looking for duly appeared. Leaving the road, I followed it down into the Atajate gorge, and then up and up, zig-zagging ever higher along an overgrown, crumbling path to reach the heights of the Cerro Bernal. Here, half a dozen paths appeared and I promptly got lost. Fortunately, not being entirely daft, I had bought a new compass in Ronda, and using that to maintain my direction, I took any path heading south, and simply bush-bashed over the sierra.

My object now was to cut off the huge sweep the main road makes round the village of Atajate and so save distance. By following a few tracks, I eventually appeared more or less on line, near a small farm, the *Casa Yunca*, which at first sight appeared deserted. Dog-wary, I was tip-toeing carefully through the farmyard when I kicked over a stone. No less than eight hairy brutes came hurtling upon me from the house, followed swiftly by the farmer, a man clearly disturbed midway through his once-weekly shave, his face a mass of foam, his hand brandishing a cut-throat razor. A great deal of shouting, stick-waving and stone-throwing then followed before the dogs were beaten off, and the farmer went off to re-lather his bristly jowl. I crept away over the hills and by four o'clock had emerged onto the main Ronda to Algeciras road, right on target at a small house, the *Venta de San Isidro*. I felt very proud of that. Some decent map and compass work at last.

From here it was no great distance down the road to Benadalid, a pretty White Town, where the town cemetery has been fitted tightly outside the walls of the ruined 12th-century castle. Benadalid looks a drowsy little place today, but it stood on the *Frontera* between Church and Moor and was often under attack. The *Moros y Cristianos* festival held here in April is said to be one of the liveliest in Spain, for the Christ Crucified is kidnapped from the church and taken to the castle, and the 'Cristianos' storm the walls to get it back; then there are fireworks and a great deal of drinking.

A small bar in Benadalid served me a beer and a ham *bocadillo*, my first substantial food of the day. It was now about five, but after checking that there were some paths offering short cuts around the sweeping bends of the road, I decided to press on for a night-stop at Algatocín, walking across beautiful, green, mountain country, covered with oak and walnut trees but quite empty of people, though dotted here and there with glittering White Towns and villages. My footpath took me high above Algatocín, and I was up on the escarpment, wondering how to get down to it before dark, when I met a man taking two donkeys to a fountain just off the path. Donkeys seem as common in Spain as they ever were. When I was learning Spanish all those years ago, the first sentence in my textbook was '*En España hay muchos burros*' – 'In Spain there are many donkeys'. This sentence used to drive our teacher mad. He would rave that Spain had modern roads, aircraft, railway engines, motor cars and all kinds of modern toys, and not only those damned donkeys. Donkeys upset him in the way that English people get annoyed when Americans think they all live in thatched cottages and wear bowler hats to walk about in the fog. Spain certainly has all the modern marvels, but if I meet my instructor again, I shall have to tell him that there still are an awful lot of donkeys.

I tailed along to help and we watered the donkeys before he led me back down into the village by a steep and stony path. The first house past the first bar in the village was a *fonda*, so by six I had rescued my feet from the boots, and leapt into the shower. My room in the *fonda* was more like a small flat. Set right at the top of the house, it had a bedroom, a bathroom and a small terrace. I was in the shower, singing away, when the señora appeared at the terrace window and handed me a cup of coffee, asking me to ignore the fact that the water was very hot and the cold tap out of order. Since she was ignoring the fact that I was stark naked, this seemed only fair. I was still coyly wrestling with hot water, a scalding coffee mug and a plastic shower curtain, when she reminded me that she had seen men before and disappeared.

Once back in the Rohan pants and trainers, I set off to explore the town. This did not take long, for Algatocín is rather small, and without a straight or level street in the entire place. The streets swoop up and down the hillside, into alleyways and under Moorish arches. The church was built in the 16th century, fell down in the 17th, and was rebuilt in the 18th. It is all extremely picturesque. I found the world's smallest supermarket packed into the front room of a house, where I stocked up with oranges and *magdalenas*, and eventually reached the Plaza Mayor where, in a small café, I waited as the sun went down, watching some old men play a very noisy game of dominoes at the next table, slapping the pieces down on the table with a great clatter. One of them clutched a huge red pomegranate to his chest, as if for luck.

Algatocín does not boast a restaurant, or if there is one I could not find it. My hostess, while worried about the effects of scalding water in the showers, did not seem overkeen to cook me a meal, so about ten o'clock I stepped into the bar next door and had a huge *tortilla bocadillo*. This had another baleful effect; I couldn't sleep a wink all night.

*   *   *

Algatocín was a chilly place next morning. A cold wind came sweeping across the terrace as I went out to take in my washing, and the water in the shower was now stone cold. I decided to skip the eye-opening *douche* for once, while accepting the señora's offer of a '*con leche* with biscuits'. We then had a long chat about my walk, and she was recounting my exploits to several of her neighbours when I came down the stairs with my rucksack a little later. We said a warm goodbye, but the effect was rather spoilt when she turned to the other ladies before I was quite out of earshot and remarked, '*Está loco*': he's crazy.

   Sweating with the climb but shivering in the wind, a steady plod then
took me up to the col at Puerto El Espino, where I sheltered from the
wind and wrote up my notes in a small café. This col, at about 800 metres
(2,500 feet), was the final high point of my walk. From now on, at least
topographically, it was downhill all the way. Low cloud now shielded the
hills ahead, but it was only a few miles now to Gaucín, where I would meet
my wife and (it says on the sign across the road) there are just sixty-nine
kilometres left to Algeciras and only another seven from there to Gibraltar.
It has been a long way from Cantabria, but the end is now getting close. It
was Sunday morning and from this point on, whenever I touched the road,
cars from Gibraltar were pouring past, usually in gaggles of three or four,
wise people getting away from the confines of the Rock into this spacious
countryside, though I doubt if they see much of it through the windscreen.
To do that, you have to go on foot. I was doing just that, walking through
more great groves of peeled cork trees, where I was sent leaping up the
bank by a great flurry of pigs which came rootling and grunting towards
me, snouting about for acorns, a score or more complete with swineherd.
   There is glorious walking country here, in the hills between Ronda and
the sea, and so, descending gently, I came by midday to Gaucín, where
I stopped by a fountain to fill up my water bottles. There I was promptly
accosted by two beautiful girls, Yolanda aged ten and Belé aged nine, who
came up on their bikes to have their photographs taken. They insisted on
this, with much posing and brushing away of hair, and who am I to refuse?
I was in the middle of taking their photos when there came a great honking
and yelling. There, leaning from a car across the road, was a family of
friends from Puerto de la Duquesa, Lito, Pilar and their children, and
waving from the back, my wife. They had come to meet me and stayed
for lunch, but when I suggested they might stay on and walk for a while,
they leapt back into the car and fled back to the Costa del Sol.

                         *   *   *

Gaucín is one of the most popular White Towns of Andalucía, a romantic
looking place, set below a castle on the slopes of a long ridge. We had a
very noisy lunch in a *venta* by the main road, and after the others had left
again for Puerto de la Duquesa, I climbed up to the castle and looked hard
towards the south. According to Ford, from up here 'The view is glorious
. . . Gibraltar rises like a tooth in the distance and Africa looms beyond'.
On this day, inevitably, there was not a sign of either, for low clouds hugged
the tops of the hills. The castle at Gaucín, El Castillo de Águila, the Eagle
Castle, was a Muslim stronghold from 1309 until 1485, and is famous in
Spain as the spot where Guzmán the Good, *Guzmán el Bueno*, was killed

by the Moors when they captured the castle in September 1309. We shall meet Guzmán the Good again later, for his descendant, the Duke of Medina Sidonia, commanded the Spanish Armada of 1588.

The country which surrounds Gaucín, between say Ronda and the coast, used to be known as *bandolero* country, bandit country, for a *bandolero* is a highwayman, and once there were lots of them preying on travellers on the road. Their descendants run hotels on the Costa del Sol. Gaucín was a centre for these bandits, but that did not discourage the hardy Britons from Gibraltar, who would ride up to Ronda for a few days' leave, and stayed at, among other places, the *Hotel Inglés*, which is now the *Fonda Nacional*. There were a number of Britons there when I arrived and the owner showed me Visitors' books going back to the last century, full of comments, mostly unfavourable, from officers of the Gibraltar garrison. 'Food indifferent.' 'People sullen, saddles an invention of the Inquisition.' Well, you can't please everyone. The *Fonda Nacional*, my last real *fonda*, charged me 1,800 pesetas for a room with dinner and breakfast and I have no complaints at all. For the moment, I was happy enough to forget the shortage of views and settle down for the night in the *fonda*, surrounded for the last time on this journey by only Spanish people.

Since Gaucín is the best-known, though not the first of the White Towns I visited on this walk, I might say a little more about these delightful places. There are a great number of them: Ronda, Olvera, Gaucín, Zahara, Arcos de la Frontera, Jimena de la Frontera, and many more. All are constantly whitewashed and kept a glittering white; all are – or were – fortified hill towns, and all are full of tiled houses, the windows protected with box-like iron grilles called *ajimeces* and set along narrow streets. The object of these sensible details, which owe their origin to the Moors, was to deflect the sun, resist the Castilians and, helped by the *ajimeces*, keep the local Don Juans away from the local virgins. Most of the town walls have gone, but the castle usually remains and the White Towns of Andalucía, which run, roughly, from Arcos de la Frontera, east to Ronda, and south from Olvera to Castellar de la Frontera, are the glory of this corner of Spain, and very beautiful.

I had been following the *Ruta de los Pueblos Blancos* from Olvera, and my route next day covered no great distance, perhaps fifteen miles to Jimena de la Frontera. This is also a famous place in Andalucía, both as a White Town and for its castle. The Algeciras road wanders to and fro across the direct route, so I decided on my usual combination of short cuts across the bends to reduce the distance, and direct cross-country compass-marches whenever the country was more open.

The east wind, the *Levantera*, was blowing hard when I left Gaucín next morning, bringing with it low clouds, spatterings of rain and more chilly winds. This being so, the first footpath, over the edge of the Sierra de Hacho, proved a rather unsteady route. The rocks were wet, the thorns sharp, and the wind strong enough to have me clutching at branches to stay upright when I finally got to the crest. Back down on the road, across the sierra, the town of Jimena de la Frontera still lay about fifteen miles away, a relatively easy walk. It was made even easier in the sheltered parts by smooth footpaths which took me through pastures where the grazing cows were well attended by white cattle – ibis, averaging three ibis per cow, the first ibis I had seen since Córdoba, but here in great numbers.

I wish I had brought a field guide to Spain, for the birdlife is outstanding and a spot of birdwatching would have enlivened the days. Another useful asset would have been a flower guide, as Spain contains more than half the wildflower species of Western Europe. Well, it's too late for that now. Maybe in my next lifetime.

* * *

I crossed the Río Guadiaro through *huertas*, orchards, full of lemon, orange and pomegranate trees, had a snack lunch in a bar, *San Pablo Buceite*, then walked out of town to a curious encounter. Walkers had been conspicuous by their absence on this journey, but my eyesight having lengthened with the years I now saw a curious vision approaching from far away down the road. The sight grew curiouser and curiouser as it grew closer. If I was *Robin del Bosque*, could this be Will Scarlett? The other walker was wearing a red tracksuit, keeping his head wrapped in a vast amount of green towelling. In one hand he held a long staff, perhaps a quarter-staff, while his feet were bare. That could be no pleasure on this wet stony road. All this I might have ignored or accepted, but over his shoulder hung (on my children's lives), a bow and a sheaf of arrows! I had to know, so I stopped and asked. Where had he come from? Los Barrios, a little town to the south, not far from Tarifa. Where was he going? Jaén. This wasn't getting me anywhere. So, er, why the staff and the bow and arrows? He always walked with a staff and a bow and arrows. I thought the English were eccentric. He was, I think, Spanish, and equally amazed that anyone should walk all the way here from Cantabria. With expressions of mutual amazement, we wished each other '*Buen viaje*' and limped off in our respective directions. When I turned round to stare back at him, he had stopped and was staring back at me.

* * *

A little while after this encounter I got my first glimpse of Jimena. This *pueblo* is a fine sight, a White Town set below the long line of yet another ruined castle which occupies much of the low sierra on which the town lies. By four I was in the *Hostal Anon* which, somewhat to my surprise, seemed to be full of British people. I was booted and ragged and faded and wan, quite out of touch with the British, and in no mood to explain myself to people who were clearly dying to know what I was about. Matters picked up somewhat when Garth, the owner of the *Anon*, told me they were a walking group from Waymark Holidays, a company with which I have had a pleasant association over many years. Garth introduced me in turn to Peter the group leader, and Peter had actually bought a copy of my book, *Walking Through France*. Fame at last.

Peter was also very keen to introduce me to his group, who would, he assured me, be delighted to meet such a well-known walker, and he invited me to join them for dinner. After a little humming and hawing on this point, we settled, thank God, for a chat over coffee, and I went off to dine alone. Just to complete my adjustment to the British I had liver and bacon (not *baicon*) for dinner, and then went in to join Peter's group. I must say that Peter gave me a good build-up. 'This is Robin Neillands . . . writer . . . journalist . . . famous walker . . . all-round good egg . . . wit, raconteur, wrote this, wrote that . . . happy to talk about his travels . . . wonderful!' I have to say the effect was less than he, or I, had hoped. If he had told them I carried the Black Death, the effect could not have been more decisive. Within two minutes the room was empty. No one actually vaulted the table to get away from my memoirs, but with mutters of 'Hello!', 'Must go', 'Rather tired', and 'Early start', the group had gone. In less than a minute, we sat there alone, stunned. 'Well, Peter,' I said at last. 'If it's true that everyone can be famous for fifteen minutes, I still have about thirteen and a half minutes to go.'

Peter later let me have a copy of his notes, so I am in his debt for much of the following information. The word *anon* is the local word for a custard apple, which my Chilean wife calls a *chirimoya*. The people of Jimena are heavily dependent on agriculture, with citrus fruits and olives as the more prominent crops. There is also horse-rearing, and bulls are reared hereabouts for the rings of Sevilla and Cádiz, though again, one of the principal sources of revenue is cork. Peter also made the point that the life here, just a few miles from the coast, is very different from that which exists on the Costa del Sol. The houses in the countryside still have no electricity or running water, and the hill-people are seemingly content to live in their traditional style, without the need to rush about, ruin their villages and make large amounts of money.

* * *

Jimena de la Frontera, and the *Hostal Anon*, is a good centre for a walking holiday and an interesting spot in its own right. The town owes its existence to the castle, which was built to protect the ford and bridge across the Río Hozgarganta, and as a midway point for travellers between Algeciras and Ronda. As at Gaucín, they say that you can see Gibraltar from Jimena, but more low clouds prevented that, so I spent a little time next morning exploring the town before setting off for Castellar de la Frontera, about twelve miles further south. Geoff was not due for another two days, so I had no need for speed or distance.

Jimena was a Muslim stronghold, well within the confines of the kingdom of Granada until 1250, when the Christians took Alcalá de los Gazules, fifteen miles to the west. This drove the Muslims back into the hills between Jimena and Castellar, both of which were then fortified. The land between them became a march, a frontier, or *frontera*, hence Jimena de la Frontera, one of many such suffixed hereabouts. These towns marked the frontier between Christian and Moor until they were eventually overrun. Jimena fell to the Christians by *coup de main* in March 1431.

> The marshal, Pedro García, left Jerez with three hundred mounted men-at-arms and two hundred foot-soldiers, and a page, Juan Rodriguez, who was a skilled climber. When they were two leagues from the town they left their horses and went on foot, taking with them a six part ladder. The first to climb was a common soldier, Juan de Jerez, and when they were within the town, the knight broke the first lock of the gate and the rest rushed in, sounding trumpets. The Arabs fought until given quarter, then left, leaving their possessions behind.

The Muslims recaptured the town in 1451, but four years later it was regained by the Catholic Kings. After the fall of Granada it crumbled away, the castle losing most of its dressed stone to the townspeople, who used it to build their houses on the slopes below. The castle was garrisoned and somewhat restored by a Spanish general during the Peninsular War, when cannon and musket loops were knocked through the walls, and in the 1830s part of the castle grounds became the town cemetery. It now serves no purpose but to stand like a beckoning signal on the sierra, a sight to bring visitors into the town, or a marvellously picturesque backdrop as you march away.

CHAPTER TWENTY

LAST LAP

*One who excels in travelling
must leave no wheel tracks.*

Tao Te Ching

I left Jimena on yet another grey, windy morning. Dawn had also revealed the sad fact that, during the night, the *Hostal Anon* had been burgled. The till and a slot machine gaped open and empty in the bar, and I thought it best to depart quickly before the Guardia Civil appeared and became officious. Peter showed me the route of the Waymark walk from Jimena to Castellar de la Frontera, along an old road, a *Camino Real*, which ran between the Río Hozgarganta and the railway line. This open track carried me south pleasantly, past cotton fields and orange groves, interspersed with eucalyptus plantations. I had a few encounters with still more British people but none of this delayed me for long and I was in Castellar by one in the afternoon, going well but ready for lunch.

Castellar is a White Town which would be much, much nicer if they threw out the crowd of hippies that now infests it. Once inside the walls I was stopped three times in the first few minutes, twice for cigarettes and once for money, and soundly cursed each time for not obliging. Even the local guidebook apologises for the hippies, so my experience was clearly not unique. Three times seems to be the quota, for I was then left alone to inspect Castellar, a town that crowns the heights of the sierra and is still enclosed by medieval walls. Apart from the present inhabitants, who seem to come from Scandinavia, Britain and the USA, and left their country for their country's good, it would be just the sort of town I like. On a good day you may get great views from here across the great dam far below, and of the countryside to the south. This countryside resembled nothing so much as the South Downs of England, not rough sierras now, but smooth, green hills, with rounded slopes all dotted with sheep. I had not known how much I would miss green countryside until I came to this arid land of Spain, but closer inspection of the valley fields also revealed orange groves, lemon trees, and more ripe pomegranates. Castellar is a most imposing place, but is best seen from a distance. Close to, the inhabitants spoil it. I soon fled and marched hard down to the valley and into the rain for Nueva Castellar, a brand new *pueblo* and rather pleasant. This is where the former inhabitants of Castellar had been moved to after the great reservoir flooded their fields, leaving the Old Town largely to the great unwashed. Nueva Castellar is really quite nice. New as it is, it has several bars, a good restaurant, a comfortable *fonda* and, best of all, no hippies. I spent a quiet evening and prepared myself for the last lap down to the Mediterranean Sea.

*   *   *

That chill *Levantera* wind was still blowing hard and the morning was therefore grey when I set out on my last lap to Gibraltar. This soon brought me to an area that was decidedly lacking in charm but well supplied with furniture factories and oil refineries. After the struggling town of Estación de San Roque, I was forced out onto the main coast road, which may not be open to walkers for much longer, as it is now being transformed into a motorway – an *autovía*. I climbed over various concrete piles and great sections of angle-iron to get to the quieter section of road between San Roque and La Línea.

San Roque occupies a hill just inland from the coast and has a varied view: to Africa, to the sierras, to the ghastly oil refineries around the bay, and even on a dark day, to the Rock of Gibraltar. It was there, when I was finally able to take my eyes off my feet, that I caught my first glimpse of Gibraltar. There it stood at last, my destination, a great, grey bulk, the mighty Rock, rearing up from the sea towards the dark clouds above, where El Tariq came ashore more than 1,200 years ago to conquer Spain for Allah. It still looked no better than the first time I had seen it, from the deck of a troop ship more than thirty years ago. It took more time to walk into La Línea and the Campo de Gibraltar, but as I reached the Bay of Algeciras and began to walk round the shoreline towards it, I could see that Gibraltar had grown and altered in the years between. There were more houses, hotels, quays and warehouses, fewer warships, only one Spanish frigate far offshore and a mass of moored oil tankers. A civil airliner came sweeping round from across the bay and landed on the airstrip that now straddles the land between the landport

and the frontier. Most of the Military have gone, the Royal Navy has
sailed away, the garrison reduced to one battalion. The great days of the
Rock of Gibraltar are over and now they are gone one can see how drab it
is. However, little scraps of glory do remain, not least on the drums and
colours of my own regiment, the Corps of Royal Marines.

*   *   *

Gibraltar came into the hands of Great Britain during the War of the
Spanish Succession, which broke out in May 1702. In 1701, Carlos II
of Spain died, leaving as his possible successors the seventeen-year-old
grandson of Louis XIV of France and the Archduke Charles of Austria.
The prospect of Louis XIV adding Spain and Latin America to his
domains appalled both England and the Dutch, so in 1702 an Anglo-
Dutch fleet under Sir George Rooke, carrying ten thousand Marines,
sailed to take Cádiz. The attempt failed but the expedition did capture
part of the Spanish treasure fleet which had just arrived in Vigo from
the Americas. The British and Dutch Marines had stormed the shore
batteries before the fleet sailed in, and taking their booty with them,
the fleet sailed home again.

By 1704, the Alliance against France had expanded and now included
England, Austria, Holland and Portugal, and yet another expedition
sailed for Cádiz, again under the command of Sir George Rooke. The
defences of Cádiz were judged to be too formidable, so Rooke sailed
on, and on 21 July 1704 a force of Dutch and British Royal Marines
landed in the isthmus, by what is now La Línea, and cut off Gibraltar
from the mainland. After six days the Rock surrendered and the British
moved in. There they stay to this day.

I once served in the Royal Marines and since 'Gibraltar' is the only
battle honour carried in the Corps' Colours, the idea of ending my walk
at Gibraltar had a natural fascination. The Royal Marines also taught
me how to cover thirty miles or more across mountains with a pack on
my back, and that you can do almost anything if you will only put your
mind to it. This single battle honour does not mean, incidentally, that
the Corps is short of glory. There simply wasn't enough space to put
the other battle honours on the Corps' Colours. When King George IV
was asked to select battle honours for the Corps in 1827, he was offered
a choice of 106 separate meritorious actions. Therefore, as the Duke
of Clarence (later William IV) told the Corps when presenting their
Colours, 'His Majesty determines that the difficulty of selecting among

so many glorious deeds such a portion as could be inserted in the space, directed that in lieu of the usual badges and mottoes of the Regiments of the Line, the Great Globe itself, encircled with laurel, shall be the emblem of the Corps, whose duties, valour and good conduct have won them glory in every quarter of the globe'.

The Royal Marines still regard Gibraltar as their signal honour, not because they took the Rock, but because they held it during the subsequent siege of 1704–5.

A French fleet appeared in the Bay of Algeciras on 1 August 1704, while the English fleet was across the Straits taking on water. The two fleets met near Malaga, fought a hard but inconclusive engagement and then, leaving the rest of the Fleet Marines at Gibraltar, Rooke retired to Lisbon. In October 1704, the Spanish appeared in force at La Línea, and another French squadron arrived offshore later that month and so invested the Rock. The Royal Marines held out until April 1705, when the French and Spanish lifted the siege and sailed away. Gibraltar was finally ceded to Britain by the Treaty of Utrecht of 1713, and now, not surprisingly, the Spanish want it back. The snag is that the Gibraltarians want to remain British. Have you noticed there is always a snag? When the matter was last put to the vote in 1967, over 12,000 Gibraltarians voted to remain British; only 44 voted to join Spain.

When I was a lad, during the last war, Gibraltar was a symbol, the 'Rock', a place that had to be held whatever the cost. This was the base for 'Force H', that squadron of fighting ships, aircraft carriers, cruisers and destroyers that harried the *Bismarck* to her watery grave and fought the convoys through to Malta. The great aircraft carrier *Ark Royal* was based in Gibraltar and the whole nation mourned when she was finally sunk.

One of the curious legends of the Rock concerns the Barbary apes. These are a remarkably unpleasant bunch of ugly, thieving monkeys that live on the top of the Rock, the only wild monkeys left in Europe. The legend has it that when the apes leave Gibraltar, then British rule will come to an end. When their number fell to a very low level during the last war, no less a person than Winston Churchill ordered that an expedition leave at once for the mountains of Morocco and bring back reinforcements. The garrison still nominates an NCO as OC Apes, whose daily task is to keep the apes fed, watered and contented. No wonder people think the British mad.

*   *   *

Legends apart, and I love legends, it has to be faced that Gibraltar lacks charm. I made my way in past the surly border guards, surly on the Gibraltar side anyway – the Spanish officials just waved me through – but then a rucksack always brings out the insolence of office. I exchanged snarls with a Customs Officer and passed through, on across the wide airport runway and through the old Landport, now heavily adorned with litter and graffiti. British they may wish to be, but in the Main Street the only language I could hear was Spanish, and though the Street has acquired some modern shops, it still reeks of the time when the Jolly Jack Tars of the Home and Mediterranean Fleets would meet here for their annual brawl. Lined with bars and little cafés serving everything with chips, Gibraltar is a grimy relic of colonial days, and rather short of Imperial splendour. I was almost tempted to drop in for the traditional Navy run-ashore joy of 'Big Eats' in a café, but on a grey day the Rock of Gibraltar can be quite depressing. I soon retreated back across the line to La Línea, resolved to meet Geoff off his plane on the morrow and finish my walk, not here, but as first proposed, at Tarifa. Tarifa, the home of Guzmán the Good, is a Moorish White Town on the very tip of Europe, and just the place to finish my walk across the Peninsula. Besides, it offered at least another day's walking, and a chance to travel with Geoff and discuss the Spanish Armada. You cannot come´ all the way across Spain and not discuss the Spanish Armada.

*   *   *

Two days later, Geoff and I were sitting crouched under a rock on the hillside high above Algeciras, eating tuna fish sandwiches.

'Well, you two really know how to look after a girl,' said Liza. 'I'm cold and wet, and the rain is running down my neck. I have ruined these trousers and they are practically new, and there is a cow up there and I don't like it.'

'Who is this woman?' I asked Geoff.

Liza was the daughter of a friend of ours, a wily gentleman who lives on the Costa del Sol and makes a fair living laundering money. Having no head for figures I have no idea how you launder money, but since it seems to involve carrying large amounts of cash across frontiers, concealing it the while inside your underpants, I can see that a good deal of laundering might be necessary. A heavy bit of money laundering was even then in hand, so Geoff and I had decided to flee into the hills, taking Liza with us as a guide. As a result we were now lost.

'We're not really lost,' said Geoff. 'There is the road, there is the Rock, and there is Africa.'

'And where are we?'

'We're up here.'
'And how do we get down? Where is the path?'
'There is a cow on the path,' said Liza.

It might have been worse. We had several cans of beer, a heap of tuna fish sandwiches and Liza, the lovely lady, had even offered to carry my rucksack. The only real problem was that it was pouring with rain and the *Levantera* was sending great drifts of spray down from the cork trees. We were all soaked to the skin, very muddy and covered with black streaks from crossing more patches of burnt matt-weed. However, there was a patch of blue away to the west and with Tarifa only a few miles away, all we had to do was get off this last sierra, cross the Algeciras-to-Cádiz road, and finish the walk at Tarifa, the town of Guzmán el Bueno.

*   *   *

The Michelin Green Guide gives a most frustrating account of the siege of Tarifa in 1292, when Alonzo Perez de Guzmán (Guzmán the Good) was holding the castle. The Moors had captured his son and duly paraded the lad before the walls, threatening to cut off his head unless Don Alonzo surrendered. Then, according to Michelin, Don Alonzo threw a dagger over the walls and shouted, 'If you need a weapon to murder my son, here is my knife'. And that's all.

'Well . . . what happened then?' asked Geoff and Liza desperately.
'It doesn't say,' I told them.

In fact, the Moors cut off the young lad's head. Some father, Don Alonzo Perez de Guzmán, but he must have had other sons before his death at Gaucín in 1309, because his descendants held great lands in this corner of Spain, and one of them was Don Alonzo de Guzmán el Bueno, Duke of Medina Sidonia, Captain General of Andalucía, who became Captain General of the Ocean Sea to Felipe II of Spain, and Commander of the Invincible Armada of 1588.

The Duke of Medina Sidonia had no wish to leave his pleasant home near Sanlúcar, a few miles to the west of where Geoff, Liza and I now sat huddled under our rock. The command was forced upon him by the death of the original commander, Don Alvarez de Bazán, the Marquis of Santa Cruz. Santa Cruz had fought at Lepanto and knew something of the sea. Medina Sidonia had only his lineage to recommend him and wrote as much to the King, when his commission arrived from El Escorial.

> My health is not equal to this voyage, I know little of the sea, and
> am always seasick and catch cold. I have no funds to expend on

this expedition and, having no experience of the sea and little of war, I cannot feel I should command this enterprise. The Adelentado Mayor of Castile is much more fitted for this post, has much experience in naval and military matters and is a good Christian too.

This was an honest letter but it did no good. No Spanish grandee, however grand, could feel slighted at the commands of the illustrious descendant of Guzmán el Bueno, and Medina Sidonia had attracted the king's attention the year before, when he led the militia of Andalucía down to Cádiz, where Sir Francis Drake was busy burning ships and 'singeing the King of Spain's beard'. Felipe II always kept a wary eye on Sir Francis, whom he rightly regarded as a personal enemy.

This bitterness between a Devon seaman and the ruler of half the world dated back to Sir John Hawkins' expedition to the Americas twenty years before. Anchored at San Juan de Ulua, near Vera Cruz on the coast of Mexico, Hawkins' squadron was treacherously attacked by the Spanish fleet. The young Francis Drake, then on his first voyage, never forgot this action and regarded the matter not simply as an act of war but as a personal affront. He sent his personal challenge and defiance to King Felipe on several occasions, and while he could ignore these letters, it did not escape the king's notice that Drake never missed a chance to do him harm. He had Drake watched and kept a file of reports which give an interesting portrait of the famous seadog.

'This Drake,' wrote Fernandez de Torquemada, 'is a man of medium stature, rather heavy than slender, merry, careful in war, suspicious. He commands and governs imperiously. He is feared and well obeyed by his men. He punishes resolutely. Sharp, restless, inclined to liberality and to ambition. Not very cruel.'

Following the action in Cádiz harbour, a Spanish friar sent another curious report to the king, stating that while the English galleons were in the harbour, he had personally seen *El Draque* conversing with the Devil on his quarter-deck. Now Medina Sidonia had command of the Spanish fleet and was to meet this feared seaman and a hundred like him in the close waters of the English Channel.

Medina Sidonia did his best, poor fellow. He left Sanlúcar and rode across Andalucía to Lisbon, where the Armada was assembling, and by the end of April 1588 he had gathered about a hundred and forty sail, great and small. The Spanish of the time called this the *felicissima armada*: the Fortunate Fleet. On 28 May 1588 the Duke's flagship, the *San Martín*, with cannon thudding salutes and pennons fluttering from every mast, led the Armada out of Lisbon into the wild Atlantic. All the world knows, or used to know, what happened after that, but history is nowhere near as well taught or understood as it used to be.

Drake may, or may not, have been playing bowls on Plymouth Hoe when the Spanish Fleet was sighted, but Garrett Mattingly has proved that it was possible and the remark, 'There is time enough to finish this game and beat the Spaniards too', is very like him. The pinnace *Disdain*, sent by Lord Howard of Uffingham, Lord High Admiral of England, met the Spanish fleet off the Lizard on 31 July and delivered the Admiral's formal challenge, and for the next two weeks the two fleets battered away at each other as they sailed up the Channel. Fire ships scattered the Armada at Gravelines, the heavy guns of the English ships pounded the light Spanish galleasses to pieces, and then, 'God breathed and they were scattered', as the legend runs on Queen Elizabeth's Armada medal. Only forty-four seaworthy ships of the Fortunate Fleet got back to Spain, and more than half the Armada was lost at sea to English guns or Atlantic gales. The loss of life was tremendous. The word 'Invincible', which was later attached to the Spanish Armada, owes more to the Spaniards' love of irony than anything else.

As for the Duke of Medina Sidonia, the loss of so many ships and men broke his heart and ruined his reputation. Practically every family in Spain had lost a son or a brother at sea and the blame for it all fell on the Duke. Only one man, his sovereign Felipe II, forgave the Duke for the defeat and had the grace to thank him for his efforts. The Duke was very ill when the *San Martín* limped in to Santander, and half the crew were already dead of wounds or typhus. The king excused him from his command and a curtained litter carried him home across Spain, to die years later, quite forgotten, at his home in Andalucía.

*   *   *

Sunny Andalucía was reluctant to appear on the last day of my walk. It was three very bedraggled walkers who finally crossed the main road to the heights above Tarifa, one of the windiest spots in Spain and therefore dotted with great power-generating windmills. We dried off in a café, found a small road and then a track and followed this across the open hillsides and through farmyards down to the walls of Tarifa.

What is there to say about the end of any walk, even this one? It is over, and you have done it and now you can go home again. That's all. I learned a lot about Spain, but nothing I can sum up in a few lines. I discovered that it is a hard land, not an easy place to love. You have to fight it, and earn its respect before it will relent and let you share its secrets. Spain gave me a run for my money and took all I had by way of tolls.

Even so, I have enjoyed this walk. Spain has reminded me again and again that most of life is pretty good if you will just keep it simple. You don't need much to be happy, and can get along with much less than you think you need. Good friends are perhaps the one thing you cannot do without, and I have a few of those. I'm very lucky and I must not forget that.

*   *   *

Tarifa is a fine town. The walls still stand and the castle of Guzmán el Bueno still occupies the headland, where there is a causeway running out to the point. Here a lighthouse welcomes mariners to the Mediterranean and the Pillars of Hercules, with the lights of Africa twinkling in the dusk, just eight miles away across the Straits. When you have come all this way, getting here to the very tip of Europe is a rather special moment, but Geoff and I have done this before, so our routine is established. We walked through the streets of the town, up to the main road outside the Land-gate of the city, and then down to the great sweep of beach, the Playa de Los Lances, which faces the Ocean, the steep Atlantic stream. As we got there the sun was just tipping below the western horizon. It was as good a time and place to finish a walk as you are likely to find.

I walked down the beach until the sea came rushing into my boots, then turned back to join the others waiting by the sea wall.

'That's it then?' asked Geoff.

'That's it,' I said.

'Where are you going to walk next?' asked Liza.

'No, that's it,' I said. 'I've done enough walking.'

Geoff has heard me say that before, but this time I mean it. You have to stop some time and this time will do. If I go off again, I might not stop until I walk off the edge of the world.

KIT LIST

The Golden Rule, as indicated by Uncle Podger, is to take everything you need and leave out anything you can do without. My kit list was as follows:

Clothing

6 pairs loop-stitched socks
1 pair Daisy Root 'Vetta' boots
1 pair trainers
2 pairs Rohan trousers (1 on, 1 off)
2 shirts (1 on, 1 off)
3 pairs underpants (1 on, 1 off, 1 in the wash)
3 handkerchiefs
1 hat
1 scarf
1 tracksuit top
1 set washing gear

All the above in one Karrimor Jaguar rucksack, with:

Equipment

2 Silva compasses
1 notebook
1 Nikon FM2 camera
6 rolls ASA 400 black and white TMX film
6 rolls ASA 64 Kodak colour film
1 Buck knife
Maps and guidebooks (various)
Water bottles 2 × 1 litre
1 mug, 1 plate, 1 plastic food box
First-Aid kit
Lip salve
Passport
Money
Credit cards
Eurocheques
English–Spanish dictionary
1 book (*Poetry, Please*)
Sunglasses

BIBLIOGRAPHY

As I Walked Out One Midsummer Morning, Laurie Lee (Penguin 1971)
The Borgia Testament, Nigel Balchin (Fontana Books 1961)
By Sea & Land: The Royal Marine Commandos 1942–82, Robin Neillands (Weidenfeld & Nicolson 1988)
Castles in Spain, Michael Buselle (Pavilion Books 1989)
Corunna, Christopher Hibbert (Batsford Books 1961)
The Defeat of the Spanish Armada, Garrett Mattingly (Penguin 1962)
Don Quixote, Miguel de Cervantes (English Edn. Penguin 1950)
Exploring Rural Spain, Jan McGirk (Christopher Helm 1988)
Gredos Mountains & Sierra Nevada, Robin Collomb (West Col 1937)
Guía de Hoteles, España 1988 (Secretaria General de Turismo)
Iberia, James Michener (Fawcett Books, New York 1968)
The Insight Guide to Spain, ed. Kathleen Wheaton (APA Publications 1988)
Marching Spain, V.S. Pritchett (Hogarth Press 1988)
Murray's Handbooks to Spain, Richard Ford (3 vols.) 1855
National Parks of Western Europe, Angus Waycott (Inklon Pub. 1983)
Northern Spain, Cedric Salter (Batsford 1975)
On Foot in Spain, J.S. Campion (Chapman & Hall 1879)
The Pilgrim Guide to Spain, ed. Patricia Quaife (Confraternity of St James 1987)
The Reconquest of Spain, D.W. Lomax (Longman 1978)
The Road to Compostela, Robin Neillands (Moorland Publishing 1988)
The Road to Santiago, Walter Starkie (John Murray 1957)
Sierra de Gredos y Picos de Europa, Jeronimo Lopez (Editorial Alpina 1985)
Spain, ed. Franz N. Mehling (Phaidon Press 1985)
Spain, Michelin Green Guide (Michelin 1980)
Spain, Hugh Thomas (Life World Library 1962)
Spain At Its Best, Robert S. Kane (Passport Books 1975)
Spain in the Middle Ages, Angus MacKay (Macmillan 1977)
Spain Off the Beaten Track, various contributors (Moorland Publishing 1988)
The Spanish, Alfonso Lowe (Cremonsi, London 1975)
The Spanish Civil War, Hugh Thomas (Penguin 1962)
The Spanish Mousetrap, Nina Epton (Macdonald 1973)
A Stranger in Spain, H.V. Morton (Methuen 1955)
Wellington's Peninsula Victories, Michael Glover (Batsford 1963)
Wild Spain, Frederick V. Grunfeld (Ebury Press 1988)

* * *

Maps

The route can be planned on the Michelin España maps scale 1:400,000 (1cm = 4km). For use on the ground, the 1:50,000 maps produced by the *Servicio Geográfico del Ejército* are the most useful.

INDEX